"It is cheaper to publish in Manchester. Staff are more loyal, more diligent and more skilful. But could you have envisaged Lord Hartwell moving to Wilmslow?"

Ben Hurren, former *Daily Telegraph* deputy northern general manager and managing director, Trafford Park Printers

"Never trust a man who works at night"

The late Norman Bennett, Manchester architect and my father-in-law

"My wife once asked me why I had to be in pubs all the time. I said it's where you meet people and dream of ideas and intros"

Gerry Dempsey of the time when he was the *Daily Express's* northern showbiz correspondent

"The great strength of the British press is to deliver a paper to the nation from the Orkneys to the Channel Islands by breakfast time, and the only way it could achieve that was by printing in Manchester"

Derek Jameson

THE OTHER FLEET STREET

Robert Waterhouse

Crowds gather outside Kemsley House, Withy Grove, to view the *Daily Dispatch/Evening Chronicle* election barometer in the 1945 General Election

CONTENTS

In memory of John Flint, Peter Hollinson, Jim Lewis, Bill Shakespeare and Brian Wood, Manchester national newspaper journalists and colleagues on *North West Times*

Acknowledgements

First encouragement to write this book came from the late John Flint. Trevor Bates then opened his contacts book to me, along with Bill Freeman, Geoff Mather, Mike Cuerden, Lynne Greenwood and Alan Mackenzie. Denis Thorpe contributed a photographer's perspective. Stanley Blenkinsop and John Knill spread the word. Ben Hurren lent me his newspaper library. Mel Harding offered media contacts.

Over at the Printworks, formerly Withy Grove, Fred Booth and Joyce Moreton made crucial introductions to the Withy Grove Fellowship as well as providing meeting space and refreshments. Albert Hartwell coordinated Fellowship members with good humour and tact. Their supply of stories – and mementoes – is the stuff of this book.

In London Richard Jones of the *Daily Mail* library and Chris Spinks of the *Daily Express* library gave me access to rarely-viewed material. Both went out of their way to help, as did Antony Schipani at Mirrorpix and Roger Tooth and Luke Dodd at the *Guardian*. I would like to thank all five, and their managements, for permission to reproduce historic images.

The same applies to Matthew Butson and Sarah McDonald at the Hulton Archive, part of Getty Images, to Bert Hardy's widow Sheila and to Manchester photographers Clive Cooksey, Denis Thorpe and Johnnie Walker.

Friendly archivists included Dr James Peters of the John Rylands Manchester University Library, James King of the Modern Records Centre, Warwick University, David Tuxford at Manchester Central Ref and all at the Greater Manchester County Record Office.

Les Thompson, designer extraordinaire, introduced me to Henry Hochland, most understanding of publishers, and Heather Stackhouse, most sympathetic of editors. Jim Hollingshead was the talented Mac specialist.

Ian Breach, friend and colleague since *Guardian* Cross Street days, brought his knowledge of newspapers and Manchester to reading drafts and proofs, along with a writer's breadth of vision and a sub's eye for detail.

Rachel McCormick and Nick Jaspan, alternating with Linda Dooley and Roger Conway, put me up and put up with me during frequent visits to Manchester, my adopted home-town but no longer my home.

What began as a lone initiative ended up a joint venture, with spontaneous contributions by journalists and specialists just too good to spike (their articles carry a byline) and a rash of newspaper stories from the likes of Bob Gray.

Jane, my wife, gave maximum support for yet another project. Anna, our daughter, chose to remember the good things about having a newspaperman as a father. Mira, our grand-daughter, born early 2003 to Anna and Hitesh, inspires us all.

Foreword

This book is a celebration of the years between 1900 and 1989 when daily national newspapers were published in Manchester. The word published means just that: a place where newspapers are originated, edited and printed. A focus for several thousand people – editors, reporters, photographers, sports writers, feature writers, theatre and music critics, sub-editors, messengers, copytakers, darkroom operatives, compositors, readers, stereo and machine-room men, publishing staff, van drivers, advertising sales and circulation departments and so on. A 24-hour, three-dimensional world driven by ambition, hope, fear, humour, lust and greed – not unlike the society it reflected. A distribution network stretching from the West of Ireland to the North of Scotland framed above a wavy line from Skegness to Aberystwyth. A "provincial" centre which was, for once, "national." The other Fleet Street.

Manchester owed its life as a national publishing centre to fast-growing daily newspapers of the early twentieth century seeking to extend into far-flung markets with up-to-the-moment news. It existed only while technology and working practices prevented London-published editions printing in the North. Despite what they at times professed, Fleet Street's barons made no other commitment.

Manchester's home-grown squirearchy, the Hulton family, having built up Europe's largest print-centre at Withy Grove, abandoned it for Fleet Street, but Withy Grove then became the headquarters of Kemsley's extensive provincial empire and enjoyed 30 good years until it fell foul of asset-stripping by Thomson and Maxwell.

For its part the *Guardian* was lucky to survive the ambition of Laurence Scott, C.P.Scott's grandson and managing director of the Manchester Guardian & Evening News Ltd from 1948-1967, to make it a London newspaper. Manchester, in the shape of the *Evening News*, funded a move during the 1960s which deprived the city of its internationally-renowned daily, starved the *Evening News* itself of development cash and killed off Manchester's other evening paper, the *Evening Chronicle*.

Guardian history is freely available. Not so for the nationals who came to publish in Manchester. The numerous accounts of Fleet Street have footnotes, at best, for Manchester. Northern editions were not systematically filed; even the British Library is light on them. When you consider the number of editions – five or six on a weekday, anything up to 13 on a Sunday – a great deal of social history has gone down the pan. Fish and chip paper, yes, but a lot more besides.

Luckily, numbers of people with strong memories survive. What are newspapers but a more-or-less ordered form of instant oral history? I have tried to collect here the stories behind the stories – from characters on all sides of the presses whose combined memory goes back to the first quarter

Manchester owed its life as a national publishing centre to fast-growing daily newspapers of the early twentieth century seeking to extend into far-flung markets with up-to-the-moment news

of the twentieth century. My apologies to those I did not manage to contact, and my thanks to those who spoke so freely and who lent precious photographs and artefacts.

Anecdotal evidence is not usually fiction, but neither is it necessarily fact. Since much of this book is reported speech I decided to attribute on page and not clog the back up with notes and sources. Those who seek them will find plenty of leads (though I have stopped short of giving out phone numbers and e-mail addresses: after all, we journalists still guard our contacts books with our lives).

Another apology. Sports enthusiasts will note straight away that their passions are woefully under-represented. Apart from a chapter on the aftermath of the 1958 Manchester United Munich crash in which eight journalists were killed along with half of the Busby Babes, and a short section on the early sporting interests of Hulton's newspapers, there is very little for you. This was a reluctant if deliberate decision. Sport is a world of its own in newspaper terms, and deserves a book of its own.

Sport apart, my approach has been inclusive but I am well aware of the myriad details which escape an overview like this. The *Daily Dispatch*, *Sporting Chronicle* and *Sunday Chronicle* – just three of Hulton's titles – each deserve proper exploration. Maybe it is only through such studies that the importance of Manchester to UK newspapers will be fully understood.

Robert Waterhouse

Nice, France

July 2004

National newspapers go national

During the final October of the nineteenth century an unmarked train steamed into Manchester's London Road Station around 4am, six days a week. Its cargo: *Daily Mail* newspapers. Alfred Harmsworth, the future Lord Northcliffe, had laid on the service from Marylebone to bring breaking news of the Boer War to Lancashire, the biggest English market outside London, in his innovative daily, established just four years earlier. Flourishing sales led to immediate investment. On February 3 1900 Harmsworth began simultaneous publication of the *Daily Mail* in both London and Manchester.

As locations go, the converted schoolroom in the industrial Manchester suburb of Gorton hardly matched Fleet Street. But it was an important moment: of the London dailies only the *Times* and the *Financial Times* declined to follow Harmsworth's initiative. For the best part of the twentieth century Manchester was the other Fleet Street, publishing between a quarter and a third of all newspapers consumed in the British Isles. Its patch embraced England north of Birmingham, Scotland for those newspapers not published in Glasgow or Edinburgh, North Wales and all of Ireland. Manchester was the means by which national newspapers became truly national.

In 1900 the private wire services subscribed to by newspapers allowed information to be assembled as well as transmitted at more than one point, but a publication's daily reach was defined by the limits of ground transportation. Over any distance that meant railways. As Harmsworth himself discovered with his London-Manchester train – and the *Manchester Guardian* already knew from its attempts to offer a Central London breakfast delivery – the four-to-five-hour journey put severe strains on distribution routines. Token editions of national and provincial dailies available at main line stations were of no interest to circulation departments or advertisers.

The concept of "national" newspapers was in its infancy. Before Harmsworth began to open things up there was the London press, headed by the *Times*, and provincial mornings serving a local readership. The *Manchester Guardian* had a morning competitor in the *Manchester Courier*; it was the same story Leeds, Bradford and Liverpool. The popular press, as we know it today, had yet to happen.

Publishing from Manchester put the important urban centres of the North (except Teesside and Tyneside) within a couple of hours by newspaper train, allowing a third edition, which went to press after midnight, or even a fourth edition to reach the distributor in time for breakfast sales. It was not 24-hour news as we know it today; but one of the ironies of media development is that the national newspapers of 2004, transmitted by page facsimile from London to print centres around the country, have earlier deadlines and fewer editions than their parallels of 50 or 75 years ago.

Ireland and Scotland, well beyond the two-hour timeframe, were a much smaller market. But Manchester, five hours closer to Glasgow than London,

The concept of "national" newspapers was in its infancy. Before Harmsworth began to open things up there was the London press, headed by the Times, and provincial mornings serving a local readership

was well-placed to hit overnight boat services from Liverpool or Holyhead. As air freight became an option the Irish markets further opened up from Ringway and Speke. Access to the West Coast, as well as the importance of Lancashire itself, explains why Leeds never proved a serious rival to Manchester – though the innovative Harmsworth had sent his Boer War editions on special trains to Leeds as well as Manchester. Starting in 1901 the *Daily Mail* was distributed from Manchester to Leeds and other points north via a new network of newspaper trains.

It was a piecemeal process, reflecting the rise and development of the penny and half-penny press in a new age of literacy and relative social change. The *Daily Mail* had the northern market to itself – along with indigenous products – until the arrival in 1909 of the small-circulation liberal *Daily News*, later to become the *News Chronicle*. That same year Edward Hulton, whose titles published at Withy Grove already included the *Daily Dispatch* – a north-only halfpenny newspaper – the *Manchester Evening Chronicle*, the *Sporting Chronicle* and the *Sunday Chronicle*, launched the *Daily Sketch* from Manchester and London. Early editions suggest that the *Sketch* was hatched in Manchester but that the newspaper's head office soon became London.

It seems that Hulton, son of the former *Manchester Guardian* compositor who founded the *Sporting Chronicle*, was himself in the process of moving south in the wake of a wife who declined to travel north of Watford. From a Manchester point of view his voyage was sadly prophetic. The *Guardian* would follow his path half a century later, though ostensibly for stronger reasons. In any case Hulton, who had picked up the London *Evening Standard* in 1916, lost a long struggle with ill-health and disposed of his empire in 1923, two years before his early death.

This celebration *Daily Mail* page, with an inset of the young Alfred Harmsworth signed by him, was prepared by Linotype Merganthaler for company publicity . Harmsworth used some of the first lino machines in Europe when he began Manchester printing in 1900. Merganthaler's mockup for Edward Hulton is on page 11

E. Hulton & Co went first to Hulton's friend and Surrey neighbour Beaverbrook, who stripped out the *Evening Standard* and sold on at the original £6 million to Rothermere, who made a quick £1.8 million himself in selling to Kemsley. Withy Grove, claimed to be Europe's largest single print hub, where some 3,000 were employed, was to become the centre of the Allied-Kemsley provincial empire. In daily newspaper terms Withy Grove increased in interest during 1940 when Camrose, looking for an alternative print centre for a Fleet Street threatened nightly by the Luftwaffe, contracted with his brother Kemsley to publish northern editions of the *Daily Telegraph* there. The *Telegraph* and the *Daily Mirror*, which arrived in 1955, were the major tenants of an increasingly creaky warren whose name changed from Kemsley House to Thomson House in 1959, then finally, in the tragi-comic era of Captain Bob, to Maxwell House.

Meantime Beaverbrook staked his Manchester claim by bringing the *Daily Express* to Great Ancoats Street in 1927, converting a corset warehouse to hold his presses. By the end of the 1930s Beaverbrook had rebuilt on site to the strong glass and steel designs of Sir Owen Williams, the third in a Black Lubyanka trilogy begun in Fleet Street (1931) and carried on at Albion Street, Glasgow (1936). Not to be outdone, Rothermere's Associated had rebuilt and enlarged the Deansgate home of the *Daily Mail*. With the *Manchester Guardian* and *Evening News* long established in Cross Street, Odhams' *Daily Herald* in Chester Street near Oxford Road and the *News Chronicle/News of the World* in Derby Street off Cheetham Hill Road, Manchester was in full swing.

The Boer War press corps in 1900. The *Manchester Guardian*'s J.B.Atkins is third from left on the top row, standing beside the *Daily Mail*'s Douglas Story, fourth from left. A certain Winston Churchill is seen second left on the seated row

Newspaper offices acquired an increasingly large complement of reporters, sportswriters, photographers and sub-editors, along with advertising sales, circulation and accounts departments. The circulation battle joined when Harmsworth first booked that newspaper train had its frenzied culmination in the 1950s; then, any town with over 50,000 inhabitants in the Lancashire and Yorkshire heartlands was deemed worth a slip edition during a cup run, a by-election or a simple promotion. Before ITV started to drain the regional advertising pot there seemed enough and more for all. It was an illusion, of course.

Absentee landlordism, Manchester's fatal weakness in the power-game of media ownership, was demonstrated decisively one November morning in 1955 when the *Daily Dispatch* failed to appear, supplanted by new northern editions of the *Daily Mirror*. Officially, the *Dispatch* was subsumed into the *News Chronicle*. In reality, many of its staff and most of its readers went to the *Mirror*. No matter that the *Dispatch's* final-year circulation was around 500,000. Kemsley, the fastidious caretaker of Withy Grove, had succumbed to the lure of contract printing. The *Mirror* was to develop a strong northern identity, but there was little reason other than expediency for the *Dispatch* to disappear.

No other country, except perhaps France, has such a centralised concept of "national" newspapers. The Manchester newspaper phenomenon celebrated in this book was an aberration, a fluke. A fast-emerging, increasingly competitive twentieth-century marketplace had to cope with nineteenth-century technology and pre-Victorian craft union practices. Look inside the mannered modernism of Beaverbrook's Great Ancoats Street creation or the understated suaveness of Associated's Deansgate: the 1940s and 1950s photographs show operatives in suits and brillo hair styles manning (women weren't in evidence) wire machines resembling torture gadgets and picture desks with nary a light box.

Now we can begin to discern the historical perspective: Manchester moved to fill a gap, the gap between the invention of the private wire, the rotary press and the linotype machine, the era of 1850-1900, and the direct-input, page composition, page fax era of 1990. Its establishment was painful, involving heavy investment and organisational commitment often on the part of people who had no wish to do time in a place they saw as uncouth and uninteresting, scarred by Industrial Revolution excess, and whose dynamism was almost exhausted. How many new recruits to Manchester must have wished they had the luck of Oscar Pulvermacher, the *Daily Telegraph's* first northern editor, who lodged at the Midland Hotel and was transported the short distance to and from Withy Grove each day in a chauffeur-driven limousine. How many – and here one includes editors as different as Arthur Christiansen and Derek Jameson – came strictly under orders but left with a healthy respect for Manchester's honesty and professionalism.

As the map on page 20 shows, newspaper offices dotted the centre of Manchester over a much wider area than Fleet Street. Each office (or factory,

The Manchester newspaper phenomenon was a historical fluke. A fast-emerging, increasingly competitive twentieth-century marketplace had to cope with nineteenth-century technology and pre-Victorian craft union practices

(DAILY.) # The Sporting Chronicle **(DAILY.)**

No. 7291.   SATURDAY, MAY 22, 1897.   FOURTH EDIT. 5·45.

MIDLAND HUNT MEETING.

NEWCASTLE AND GOSFORTH PARK

FOR SPECIAL REPORTS

Saturday's Sporting Events

READ THE

SUNDAY CHRONICLE

THE BRIGHTEST, BREEZIEST AND BEST

SUNDAY PAPER.

MANCHESTER EVENING CHRONICLE

WEDNESDAY NOVEMBER 10, 1897

PRICE ONE HALFPENNY

NO WIRES OR INNER TUBE.

THE "WARRY" TYRE.

SIMPLEST AND BEST.

TUCK & CO., LTD.,
42, CHAPEL STREET, LIVERPOOL.

No. 638.

THE SUNDAY CHRONICLE

SUNDAY, NOVEMBER 7, 1897

FOURTH EDITION

PRICE ONE PENNY

DEMOCRACY AND PATRIOTISM.

NOTES AND NOTIONS.

THE URIAH HEEPS OF POLITICS.

(Fide Mr. CHAMBERLAIN at GLASGOW.)

TURTLES AND SOUP.

WHENCE AND HOW THEY COME.

Some Points for the Curious.

The Athletic News

'D CYCLISTS' JOURNAL.

MONDAY, NOVEMBER 8, 1897.

PRICE ONE PENNY

No. 1153.

EN PA...

PEACE WITH HONOUR.

FOOTBALL FEDERATION

	Winner	Lower
WEST BROMWICH A. v LIVERPOOL.		
ASTON VILLA v EVERTON		
DERBY COUNTY v SHEFFIELD U.		
SHEFFIELD W. v BLACKBURN R.		

Name ....

Address ....

as it was in effect) had its own watering holes, even its own clubs in the case of Withy Grove. There was not much exchange between the *Daily Mail* on Deansgate and the *Daily Express* nearly a mile away on Great Ancoats Street. From time to time rival news editors would organise "raiding parties" of home pubs to find out what their competitors were up to which ended, inevitably, in communal drinking sessions. *Daily Telegraph* and *Daily Mirror* journalists, though they shared the same building, tended to keep to their own. The *Guardian*, stuck in the middle of them all at Cross Street, was notoriously self-absorbed (and aloof from the *Evening News* on the floor below). As in Fleet Street and other provincial locations, such factories were fast becoming city centre anachronisms: true to form, the *Guardian* was in the van of change when the Scott Trust left Cross Street in 1970 to make way for Boots and the Arndale Centre.

Manchester was always less costly than Fleet Street – wages were some 30-50 per cent lower for much the same job – but newspaper proprietors did not invest there for the cheap option, or to escape trades unions. The Typographical Association, the TA, grew out of the Manchester Typographical

Withy Grove in its early twentieth-century heyday, with the principal Hulton titles established and flourishing. Newsprint carriers line up on Shude Hill waiting for delivery carts to emerge from the publishing room bays (see overleaf)

Society, the MTS, founded by Manchester compositors in the eighteenth century. In the 1797 the MTS set out its rules – seven years' servitude (or apprenticeship); exclusion of 'foreigners' (predating a Fleet Street practice); apprentice restrictions; regulation of wages and hours; punishment of 'rats'. There was also a benefit society to fund strikers. By 1865 Manchester had become the national headquarters of the TA, controlling compositors' chapels around the country except in the capital, where the London Typographical Society, the LTS, held sway.

In 1868 the secretary and treasurer of MTS, W.H.Wood and S.S.Nicholson, as secretary and president of the Manchester & Salford Trades Council, were responsible for summoning the First Trades Union Congress, which took place in Princess Street, Manchester. Before the 1965 amalgamation of the two compositors' unions as the National Graphical Association, the NGA, the LTS was in continual dispute with the TA, which it accused of poaching members in towns like Reading on the London fringe. Yet it was the LTS, through its then general secretary Bill Keys, which dominated the new NGA, headquartered at Bedford. NATSOPA, the main general print union, had a strong Manchester branch from 1904 but was always run centrally from London.

In the papers of Robert Willis, LTS's general secretary during the 1950s and 1960s, now lodged along with many other trades union documents in the Modern Records Centre at Warwick University, the cultural differences between London and the trade union world outside soon show themselves. Willis's diary is dotted with appointments – drinks with the Newspaper Proprietors' Association, an interview with the Labour Party leadership, a commemorative event at the Royal Albert Hall, lunch with Cecil King – which distance and contacts denied the TA in Manchester. However difficult life became, the LTS remained part of the London scene. Its loyalties lay to its London-based members, not to the print unions as a whole. The developing crisis in Fleet Street was seen through its eyes, though Manchester was closely affected by London disputes. If copy or pictures failed to materialise for the edition there was little Manchester could do.

When attempting to trace the history of national newspapers in Manchester it becomes obvious that the five or six editions published there by each newspaper night after night – and there could be 12 or 13 editions on a Saturday night – have largely disappeared from the face of the earth. Nothing is more outdated than yesterday's news, but the newspapers themselves, of course, had a practice of keeping editions on file and then creating bound volumes, normally of the final edition. At some point, depending on management policy, bound volumes were microfilmed – and the volumes themselves often junked.

What has survived is almost a lottery. Bound volumes of most northern final editions of the *Daily Telegraph* are to be found in the Greater Manchester

C.P. Scott near the beginning of his editorship and in 1921. Scott was editor of the *Manchester Guardian* from 1872-1932, becoming proprietor in 1907

County Record Office, along – very helpfully – with the *Daily Telegraph* northern cuttings library and bound volumes of the *Daily Dispatch* and *Manchester Evening News*. The *Daily Mail* itself keeps bound volumes of northern editions, along with the Manchester picture library, in a North London store while the *Daily Express* has sundry northern editions on microfilm at its South London store. *Daily Mirror* history is similarly stored at Watford. Such stores are not open to the general public

At Colindale, the British Library's newspaper collection in the London suburbs, one can track down northern editions of the *Guardian*, the *Daily Mail* and the *Daily Sketch* (between 1911-1920), along with editions of the evening newspapers, the *Daily Dispatch*, the *Sunday Chronicle* and *Empire News*. But that seems to be the sum total in a library which purports to be the reference base for newspapers in the English language worldwide. It's clear that northern editions were not collected systematically. Perhaps worse still, newspaper collection in the Social Sciences Library at Manchester Central Reference Library has become a haphazard process, affected by financial squeeze. The library lost its bindery and hard copies were disposed of after microfilm sessions. In some cases Manchester bought microfilm from Colindale. That's the case for the interesting period of *Daily Express* history described in Chapter 3 when Arthur Christiansen was despatched to Manchester by Beaverbrook to make northern editions pay. Central Ref holds the London editions of the *Daily Express* for 1932-33 and we are the poorer for it.

You can dispose of a business, sell-off the presses, pull down buildings, transfer readership from one title to another – but you cannot efface the memories of those whose working lives revolved around newspapers. This book makes no apology for majoring on such people – from Sam Marsh, still very much alive at 94, who started in the publishing room at Withy Grove in 1924, the year after Hulton sold out, to Michael Kennedy, northern editor of the *Daily Telegraph* between 1960 and 1985, friend of Beecham and Barbirolli, himself an internationally-renowned music critic and author. Other chapters retail stories, true and apocryphal, of journalists in pursuit of business and/or pleasure matched by the army of more-or-less skilled night-workers who had their own agendas.

What emerges – strangely, perhaps, to those unfamiliar with the press – is a strong sense of involvement, not just with fellow workers but with the companies which employed them and the callings they followed. Former *Daily Express* journalists remember 'The World's Once-Greatest Newspaper'. Rival showbiz correspondents reminisce, nearly 40 years on, about the Manchester Palace Theatre premier of Alan Bennett's play 'Forty Years On'. Football correspondents describe the bleakness of Old Trafford after the 1958 Munich Disaster. Compositors, readers and publishing staff tally their despair at the way Thomson stripped Withy Grove of its place in the Kemsley provincial empire and disgust at Maxwell's purloining of the building as well as their pension fund.

Not for nothing is the association of former workers there called the Withy Grove Fellowship. Some 16 years after the building's closure, the Fellowship has a growing membership who meet three times a year to keep in touch and discuss old times. The Fellowship has been actively encouraged by Fred Booth, centre director of the Printworks, the leisure complex created from the ruins of Withy Grove. Booth won Fellowship hearts by ensuring that the Hulton and Kemsley Rolls of Honour for employees who died in the two world wars were formally reinstated at the Printworks. He makes meeting rooms available to the Fellowship and plans to create a memorabilia museum in the management suite.

The Printworks claims to be Manchester's premier drinking haunt, with dozens of bars and restaurants supplementing the multi-screen cinemas, health club and casino. Little changes. Withy Grove was surrounded by pubs and clubs, some of which star in this book. As one former night-worker's wife remarked to her husband, "I'm glad to hear the old place is a leisure centre once again."

You can dispose of a business, sell-off the presses, pull down buildings, transfer readership from one title to another – but you cannot efface the memories of those whose working lives revolved around newspapers

A Manchester newspaper timeline 1821-1989

1820

1821   *Manchester Guardian* founded

1825   *Manchester Courier* founded

1840

1845   *Manchester Examiner* founded

1860

1865   Manchester becomes national HQ of Typographical Association

1868   *Manchester Evening News* founded

1870

1871   *The Tissue* founded by Edward Hulton 1

1873   *The Tissue* becomes the *Sporting Chronicle* Withy Grove works opened by Edward Hulton 1

1880

1885   *Sunday Chronicle* founded by Edward Hulton 1

1886   *Manchester Guardian* and *Manchester Evening News* new building, Cross Street

1890

1894   *Manchester Examiner* closed

1897   *Manchester Evening Chronicle* founded by Edward Hulton 1/2

1899   *Daily Mail* nightly newspaper train from London

1900

1900   *Daily Dispatch* founded by Edward Hulton 2 *Daily Mail* Manchester publishing, Gorton

1901   First newspaper trains from Manchester

1902   *Daily Mail* published from Deansgate site

1904   *Manchester Courier* bought by Northcliffe

1909   *Daily Sketch* founded by Edward Hulton 2 (Manchester & London publishing) *Daily News* Manchester publishing

1910

1916   London *Evening Standard* bought by Edward Hulton 2 *Manchester Courier* closed

1917   *Empire News* (formerly *The Umpire*) bought by Edward Hulton 2

1920

1923   E.Hulton & Co sold by Edward Hulton 2 to Beaverbrook, who strips out the *Evening Standard* and sells the remainder to Rothermere

1924   Rothermere sells Hulton empire to Camrose and Kemsley who form Allied Northern Newspapers, headquartered at Withy Grove

1927   *Daily Express/Sunday Express* Manchester publishing at Great Ancoats Street

1928   *News Chronicle* publishing at Derby Street *News of the World* published on same presses

1929   Withy Grove remodelled and enlarged by Allied

1930

1930   *Daily Herald* and *People* Manchester publishing at Odhams, Chester Street

1937   Kemsley acquires Camrose shares in Allied

1938   New *Daily Express* building opened at Great Ancoats Street

1940

1940   *Daily Telegraph* Manchester publishing at Withy Grove *Sunday Times* Manchester publishing at Withy Grove

1943   Allied becomes Kemsley. Withy Grove named Kemsley House

1950

1954 *Daily Sketch* joins *Daily Mail* stable

1955 *Daily Dispatch* closed

Daily Mirror and *Sunday Pictorial* Manchester publishing at Withy Grove
Sunday Chronicle merged with *Empire News*

1959 Thomson acquires Kemsley. Kemsley House renamed Thomson House
Manchester Guardian renamed the *Guardian*

1960

1960 *News Chronicle* closed; printing of *News of the World* transferred to Thomson House. *Empire News* closed

1961 *Guardian* London publishing at Gray's Inn Road Manchester Guardian and Evening News Ltd gains control of *Manchester Evening Chronicle*

1963 *Manchester Evening Chronicle* closed

1964 *Guardian* editor moves to London
Daily Herald renamed the *Sun*
Sunday Times stops Manchester publishing

1965 *Daily Mirror* facsimile printing in Belfast from Manchester
Typographical Association merged with London Typographical Society to become National Graphical Association (NGA) headquartered at Bedford

1968 *Scottish Daily Mail* published from Manchester

1969 *Sun* relaunched by Murdoch, Manchester production stops
People printed on *Daily Mail* presses

1970

1970 *Daily Mirror* Belfast plant destroyed by IRA bomb
Guardian and *Manchester Evening News* move from Cross Street to Deansgate. Presses shared with *Daily Mail*

1971 *Daily Sketch* merged with *Daily Mail*

1974 *Scottish Daily Express* published from Great Ancoats Street

1976 *Guardian* starts facsimile printing from London; live Manchester production halted

1978 *Daily Star* launched at Great Ancoats Street

1980

1983 *Sporting Chronicle* closed

1985 Maxwell acquires Withy Grove.
News of the World publishing halted.
Daily Telegraph publishing halted (December 31)

1986 *Daily Telegraph* facsimile printing from London to Trafford Park (Jan 1)

1987 *Daily Mail* publishing halted at Deansgate
News on Sunday launched and closed

1988 *Daily* and *Sunday Mirror* publishing halted at Withy Grove. Facsimile printing from London to Oldham
North West Times launched and closed
Post launched and closed
Sport launched

1989 *Daily Express* and *Daily Star* publishing halted Great Ancoats Street

END

Press barons and Manchester **A chronological list**

John Edward Taylor 2	Owner of the *Manchester Guardian* and *Manchester Evening News* at the time of growing national newspaper interest in Manchester. Made C.P.Scott editor of the *MG* in 1872
Edward Hulton 1	Founded the *Sporting Chronicle*, the *Sunday Chronicle* and the *Manchester Evening Chronicle*. Created Withy Grove, the country's largest newspaper print centre
Edward Hulton 2	Founded the *Daily Dispatch* and the *Daily Sketch*. Acquired the *Empire News*. Developed Withy Grove as a publishing centre for annuals and books as well as newspapers. Transferred the head office of E.Hulton & Co to London before the First World War. Sold E.Hulton & Co to Beaverbrook in 1923 for £6 million
Edward Hulton 3	Used inheritance from E.Hulton & Co to acquire *Picture Post,* which became the leading photo-news weekly. No direct links with Manchester
Northcliffe	Set up nightly newspaper trains from London to Manchester in 1899 for distribution of the *Daily Mail* throughout the North West. Published the *Daily Mail* in Manchester from 1900. Bought the *Manchester Courier*. Deansgate became the company's second centre
C.P.Scott	However untypical of the species, Scott became a press magnate in 1907 when, by raising £247,000 (including £37,000 of his own) he acquired the *Manchester Guardian* after protracted negotiation with trustees of the late John Edward Taylor's estate. The *Manchester Evening News*, which had also been owned by Taylor, was bought separately in the 1920s. The Scott Trust was formed in 1936 when John Scott renounced all financial interest in the company to avoid paying punishing death duties after the sudden demise of his brother Ted
Beaverbrook	As a neighbour of Edward Hulton 2 facilitated the ailing Hulton's sale of his company (taking Hulton's London *Evening Standard* as his prize). Launched northern editions of the *Daily Express* and the *Sunday Express* in a converted Great Ancoats Street warehouse, 1927. Opened the purpose-built "Black Lubyanka" *Daily Express* offices and printworks on the same site in 1938, similar to buildings in Fleet Street and Glasgow
Rothermere	Acquired E.Hulton & Co from Beaverbrook in 1923 then sold it on to Kemsley & Camrose at a reputed £1.8 million profit
Kemsley	Together with his brother Camrose acquired E.Hulton & Co from Rothermere. Made Withy Grove the nerve-centre and registered office of Allied Northern Newspapers. Redeveloped and enlarged Withy Grove. Brought the *Sunday Times* to Withy Grove in 1940. In 1943 gained full control of Allied, renamed Kemsley. Closed the *Daily Dispatch* in 1955 to make press space for a contract to publish the *Daily Mirror* and *Sunday Pictorial*. Merged the *Sunday Chronicle* with the *Empire News*. Sold Kemsley, including the whole Withy Grove site, to Thomson in 1959

Camrose	Brought the *Daily Telegraph* to Withy Grove in 1940, contract-printed by Kemsley
Cadbury family	Stop-start publishing of *Daily News*/ *Daily Chronicle*/*News Chronicle* in the North, continuous in Manchester from 1928-1960. Closure of *News Chronicle* meant transfer of *News of the World* to Withy Grove
Thomson	With 1959 acquisition of Kemsley became reluctant owner of Withy Grove. Closed *Empire News* (1960) and washed hands of *Manchester Evening Chronicle* (1961) to focus on contract printing, but maintained *Sporting Chronicle* until 1983
Laurence Scott	(Scott Trust) Grandson of the great C.P., became managing director of Manchester Guardian & Evening News Ltd in 1948. Responsible for dropping Manchester in the masthead (1959), starting London printing (1961) and closing the *Evening Chronicle* (1963). "Retired" after abortive attempts to merge the *Guardian* with the *Times* (1966) and the *Observer* (1967)
King/Cudlipp	As IPC directors brought *Daily Mirror/Sunday Pictorial* to Withy Grove in 1955. Acquired *Daily Herald* from Odhams in 1960. *Herald* relaunched as the *Sun* in 1964, sold to Murdoch in 1969
Rupert Murdoch	Relaunched *Sun* as London-only tabloid in 1969 edited by Larry Lamb, poached from Deansgate. No interest in Manchester, but opened print centre at Knowsley and took share in Trafford Park Printers
Victor Matthews	(Trafalgar House) Launched *Daily Star* from Great Ancoats Street in 1978
Robert Maxwell	Acquisition of Mirror Group in 1984 forced new regimes at Withy Grove, which he bought from Thomson Organisation in December 1985. Closed WG in May 1988 along with live publication in Manchester of *Daily* and *Sunday Mirror*
Eddy Shah	Confrontations with the NGA at Stockport and Warrington in 1983 led to revolution in Fleet Street and Manchester. His *Post*, launched Warrington November 1988, lasted a few weeks
David Sullivan	Porn king, successfully launched the *Sport* in 1988
Richard Desmond	Porn king, acquired Express Newspapers in 2000 and has overseen transfer of production back to the North (Broughton)

Manchester's principal newspaper offices

The 1896 Ordnance Survey map shows the offices' proximity to four mainline rail terminals:
London Road (Piccadilly), Victoria, Exchange and Central

1 Cross Street

Manchester Guardian 1886-1959
Manchester Evening News 1886-1970
Guardian 1959-1970

2 Derby Street

News Chronicle 1928-1960
News of the World 1928-1960

3 Chester Street

Daily Herald 1930-1964
Sun 1964-1969
People 1930-1969

4 Great Ancoats Street

Daily Express 1928-1989
Sunday Express 1928-1989
Scottish Daily Express 1973-1980
Daily Star 1978-1989

5 Deansgate

Daily Mail 1902-1987
Scottish Daily Mail 1968-71
Daily Sketch 1954-1971
People 1969-1988
Guardian 1970-1976
Manchester Evening News 1970-to date

6 Withy Grove

Sporting Chronicle 1873-1983
Sunday Chronicle 1885-1955
Manchester Evening Chronicle 1897-1963
Daily Dispatch 1900-1955
Daily Sketch (Daily Graphic) 1909-1954
Empire News 1917-1960
Sunday Graphic 1927-1955
Sunday Times 1940-1964
Daily Telegraph 1940-1985
Daily Mirror 1955-1988
Sunday Pictorial (Sunday Mirror) 1955-1988
News of the World 1960-1985

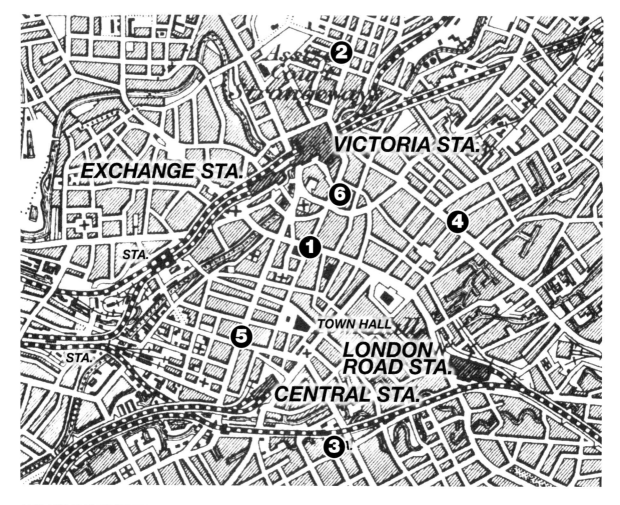

Editions published from Manchester

The four principal *Daily Telegraph* nightly editions from Manchester in March 1985. Nationals shared newspaper trains and road services. Sunday newspapers editionalised more heavily

The table below shows scheduled transport departures (times for vans leaving newspaper offices were typically 20 minutes earlier)

23.30	Eire air service
	Ulster air service
	Carlisle road service
23.45	Victoria Station-Scotland
	(incl Euston-Inverness link at Preston)
00.35	Victoria-Newcastle, Darlington
00.42	Piccadilly Station-Shrewsbury,
	Oswestry, Hereford
00.45	Victoria-York, Scarborough, Hull
00.50	Victoria-Penrith
01.00	Ashbourne road service
01.20	Piccadilly-Doncaster, Barnsley, Grimsby
01.25	Victoria-Chester, North Wales
02.10	Piccadilly-Sheffield, Gainsborough
02.15	Victoria-Huddersfield, Leeds
02.22	Victoria-Bradford
02.28	Victoria-Lancaster, Carnforth, Barrow
02.30	Chester road service
02.50	Piccadilly-Crewe, Stoke-on-Trent
03.00	Leyland road service
03.15	Victoria-Southport, Wigan
	Burnley road service
03.28	Victoria-Liverpool,
	Birkenhead
03.30	Surridge Dawson
	Manchester No 1
03.35	Victoria-St Helens
03.45	Victoria-Blackburn
	Suburban road services
04.30	Isle of Man air service
	WH Smith Manchester
	Surridge Dawson
	Manchester No 2

Withy Grove to Deansgate via Cross Street

There is no definitive account of the Hulton Manchester publishing empire. We must rely, for the early years at least, on what amounts to word of mouth, passed down between generations of employees. Ned Hulton had started life as a *Manchester Guardian* compositor before being sacked for a bit of private enterprise and then founding, in 1871, what became the *Sporting Chronicle*. His son, Sir Edward Hulton, proprietor of the *Daily Sketch*, the London *Evening Standard* and the *Sunday Chronicle* among other dailies and Sunday papers, received a baronetcy two years before his early death in 1925. The third Edward Hulton, educated at Harrow and Oxford, with a penchant for Russian princesses, was to found *Picture Post* in 1938 and Eagle comic in 1950. The Hulton Archive, based on the celebrated *Picture Post* archive initiated by Tom Hopkinson, is the one extant reminder of the Hulton name. All the same, the third Edward Hulton's nephew is none other than Sir Jocelyn Stevens, the former *Daily Express* managing director beloved of *Private Eye*. Stevens played a typically controversial role in the Express Newspapers' Manchester operations during the 1970s.

It is indeed notable that the city where national newspapers chose to publish was also home both to the *Manchester Guardian* and to E.Hulton & Co of Withy Grove. Other provincial cities published dailies, even Sundays, but other cities had not given birth to a morning newspaper renowned throughout the world, or to what was to become Europe's largest newspaper printing office. The arrival of the nationals and their interaction with indigenous titles makes the story of Manchester newspapers in the late nineteenth and early twentieth century a complex mosaic. So let's begin near the beginning.

Ned Hulton's job with the *MG* back in the 1860s involved making up the contents bills supplied each weekday to newsagents. On the side he started a racing form sheet distributed to pubs, clubs and illegal backstreet bookies. It was hardly surprising that, when discovered, he was summarily dismissed (the *Guardian* eschewed racing coverage until the 1960s). Undaunted, Hulton persuaded a Manchester cotton merchant, E.O.Bleackley, to back him, buying a small press in a cellar off Oldham Street. There, Hulton published *The Tissue*, a one-page paper of handicaps and results accepted as gospel by the racing fraternity. It was to become, through mutation, the *Prophetic Bell* and then, by April 1873, from new premises at Mark Lane, Withy Grove, the *Sporting Chronicle*. The paper's size and scope had extended to interests like hare-coursing, shooting, dog racing and pigeon fancying. In a splendid affirmation of the workingman's lifestyle (as quoted in a 1953 bookmakers' magazine by Teddy Dawson, a journalist at Withy Grove for 50 years and whose father, another Edward, was a compositor with Hulton from the start) the *Sporting Chronicle* of the time promoted "our popular series of anti-teetotal articles, giving the mawworms of society no quarter." Was Ned Hulton taking a side-swipe at the principled young C.P.Scott, who became editor of the *Manchester Guardian* on New Year's Day 1872?

Other provincial cities published dailies, even Sundays, but other cities had not given birth to a morning newspaper renowned throughout the world, or to what was to become Europe's largest newspaper printing office

Soon Hulton had added the weekly *Athletic News*, offering mainstream cricket and football reports as well as athletics coverage, while the *Sporting Chronicle* built up a readership throughout the North, the Midlands and further south. It was in effect Manchester's first national newspaper, the racing fraternity being as interested in events at Exeter as at York or Musselburgh.

Dawson recalls that part of the paper's appeal came from a direct involvement with sporting events of any shape or size, and with the bets which inevitably accompanied them:

"We reported everything of sporting interest from pitching pennies into a pint pot, a popular public-house pastime, ring-throwing, darts and air-gun shooting.

"Editors in those days were the stake-holders for many kinds of wagers, such as billiards, hop step and jump, one-legged races and knur-and-spell contests, and as reporters acted as the referees the sporting journalist needed to be a versatile fellow indeed." Journalists obviously inspired more trust then than they do now.

The *Manchester Evening Chronicle*, whose sister paper was the north-only *Daily Dispatch*, was head-on competition for the *Manchester Evening News*

Overleaf: A presentation panel indicating the strength and self-esteem of the "night companionship" – the Manchester Typographical Society compositors employed by E. Hulton & Co on the *Sporting Chronicle*, the *Daily Dispatch*, the *Sunday Chronicle* and the weekly *Athletic News* at New Year 1906, not long after the first Edward Hulton died

FRATERNAL GREETINGS from the NIGHT COMPANIONSHIP 1905-6.

T. STINTON. L. RYAN. F. M. ASHWORTH. J. C. TAIT. W. WEDGWOOD. J. WOOD.

W. CLAPHAM. W. LOWE. T. V. HOWELL.

S. JOHNSTON. C. H. TOWNLEY. F. HILL. T. DAWSON.

H. WAY. W. STRONG. J. BASTIN.

P. WALLACE. J. READY.

C. OLDHAM. J. COPE. F. ALDHOUSE. R. W. HUGILL.

J. CRAWFORD. G. PROSSER (Clerk). F. S. ROBERTS (Father). C. J. CAREFULL.

F. HOBSON. T. DODSWORTH. J. BENNETT. W. KIRTON.

E. WILLIAMS. J. SIMPSON. J. BILL. J. DIGGLE.

G. WILLIAMS. WILLIAM K. MACKAY. J. T. FLETCHER.

T. EVEREST. F. C. DODGSON. W. G. TAYLOR. W. A. HAYDOCK. P. NICHOLSON. E. RIDGWAY.

B. PILLING. G. R. WALKER. W. D. RUSSELL.

W. R. HILES. J. B. STEAD. T. ARCH. I. N. VICKERS. T. K. SETTLE.

T. HANLEY. H. BIRD.

H. HANLEY. J. CONWAY. J. DICK. W. LANCASHIRE. H. W. THORNE.

W. H. ACKLAND. S. JONES. W. BROWN.

W. J. SMITH. A. MORLING. E. C. BELL. J. PEEK. T. ROSE. COJEEN.

H. FOX.

SPORTING CHRONICLE, DAILY DISPATCH, SUNDAY CHRONICLE, ATHLETIC NEWS
MANCHESTER.

So was the Hulton empire born. In 1885 the *Sunday Chronicle* appeared, to be edited with a national remit by the social reformer Robert Blatchford, who wrote under the nom-de-plume of Nunquam. He, along with A.M.Thompson (Dangle), Hubert Bland (Hubert) and E.F.Fay (The Bounder), set about creating a substantial newspaper whose views were not necessarily those of their proprietor. Blatchford was to found the Socialist weekly, *The Clarion.* In 1897 the *Manchester Evening Chronicle* was launched as a direct competitor to the *Manchester Evening News*. By then, Hulton's son Edward was involved. He, too, oversaw the 1900 launch of the *Daily Dispatch*, a half-penny daily aimed at a broad northern readership. Withy Grove also published an increasing number of popular weeklies, monthlies and annuals marketed on the back of the newspapers. It was becoming a very confident operation.

A couple of hundred yards away, just the other side of Market Street, the world of the *Manchester Guardian* was an astonishing contrast. We know a lot about it thanks to the punctilious research and exemplary descriptive style of the late David Ayerst, the former *Guardian* journalist and historian who, during the 1960s, was taken back on staff for six years to write the official biography, "*Guardian.*" An act of contrition by the Scott Trust, then currently overseeing the wholesale transfer to London? Perhaps, but the *Guardian* has ensured that its history, with all the creativity and controversy that accompanied it, is open to those seriously interested. The Guardian Archive is to be found in the John Rylands University Library of Manchester, which holds the correspondence of C.P.Scott along with much else. Researchers will soon discover that Ayerst was first to the cherry-picking.

As Ned Hulton was pouring his energies into developing Withy Grove in celebration of the common man, Scott turned for commercial impetus to George Binney Dibblee, a Fellow of All Souls (having tried, without success, to lure three other Oxford men). Dibblee joined the *MG* in 1892, aged 24, after a few months' work experience on the *Scotsman* in Edinburgh. In Ayerst's charitable view, Dibblee proved himself "thoughtful, if too sanguine." One of his first tasks was to cost the idea of a North Wales edition: the *MG* was already considering ways to break out of its Manchester-Lancashire circulation area and the North Wales coast was considered good Liberal territory. What seems to have been forgotten was that Welsh loyalties, then as now, were to Liverpool. Dibblee's costing, written on the inside of a folded one-sheet A4 letter to Scott, assumed an annual profit of £350 on a North Wales circulation of 8,000 daily compared with only 600 in 1892 (and an estimated 4,500 sold by Liverpool papers across the Dee). On this slim projection the edition was launched, adding only 2,000 to *MG* circulation and losing £562 in 1893 and £76 in 1894. It was hardly the answer; a later initiative in the direction of Stoke-on-Trent was dropped. The *MG's* owner, John Edward Taylor, got more badly burnt by the *New Weekly*, an attempt at

The Guardian has ensured that its history, with all the creativity and controversy that accompanied it, is open to those seriously interested

radical popular family journalism launched in January 1894, much the same time as Hulton's weekly *Ideas*; it had lost over £10,000 when it folded in May 1895. Dibblee compounded its problems by trying to enter the London market and calling himself "managing editor", assuming editorial responsibilities.

Hulton obviously worried the *MG* – as much in the staff likely to be tempted away from Cross Street as in the proliferation of titles – but rumours surrounding Harmsworth's *Daily Mail* caused Dibblee, as early as December 1897, to offer Scott costings for a new halfpenny paper aimed at taking the competition head-on. It was an even more desultory exercise than the North Wales edition. Again on the inside of an A4 sheet in a letter to Scott from Edinburgh, Dibblee projected selling 30,000 copies of an 8-page paper produced by an editorial team of six, including two sub-editors. The editor would be paid a princely £600 per annum. There's no evidence that Scott or Taylor took the proposition seriously. When the *Daily Mail* eventually arrived by overnight train from London in the autumn of 1899 it was Hulton who was preparing to launch against it – the *Daily Dispatch*, which would certainly have seen off the half-penny Cross Street effort. Ayerst goes further in concluding that such a launch could have put the *Guardian* itself at peril. The *Dispatch* hit the streets early in February 1900, a few days after the *Daily Mail* began printing in Manchester. State-of-the art quadruple Hoe presses installed at Gorton were an indication of Harmsworth's intentions: by 1902 he had opened the Deansgate office from where, with sundry extensions and alterations, the *Daily Mail* would be published for 85 years.

Just before Christmas 1899 Dibblee wrote to Scott, who was in Rome: "The *Daily Mail* competition is not terrifying at all, in fact I like the interest which rivalry throws into the business… I had a curious proof last week of the direct harm it has done to our circulation, which I had only surmised before. Twice during the last weeks the DM train has been late and immediately demands come in for us from the newsagents with the comment that they can sell a great many more *Guardians* when the *Mails* do not arrive. You see, for some people we are already become the second paper."

Dibblee estimated that the *Daily Mail* was, even before Manchester printing selling twice as many copies as the *MG* in its limited Northern circulation area. However, he comforted himself with the "inevitable" death of the *Manchester Courier*, a rival Manchester morning. He was proved wrong there, too, since Harmsworth acquired the *Courier* in December 1904 to further his own political ends with Balfour and Churchill. It was never a serious competitor, or serious propagandist weapon, despite having Nicol Dunn of the *Morning Post* brought from London to edit it, and was killed off by Associated in 1916. However, the *Manchester Guardian*'s net daily circulation dropped from 48,756 in 1898 to just over 46,000 in 1900 and to 43,500 in 1901 – hardly a healthy sequence, and one which Dibblee sought to explain by criticising, to Scott, the paper's Anti Boer War stance.

Taylor had himself written to Scott just before Christmas 1899, also worried about the future: "I am to some extent relieved to see that you are really becoming alive to the new condition of things which is developing in the keen competition which is near upon us. I sincerely hope that you will tackle the many defects which exist in our organization and let us at least make the best defence of our position which we can." Of such frustrations are editors' lives made up, even if your name is C.P.Scott and you are conducting one of the most-celebrated campaigns in press history. Readers interested in the War of the Taylor Succession, as Ayerst calls it, should track down his book, sadly out of print like so many other press monographs.

But what of the *Daily Mail*? Harmsworth, soon to become Northcliffe, had the sense to send to Manchester his assistant and all-round hard man, the journalist Kennedy Jones, to take charge first of the makeshift printing operation in Gorton, and then of the move to Deansgate almost three years later. The Gorton press was constructed in the former Tank School built for children of workers at the nearby L&NWR wagon facility. Together with an assistant called McRae, Kennedy Jones pioneered two-centre transmission by devising a code system which allowed London to wire page headings and positions. The Hoe presses mentioned by Dibblee were fed by ten linotype machines, the Ottmar Mergenthaler invention allowing automated setting of lines or slugs of metal from a 90-character keyboard which would be the industry standard throughout Manchester's national newspaper years (according to a later *Daily Mail* account, two of these linos were amongst the first 50 ever made). Years afterwards, the floor of linos producing the *Daily Mirror* and *Daily Telegraph* at Withy Grove was claimed to be a quarter of a mile long. Manchester became very important to Linotype and Machinery Ltd, who opened their European assembly and repair works at Altrincham.

Harmsworth intended the eight-page northern *Daily Mail* to be an exact replica of the London edition, simply using the advantage of printing in Manchester to promote its claim to be the first truly national newspaper. Newspaper trains from Manchester started in September 1901, carrying copies of the *Daily Mail* along with the *Manchester Guardian*, the *Daily Dispatch* and the *Sporting Chronicle* to Yorkshire. The elaborate distribution network described in a later chapter was under way. But, of course, the *Mail* did not remain editorially static. The temptation of being first with northern news and opening a dialogue with northern readers proved irresistible. A *Daily Mail* promotional article of May 13 1912 recalls the process:

"A new era was inaugurated in British journalism when in February 1900 The *Daily Mail* began publication of a special Manchester edition. The remarkable feature of this was that it gave its North of England readers the complete London *Daily Mail*, with all the national news.

"This system of special editions has now been vastly extended and developed

Harmsworth intended the eight-page northern Daily Mail to be an exact replica of the London edition, simply using the advantage of printing in Manchester to promote its claim to be the first truly national newspaper

The *Manchester Guardian* building, Cross Street, in 1902 at the time C.P.Scott's son John took over as commercial manager

until the *Daily Mail* is today publishing from its offices in London and Manchester no fewer than eight separate and distinct local editions, each of which contains the complete London edition with two pages of additional local news – eight separate local newspapers, in fact, which are supplied to our readers in the various districts for the price charged for the London *Daily Mail*.

"These editions are as follows: Greater Manchester, Liverpool, Lancashire, Yorkshire, North Wales, Birmingham and the Midland Counties, Staffordshire, West of England, and South Wales."

It seems that the two-page Midlands edition was printed in Birmingham; the report gives no clues on the printing of the West of England and South Wales editions. So the *Mail* was already editionalising for Liverpool, Lancashire and Yorkshire from its Deansgate offices.

An example of local involvement was published in the *Daily Mail* of December 19 1912, giving results of a poll in which over 5,000 Manchester readers took part, vying for ten prizes of £5. They were set 20 questions, but only ten had to be answered so that all might get a fair chance to offer considered opinions. And what a prudish lot they proved. Their top verdicts (counted strictly by numbers): No Mixed Bathing (in corporation swimming pools); No More Picture Palaces; Clubs Must Close at Public-House Times. But, and here's the softener, No Whist Drive Prosecutions. Mixed Bathing was a highly controversial subject; 1,522 voted against, 1,177 for. Among comments: "yes, under proper supervision"; "no, woman is everywhere, let man rest somewhere." Readers voted decisively against more picture palaces – 2,547 to 166 – and almost as strongly against drinking clubs opening beyond pub hours – 2,759 to 302. But those supporting whist drives outnumbered those against by 1,685 to 376. Were they ever illegal?

The city's best-known person turned out to be Bishop Welldon, Dean of Manchester. He won a comfortable 1,500 majority over Robert Peacock, the chief constable. Readers felt, the *Mail* reported, that: "he is as popular in the street as in the pulpit. He has always a cheery word for his friends of all classes, and is specially liked by the lorry drivers and 'nippers' and tramway servants. Recently he became a 'Buffalo'. In his desire to find out how workers spend their lives he descended a coal pit at Pendleton."

If the concept of a London daily plus a local paper did not survive, tacking on a bit of local colour in the form of what amounted to an advertising come-on became a favourite pastime. In 1968, for instance, the *Daily Mail* published a weekly "North West Extra" of which, according to the blurb, "Readers are demanding to see more often; rivals are envious; and advertisers are clamouring for space." The northern editor of the time, one Larry Lamb, told *Campaign,* the advertising industry weekly: "It has quickly established itself as a good local ad medium. It pays very well for us as it doesn't cost anything to produce" (there's honesty for you). In the twilight of Manchester publishing the *Guardian* carried a page or two entitled News of the North, while the *Daily Telegraph* celebrated its 1986 move to Trafford Park with a weekly supplement called Looks North.

Manchester merited a bit of attention. Addressing 800 guests, mainly Associated staff, gathered in the Free Trade Hall for lunch on Sunday May 21 1921 to celebrate the 21st anniversary of *Daily Mail* Manchester publishing (it was held on a Sunday so that night-workers could attend), Northcliffe himself, already a sick man not much more than a year from his death, had this to say (as reported in the next day's *Mail*):

"We are very proud of our success in coming to the greatest business centre of the assemblage of nations called the British Empire, and being able to establish ourselves with such very able and efficient people as are to be found in Lancashire.

"We are very proud of our success in coming to the greatest business centre of…the British Empire, and being able to establish ourselves with such very able and efficient people as are to be found in Lancashire"

"When we came here we were told that there were too many newspapers, and, what is quite true, you have one of the most distinguished newspapers in the world, as well known in Europe and the United States as it is in this city – the *Manchester Guardian*. (Applause.)

"We were told that it would be better to pack up our traps and go home, but we stayed, and we give you warning that not only are we not going away, but that we are enlarging our premises very rapidly, and in the course of a few months shall have installed machinery in this town to meet the demands we are getting from Yorkshire, Lancashire, Northumberland, Durham, Cumberland, Westmorland, Derbyshire, Cheshire, Staffordshire, Shropshire, Scotland, Wales and Ireland, which are all served from this city. (Applause.)

"We hope we shall be able to drive home some of our ideals for national improvement, national economy, increased production, farm produce and all the other campaigns we wage every day." (Applause.)

Northcliffe had tailored his speech for what he thought was the local audience, throwing in North Country colloquialisms like "jannock" and "gradely" which must have confused Mancunian print-workers, embarrassed journalists and shocked the organisers (food by Messrs J. Lyons, decorations by Messrs Harrods). Yet as a commitment to Manchester publishing at a time of national downturn – "last year was the worst year we ever had", Northcliffe admitted – it could hardly have been stronger. Manchester was always an opportunity, never a problem, for both Northcliffe and Beaverbrook.

The *Daily Mail* espoused and marketed modernity – motor-cars, aeroplanes, ideal homes, and the wonders of newspapers themselves. It also, of course, espoused the monarchy. In a report of July 15 1911 the *Mail* elaborated to northern readers how it had spared no effort to bring them, the morning after

Patent medicines and health cures were a staple advertising source for Hulton

the ceremony, "a complete record in pictures" of the Prince of Wales's investiture at Carnarvon.

"The ceremony did not commence until half-past two on the Thursday afternoon, and Carnarvon is 108 miles by railway from Manchester. Pictures of the early morning scenes and of the arrival of the guests were despatched by motor-car to Bangor, and then by ordinary train. The real struggle against time began with the arrival of the King and Prince.

"For the despatch of the later photographs a special train was chartered to leave Bangor at 4.50 p.m., and a fleet of motor-cars brought the photographs from Carnarvon to the train. The plates were hurriedly developed on board the special as it dashed along at fifty miles an hour. Manchester was reached at 7 p.m., and the work of making the blocks was carried out with such rapidity that the pictures of the ceremonies were in the edition of the *Daily Mail* on sale in places as far distant as Belfast and the north of Scotland."

Thus the advantage of Manchester production.

Across town, Hulton was certainly not marking time. A colour brochure, published about 1912, marvels at the majesty of Withy Grove.

"In the world of modern industry there is no higher example of organized effort than that which is needed in the making of a great daily newspaper. Yet even more wonderful is the enterprise which has brought into existence such a vast and complex newspaper publishing business as that of E.Hulton & Co. Ltd..... In no other office in the Kingdom will one find such an extensive installation of printing plant.... An organization of the magnitude of E.Hulton & Co. Ltd. not only has a large staff of reporters, prepared to rush off at a moment's notice to any part of the Country, to take the speech of a cabinet minister or investigate a mystery or crime... Across the corridor from the editorial rooms is the wire room...... On a busy day Manchester staff will receive as many as 120,000 words from London... The private wire stretches the whole 200 miles between Manchester and London, and is one of the most marvellous achievements of telegraphy... Just imagine! It can deliver two messages in Manchester while it is transmitting one to London... The capacity of the printing room is 624,000 twelve or sixteen-page papers per hour, or 1,248,000 four-page or eight-page papers per hour. The paper travels through the machines at the amazing speed of 800 feet per minute...."

And so on. But Manchester beware. The brochure accentuates Withy Grove's efficiency at being on the receiving end from Fleet Street. Edward Hulton had more than a premonition of the contract print centre Withy Grove was to become.

"On a busy day Manchester staff will receive as many as 120,000 words from London...
The private wire stretches the whole 200 miles between Manchester and London, and is one of the most marvellous achievements of telegraphy..."

Manchester's newspaper dynasty

The Hulton family grave is to be found in Brooklands Cemetery, near Sale, South Manchester. For an Edwardian tombstone the grey and pink marble freestanding edifice is not particularly imposing. The grave shows no sign of recent tending. It holds the remains of Edward Hulton, the founder of E.Hulton & Co, who died at his home, Oakfield House, Ashton-on-Mersey, on March 28 1904, aged 65; of his wife Mary, who died at Monaco in March 1912 aged 72 and was interred at Brooklands later that month; and of a nephew, Lt Edward Hulton Taylor, killed in action at Flanders during the First World War. It also bears a memorial to James, the Hultons' eldest son, who died at Oakfield House on January 20 1889, aged 25.

All graves tell a story. Let us try to read this one. The Hultons were a tight-knit, god-fearing family, Catholics as it happened but not the sort to sprinkle cherubs or Virgin Marys around. Their fortunes were already substantial by the time James died. Oakfield House was a long way in social terms from the Hulme terrace where Ned Hulton, the former *Manchester Guardian* compositor, was born. But Hulton was more interested in developing his business than in flaunting his wealth: he might easily have moved to Bowdon or Alderley Edge by the turn of the century. His widow was happy enough to seek the solaces of the Côte d'Azur. The early death of James left the way open for their second son Edward to take over from his father. Brooklands offers no sign of this Edward, Sir Edward Hulton Bt, who died at Leatherhead, Surrey, in 1925, or any subsequent Hulton. By then, like Withy Grove and Manchester, the grave had been left behind.

Ned Hulton, the patriarch, had passed effective control of his empire to Edward by the turn of the century. His legacies, apart from the magnificent Withy Grove site and a booming business, were a deep involvement in sport

The patriarch. Edward Hulton 1, founder of Withy Grove. Right: the young Edward Hulton 2 is seen standing beside his father and his sister

and sporting events, a loyal (and largely Catholic) workforce, a strong visual ability (that applied to all three Hultons), a conservative view of the world (not always reflected in the *Sunday Chronicle*) and straightforward commercial nous. He had created two national titles, the *Sporting Chronicle* and the *Sunday Chronicle,* without showing any interest in leaving Manchester. His son was to change all that.

Perhaps the best clues about Sir Edward's motives are to be found in "When I was a Child", the short autobiography which his son, the third Edward, published in 1952. Born 1906 in Harrogate, Edward Hulton the third was brought up in semi-rural Surrey and fashionable London surrounded by the full panoply of butlers, footmen, chauffeurs, maids, governesses and tutors. He called his father Dada, his mother Mama, his nurse Nana and his maternal grandmother Gaga. He was never to meet his Hulton grandmother. Mama refused to go north after his birth. Edward describes how Mama thought civilization began south of the Trent though Dada, throughout his life, "remained at heart a Man of the North." Among many sporting interests (he bred horses at Newmarket, winning the Derby and the Oaks in 1916 with Fidelia) Dada was captain of Royal Lytham & St Anne's golf club "but Mama considered St Anne's, no less than Blackpool itself, like all Northern institutions, not only bleak but barbarous." Even so, Dada stayed a keen patron of northern institutions like the Waterloo Cup.

From the perspective of 1952, and taking a few liberties with history, Hulton wrote: "Dada and his father were both stern disciplinarians inside The Office. I remember hearing that grandfather, though a benevolent and, on the whole, easygoing man, unlike his wife, would not countenance smoking at Withy Grove, the great building (still the largest newspaper office in the world), which he had erected on the site of the shed he had built when a penniless boy. On one recorded occasion he encountered a leading journalist upon the back stairs leading to the lavatories. 'You have a pipe in your mouth!' he observed severely. The great journalist rejoined: 'Did you expect me to have it in my bottom?'" This story does not tell us whether Ned Hulton was prepared to accept such backchat, even from leading journalists.

We learn from the book that "in earlier years, my father spent a good deal of his time at The Office at Withy Grove, in Manchester. This distressed Mama, who gradually persuaded him to make the headquarters of his papers at Shoe Lane, off Fleet Street." It's hard to put a date on this. When Hulton launched the *Daily Sketch* on March 15 1909 as a picture paper rival to the *Daily Graphic* the leader page offered three addresses – 118 Fleet Street; Mark Lane, Manchester; and Boulevard des Italiens, Paris. London? Paris? Sheer bravado, perhaps. In the two-week pre-launch dummy phase northern stories outnumber southern ones by a margin, while advertisers also have a strong northern bias. But only three years later, in April 1912, when the

Sketch scooped other dailies in its coverage of the Titanic tragedy, there were separate London and Manchester editions. By 1914 the *Sketch* lists its London headquarters as Shoe Lane. So it seems likely that Hulton's own switch to the capital took place in the years before the First World War. In 1916 he underlined his London credentials by acquiring the *Evening Standard*.

Reporting to the Royal Commission on the Press 1947-49, the managing editor of Kemsley's Manchester operations said that *Daily Dispatch* leaders had been written in London "for a long time" before Allied's takeover in 1924, but that the practice had reverted to Manchester under Kemsley. In other words, Edward Hulton was controlling the policy of his north-only morning paper from his London office. The enormous Kemsley empire was more relaxed in this matter.

Something of the balance of manpower between the two Hulton offices, and the strength of various departments, can be read from the war memorial to employees who died in the First World War – a memorial which is found today near the entrance to the Printworks, the former Withy Grove complex. The roll of honour lists four London office journalists, two photographers, three from the accounts department, a cashier, a works man, a reader, two compositors, six from the engraving department, three machine room men, an engineer and twelve from publishing, or some 36 in all. The Manchester office is remembered for eight journalists who gave their lives, along with four employees from the advertisement department, three from the accounts department, two compositors, two from engraving, eight from general printing, an engineer, 31 from the machine room, five from stereo, 24 from publishing and two cleaners – or 90 employees in all. London was the head office, Manchester the powerbase.

Now, Edward Hulton the third's childhood appears to have been extremely fulfilling, and his father, in love with a beautiful, vivacious society woman, was no doubt right to follow her where she was happiest. The London move concerns us only in its implications for Manchester. Hulton was a natural entrepreneur, with his eyes open to opportunities London brought along. So far as Manchester is concerned, the *Daily Sketch* was his final half-fling. Editors of the *Daily Dispatch*, the *Sunday Chronicle*, the *Sporting Chronicle*, the *Evening Chronicle* and the *Empire News* had to learn to deal with an absentee boss, one moreover who was coming under the spell of his friend and neighbour at Leatherhead, Lord Beaverbrook. The families intermingled, socialising with the Duff Cooper set. Through Beaverbrook, Hulton met Bonar Law, Lloyd George and Churchill. Political compacts were passed on to his editors. Hulton's first interests remained in the turf, and in coloured prints – his was said to be the finest private collection in Britain.

A Manchester consultant had diagnosed Bright's Disease for Hulton back in 1907, giving him six months to live then. He died, aged 56, on May 23 1925 after long illnesses. Beaverbrook accorded him front page treatment in the

Mama and Gaga (Edward Hulton 3's mother and grandmother) with Tiny. Below: Edward Hulton 3 with his sister Betty in 1917. She was to die shortly after giving birth to Jocelyn Stevens in 1932

next morning's *Sunday Express*. His tribute, heading the leader page, was simply titled 'EDWARD HULTON' by Lord Beaverbrook. He wrote about his neighbour as a reserved, perhaps too reserved, man who found it hard to make friends but held true friendship sacred. He would "observe rather than hold centre stage." He examined issues thoroughly before taking a decision, which would then be "backed by an iron will and carried through implacably."

Beaverbrook most admired the courage Hulton showed in his final illness. "The wit and humour which he displayed in the face of the inevitable was most remarkable. It is not easy to look at death with clear eyes."

Beaverbrook concluded rhetorically. "Was he a great man? In character and ability 'Yes' – in actual fruition 'No'; His body failed him just as his mental powers were reaching maturity... He died too young to hold the place to which his greatness entitled him."

History must think otherwise. Northcliffe was much the same age as Hulton when he died; critics might question Northcliffe's sanity, his methods and his personal behaviour, but not his greatness. Northcliffe also lived with illness, his energies increasingly sapped. Hulton was denied greatness by lack of judgement. Beaverbrook's obituary mentioned the *Evening Standard* in passing, but said nothing about the Withy Grove empire Hulton had inherited, added to – and thrown away. Beaverbrook could afford to be generous in praise of Hulton's human qualities. Two years earlier he had concluded a £6 million deal to buy Hulton out, which allowed him to assume control of the *Evening Standard* for nothing by passing E.Hulton & Co minus the *Standard* on to Rothermere at the same price. It seems Beaverbrook, the apparent true friend, had taken advantage of being the only press baron Hulton would deal with. Northcliffe had seen it coming. Six months before his own death in 1922 Northcliffe told one of his editors "Watch Beaverbrook. He is swallowing Hulton. Hulton will be absorbed. I can see it. Beaverbrook has him hypnotised" (as quoted by S.J. Taylor in 'The Great Outsiders'). Then Rothermere quickly took his cut (with the full approval of Beaverbrook) by selling the Hulton concern minus the *Daily Sketch* and the *Illustrated Sunday Herald* to the Berrys for an estimated £7.8 million.

The ticket put a full value of around £10 million on the business, say £400 million at today's prices. Allied Northern Newspapers, the company set up by the Berry brothers after the deal, was soon offered the *Daily Sketch* – which Rothermere had judged no competition for the *Daily Mirror* – and the *Illustrated Sunday Herald*, a London paper Hulton had started in 1915 and which merged with the *Sunday Graphic* in 1927 and later printed in Manchester. Allied added a string of provincial titles. Allied was to post profits of around £1 million a year in the late 1920s. That would value it conservatively at around £650 million today.

Pears soap advertisements were schemed in pre-launch editions of the *Daily Sketch*

In such a fashion was Edward Hulton, just 17 at the time of the deal, deprived of his birthright (he inherited £2 million at a later date; Jocelyn Stevens, whose mother Betty, Edward's sister, died in childbirth aged 22, received £1 million on his majority). Withy Grove became a provincial print-centre. The Hulton family newspaper empire, so substantial, so confident and so profitable, had been dissolved after barely half a century of existence. It was a tragedy.

There was another matter. Because, according to A.J.P.Taylor, Edward had been born out of wedlock, the Hulton baronetcy, created only in 1921, died along with his father. Taylor recounts in "Beaverbrook" how, at his neighbour's suggestion, Hulton had pledged his newspapers' support for Lloyd George in the 1918 General Election over dinner with the prime minister at Downing Street, also attended by Beaverbrook and by Rothermere, who committed the *Daily Mirror*. In return, Lloyd George promised, Rothermere would become a viscount, Hulton a baron. George V apparently baulked at the Rothermere nomination, which was then backed up by Bonar Law. But the most the monarch would award Hulton was a baronetcy. Hulton concurred on the understanding that the title be remaindered on his son. This commitment was conveniently overlooked by Stanley Baldwin, prime minister in 1925 when Sir Edward Hulton Bt died. The murky world of Realpolitik had judged the not-so-clever Man of the North. For his part, C.P.Scott declined political honours offered by Lord Rosebery in 1895, by Lloyd George in 1921 and by Ramsay MacDonald in 1924 and 1929. He knew better.

Hulton's son and "heir" eventually received a knighthood of his own. Despite inheriting just one third of a knock-down deal he had enough in his piggy-bank to buy and develop one of the most important and influential magazines of the century, *Picture Post*. Its radical views were not particularly to his taste, and eventually led to the departure of Tom Hopkinson, his oustanding editor, after which the weekly went into a decline hastened by the arrival of television news. Its residue, the Hulton Archive, now part of Getty Images, is a priceless image bank of contemporary history.

Some day the history of the Hulton dynasty may be written. It will prove hard to rank the three Edwards. Ned, the grandfather, a Manchester compositor from a humble background, had the foresight and drive to start his own sporting papers, paving the way for the biggest regionally-based publishing operation in Europe at Withy Grove. Sir Edward Bt, his son, added daily and Sunday titles, established a Fleet Street office, and created what might have become a national empire to rival Rothermere or Beaverbrook. His grandson, Sir Edward, showed the most imagination of the three but operated in the more restricted arena of periodicals. The difference between the Hultons and other press dynasties is not that their creative genius was flawed but that it survived fully three generations.

Annuals, produced by the general publishing arm at Withy Grove, were a long-running moneymaker. These examples were used by the payments department to mark up contributors' fees

Hulton's *Sporting Chronicle*: a journalist remembers

Until the First World War at least, the Hulton Withy Grove culture represented a Manchester in stark contrast to the earnest world of Scott's Cross Street. It, too, was a Manchester which attracted top journalists from around the country, and which looked far beyond the confines of the city. The best account of this period comes from 1953 by Edward (Teddy) Dawson in an article for *Banyan*, the official organ of the National Bookmakers' Protection Association. Dawson, as mentioned in Chapter 1, was writing from retirement after half a century as a journalist on the *Sporting Chronicle*, where his own father had started work as a compositor in the 1870s. Ned Hulton is referred to here as 'Mr Hulton'; his son as 'Sir Edward'. Dawson offers us a unique glimpse of the relaxed but demanding Hulton hands-on style, of the people attracted by it, and of the perils attached to front-line sports writing.

The article is worth quoting at length, caustic asides and all.

"In racing 'Kettledrum' has always been the nom-de-plume of the leading writer in the *Sporting Chronicle* and the earliest I can remember was William Vickers who, I believe, also owned race horses. William Stinson was an early Racing Editor (his son Fred was well known in the North later as a racing reporter) and John Hulton, a cousin of the late Sir Edward, was a very entertaining writer on racing and racing personalities.

"Others who followed on as 'Kettledrum' were T.W.Gale, a bluff Newcastle man who was also well known in boxing circles, and at one time a great friend of Dick Burge, Charles Warren, a charming writer who was lured from the *Sporting Life* by Mr Hulton at what was then a princely salary of £12 per week. Then followed Willie Standring, who graduated from sparkling reports of Association football and coursing. Willie Standring never believed in gossip and only recorded the impressions of what he himself saw. As 'Donald' he brought a new journalism to coursing which replaced the former stilted style of the expert.

"On the course he had a wonderfully keen eye for race reading. His style would now be labelled old-fashioned, but while he was not a lucky tipster there was much to be learned from his comments on running.

Edward Hulton 2 was an avid sportsman. He was captain of Royal Lytham & St Annes Golf Club; his greyhounds won the Waterloo Cup in 1908 and 1916; and in 1916 his horse Fidelia won both the Derby and the Oaks

"It may have been just before Standring's time that Mr Hulton secured the services as 'Kettledrum' of the Hon. Francis Trevelyan, who came from a Midland family, but was first under notice as the New York correspondent of the *Sporting Chronicle*. I fancy a rather early death put an end to this very versatile and brilliant writer.

"In the meantime Jimmy Park, a slightly-built fresh-faced youngster, had come to the office from Edinburgh, and after gaining experience he became "Gimcrack" of the Sketch when that paper was first taken from Manchester to London."

Dawson then cast his professional eye back to editors:

"Following the death of the first Editor under whom I served, Mr W.H.Mountsey, came Mr J.A.H.Catton. He was a versatile writer of Cricket and Association football, and a universally acknowledged authority on those sports, but I do not think his heart was ever in Racing. As he himself said, he came from a family of preachers. His successor was Mr W.L.Sinclair ('Chick'), an Edinburgh man and a most prolific writer on sport of all kinds, for he could turn out a daily article on almost any sporting topic with his chief leanings towards Rugby, golf and professional and amateur running. Old peds will recall 'Chick' Sinclair's candid comments on professional running and his yearly visits to Powderhall.

"He was succeeded by Dick Reading, a young Birmingham journalist who captured the heart and the imagination of the late Sir Edward, who made him the youngest editor I can recall, and he might have been in the Chair to this day had not the war intervened. He volunteered his services to Britain, but was not accepted. He thereupon joined the League of Frontiersmen, but that association did not appeal to the authorities and he went over to Belgium and served the Army there. He was wounded very badly in the very early days of the German invasion of that country, having both legs smashed. After a partial recovery he could not settle down in Manchester again and went to Australia, where his death at a comparatively early age was due to the drain of his vitality by war wounds."

Dawson goes on to offer an insight into how the *Sporting Chronicle* developed in tune with a changing society:

"From the early 1890s the *Sporting Chronicle* rapidly increased in popularity and circulation as a penny paper; the Saturday edition was a particularly fine production, and all the sub-editor-reporters had each to contribute a column on one of their pet subjects. There were no real specialists in those days; we were expected to tackle anything in the way of writing.

"Still the character of the paper, while making racing its chief interest, gradually changed, for the police banned some of the old-fashioned sports, and the claims to cricket and football became stronger. Once upon a time the

"From the early 1890s the Sporting Chronicle rapidly increased in popularity and circulation as a penny paper; the Saturday edition was a particularly fine production, and all the sub-editor-reporters had each to contribute a column on their pet subjects"

whole back page on a Monday was devoted to what were called the minor sports at the grounds, but some passed out of favour, knocked out by the law or public opinion.

"The authorities even began to frown on boxing. For a long time, the word 'fight', as frequently used now in newspapers, was banned. It had to be called 'contest' and there must be no mention of side stakes in a match. This also applied to professional bowlers who always advertised a match as a cup. I think the same cup was used over and over again.

"Trotting, once a very popular pastime, fell upon evil ways like professional running, mostly ruined by 'the gaffers." Well, the boys had to have their sport, and so their ideas were turned to other channels, like the dogs, but whatever came along the *Sporting Chronicle* saw to it that the new sport had fair play."

Finally, Teddy Dawson turns to his own role in the early days:

"I suppose I must have been considered a useful hack to stay so long with the firm, as neither Mr Hulton senior, nor the late Sir Edward, kept idlers around. At the age of 17 I was attending Old Trafford and saw W.G.Grace a few times in the days of the captaincy of Mr A.N. (Monkey) Hornby. My first race meetings were Burgh-by-Sands on Solway Firth and Cark-in-Cartmel on Morecambe Bay before 1900, and in that year I had a west country trip which took in Devon and Exeter, Dawlish and Bridgwater meetings.

Shoe Lane, Hulton's London office, in 1917

"Sometimes most of my winter was taken up with professional billiards and I have refereed long matches played by John Roberts, Teddy Diggle, W.H.Stevenson, W.Cook junr, Charles Dawson, Billy Mitchell, Joe Mack and many others, and I once took charge of a public house game which I knew privately was for 'a monkey' aside." (*Special thanks to Ted Grey, Teddy Dawson's grandson and wire-room man at the Daily Mail and Daily Express, for this account).*

Neville Cardus, whose writing on cricket and music was to make him one of the best-known journalists of the century, had a different perspective of Manchester. In his autobiography he noted that as an 18-year-old, around 1908, "I often performed a ritual known only to myself. I would go and stand at the corner of Cross Street and Market Street, opposite the *Manchester Guardian* building. I would look at the lighted windows and imagine that behind any one of them Montague was at work on a dramatic notice; that Agate was putting a finishing touch; that Samuel Langford, greatest of all writers on music, was meditating on Brahms over his desk."

Two worlds, two hundred yards apart: who would have believed, in 1908, that the *Manchester Guardian*, as the Guardian Media Group, would end the century a major power in British publishing with E.Hulton & Co long forgotten?

Daily Sketch launch – dummy editions and launch issues

The launch of the *Daily Sketch* on Monday March 15 1909 was preceded by two weeks of dummy editions. These are to be found on microfilm at the British Library Newspapers, Colindale. A selection of headlines, picture subjects and advertisements taken from these dummy issues and listed below suggests that – although the Sketch boasted a London (and Paris) address, as well as a Manchester one, in the first "live" edition – its powerbase was Manchester. Eclectic topics, national and international, are leavened by local interest – and picture availability.

The dummy editions reflect an (unhealthy?) Edwardian obsession with the new woman's demeanour. The article "Should Ladies Ride Astride?" is repeated several times as a make-weight (not unusual in dummies), followed up by a picture of Ladies riding Astride in Rotten Row. An article "Why Girls should not play Hockey", also used on several occasions during the dummy period, was printed in the first "live" issue of March 15 but was followed, only a week later, by a report and three pictures of a women's county hockey match at Brooklands, near Manchester, where Lancashire beat Cheshire 9-1.

The editors also indicated a particular interest in events in Berlin; with immigrants or so-called aliens; and with suffragettes. The Berlin sequence of the first dummy issue, March 2, includes a story on nudism (but no pictures of the marching schoolgirls).

The first dummy is dated Tuesday March 2 1909

Front page
BY-ELECTION IN SCOTLAND
Forfarshire & Glasgow district

Page 3
London 118 Fleet St, Manchester Mark Lane
Weather – all over country
Leader – What is wrong?
"We are becoming a flabby race. We are not the men our fathers were.." etc

Page 4
Shrove Tuesday football at Ashbourne, Derbyshire – picture
German stories:
RED TAPE RUN MAD
A German rival to our War Office
German Foreign office ˋ

CLOTHES TABOOED
Colony for People who do not Dress; Schoolgirls' Parades
Page 6
Revolving staircase for Railway Station - picture of the Paris Metro
Feature:
SHOULD LADIES RIDE ASTRIDE?
Space for Wincarnis, Pears soap ads etc (but no ads as yet)

No 2 Wednesday March 3
Page 7
THE EVER-OPEN DOOR
More Aliens and a Woman who had some Russian Jews from St Petersburg
SITTING ASTRIDE IN ROTTEN ROW – picture

Page 10
Cockermouth Beagles in Buttermere – picture
Page 12
STOCKPORT WINDOW CORRECTED BY PRINCE
Prince of Wales noticed a problem with his Coat of Arms when he opened a stained glass window in his honour at Stockport Town Hall. Now corrected!

No 3 Thursday March 4
Front page
WELCOME HOME OF THE US FLEET
Page 14
First real-looking ad – HP Sauce

No 4 Friday March 5
Front page
SUFFRAGETTES TAKE AN ACTIVE PART IN TWO SCOTTISH CONTESTS
Page 5
"Have a coffee" movement to make the Beverage Popular in England
Page 9
"ABODE OF LOVE"
BISHOP TO UNFROCK PIGGOTT

No 5 Saturday March 6
Front page sub-title
The ALL-PICTURE MORNING PAPER
SALOON SMASHER IN MANCHESTER (with picture)
Miss Carrie Nation addresses Hulme meeting
Page 2
UNEMPLOYED CENSUS AT MANCHESTER NIGHT SHELTER
(Wood Street Mission, *Daily Sketch* flashlight photo)

No 6 Monday March 8
DOCK DAM BURSTS AT
BIRKENHEAD
Page 7
Birkenhead Dock disaster 14 drowned!
Negro owes his life to premonition
of disaster
First almost full page of ads
TRILENE – ALL FAT PEOPLE CAN
BE CURED BY TAKING "TRILENE"
REDUCING TABLETS
Phospherine – The Greatest of all
Tonics, the Remedy of Kings
"Room to Room" Patent Cinder Shifter
Daily Sketch Gift (offer)
Early Morning – Goring-on-Thames
By B.W.Leader RA
Free at 63 Baker Street or send 4d
stamps for postage anywhere in the
world but reader has to fill in name
and address
SHOULD LADIES RIDE ASTRIDE?
(reprise)

Quarter page promotion for the
Sunday Chronicle
Appeals to:
The Ordinary Man & Woman
The Social Re*former*
The Politician
The Athlete
The Investor
The Amateur Gardener
The Sportsman
The Man Who Keeps Fowls

Front page of the first *Daily
Sketch* dummy edition, preserved
as a fragment at Colindale. The
edition improbably leads on
Scottish by-election contests

No 7 Tuesday March 9

Ads for: Billiards at Home
Chivers Jellies
Ju-Vis Beef Tea
I cure catarrh
Dainty Jewellery
Page 3
DECORATED BY THE KAISER
Fr Rita Sacchetto, an opera singer
Picture spread:
Young England at play: Eton College
steeplechases

No 8 Wednesday March 10

Page 4
PICTURE BIBLE CAUSES
SENSATION IN BERLIN
Page 5
JEW'S HORRIBLE END
Hermann Cohen, a Jewish
moneylender, 30, found battered
and dying by friends at Harold
Street, Sunderland
Page 6
MRS NATION AT THE
MANCHESTER REFORM CLUB
SEEKING TO DISCUSS THE
LICENSING BILL

No 9 Thursday March 11

Page 4
Picture of murdered money lender
outside his Sunderland terraced house
MR CHURCHILL'S HOUSE HUNT
ENDED: picture of Queen Anne's
Gate. Churchill to be neighbour of
Grey and Haldane
FAMOUS ACTOR SPEAKS FOR
SUFFRAGISTS
SNOW CARICATURE OF GERMAN
CHANCELLOR
WHY GIRLS SHOULD NOT PLAY
HOCKEY

Front page of the launch issue. Note the changed masthead and much more newsy use of pictures

Daily Sketch launch issues
A few tasters of the launch after two
weeks of dummies:

Monday March 15 1909
Leader – CHEER UP!
Cartoon of the globe sitting for his
portrait by the *Daily Sketch*: "Here
you are sir. All your features faithfully
portrayed. Look towards me, if you
please."
Page 14
WHY GIRLS SHOULD NOT PLAY
HOCKEY
WHAT OTHER NATIONS ARE
DOING WITH WAR MOTORS

SOME MODES OF TOMORROW
Page 16 – back page
The New All-Picture Morning Paper
Daily Sketch welcome snapshot of
Buxton Station
London – 118 Fleet St
Manchester – Mark Lane
Paris – 32 rue Louvre le Grand
Boulevard des Italiens

Wednesday March 17
Launch of *Daily Sketch* Bon Marché
Form for the Private Advertiser:
Bargains, Seaside & County,
Gardening, Tuition

Tuesday March 23
THREAD KING'S DAUGHTER
MARRIES MARQUIS TODAY
Miss Lillian Maud Coats and the
Marquis Douro, heir to the Duke of
Wellington
Women's hockey report plus
pictures:
Lancashire 9, Cheshire 1 at Brooklands

Wednesday March 24
SHACKLETON'S EXPEDITION TO
THE SOUTH POLE, GETTING
WITHIN 120 MILES
Front page and centre spread
pictures

Thursday March 25
SHEEP DOG TRIALS AT BELLE VUE
Military airship passing over Berlin –
picture – with Prince Henry of Prussia
on board

Friday March 26
SCILLY ISLAND FLOWERS

Ode to the British Indian Excluded from the Transvaal

From the *Sunday Chronicle*, January 19 1908, page one

We have planted Faith & Freedom -
Though they swore they didn't need 'em –
In the breasts of Boer & Bushman & Babu,
So Britannia is their mother,
And you plead, as man and brother,
If they're loyal to the Empire, so are you!

You're a countryman of Ranji's
From the region of the Ganges,
And we feel some perturbation at your shout
That it's not Imperial cricket
When they clap the alien ticket
On your back, and from the Transvaal kick you out,
Kick you out,
When your brothers of the Empire kick you out.

Are you put the pointed query
Is our Freedom but a theory
Or are British subjects one Imperial kin?
We evade that awkward question
With the delicate suggestion
That you've got a little defect; it's your skin
That's your sin
Many people have the colour of your skin.

We are Brothers – in a manner,
Under one illustrious banner,
But, dear Brother, let us whisper in your ear,
All those Colonies resplendent
Are so jolly independent
That they snub us if we care to interfere,
You must clear!
For they warn us that we mustn't interfere!

In our homes at Bow or Putney
We enjoy the spicy chutney
And the tea and silks you send us o'er the foam;
We're an Empire democratic,
But the Cape is most emphatic
Crying 'let the Asiatics stay at home – stay at home,
You are free beneath the flag – to stay at Home!'

Newsreel link to the *Daily Sketch*

All three Hultons combined an unusual visual awareness with an instinct for exploiting the media potential of the image. Edward Hulton the first, a compositor by trade, did not need to employ a typographer when he started *The Tissue*, the racing sheet which became the *Sporting Chronicle*. His grandson Edward, as proprietor of *Picture Post*, presided over the innovative and celebrated photographic weekly which defined the bounds of photojournalism in the late 1930s and 1940s. Edward Hulton the second, the most entrepreneurial of the three, founded the *Daily Sketch* as a picture-paper to rival the *Daily Graphic* and *Daily Mirror* as well as creating a whole series of pictorial annuals around his newspapers. When, after the First World War, he acquired the British newsreel producer Topical Film Company, he cunningly tied in events coverage to *Daily Sketch* promotions.

Luke McKernan, film archivist and historian, writes:

"Newsreels were a regular feature of cinema programmes between 1910 and 1970. Among the first to be established was Topical Budget, formed in September 1911 by the Topical Film Company. The bi-weekly newsreel was take over by the British government in 1917 and operated as a propaganda reel. It came under the management of Lord Beaverbrook's Ministry of Information, and it is likely that Beaverbrook indicated to his friend Edward Hulton the advantages of adding this new form of visual news-telling to his existing news empire when the company was offered for sale in February 1919.

"Hulton purchased the company and put members of his newspaper companies on the board of directors. The newsreels had their original inspiration in illustrated newspapers such as the *Daily Sketch* and Hulton became the first to demonstrate how the two media could operate profitably alongside each other.

"Hulton remained in charge of Topical Budget until his death in 1925, though ill-health lessened his involvement after 1923. The years 1919-1923 were the most vital and creative of Topical Budget's history. Hulton built strong links between the newsreel and his *Daily Sketch*, with cameramen and photographers going on the same assignments. Newspaper and newsreel held a common interest in light, visual news,

Edward Hulton 2 tied ownership of the Topical Budget newsreel company into promotion for his *Daily Sketch*, as in the 1922 stunt followed at length in the Sketch to create a star out of a "shop girl from Brixton." The girl, Margaret Leahy, is seen here with filmstar Norma Talmadge (left) at the start of a US tour. It was not particularly successful. although Talmadge, Buster Keaton's wife, did her best to help

with a particular emphasis on royalty and sport (Topical had the exclusive rights for the filming of the FA Cup Final 1921-1923).

"The newsreel featured *Daily Sketch* competitions, and between September 1922 and August 1923 it was known as the *Daily Sketch* Topical Budget. This creative cross-media ownership was emulated by Beaverbrook, who acquired a half-share in the Pathe Gazette newsreels during the 1920s, and paved the way for subsequent newspaper/newsfilm ownership, including the part-ownership of British Movietone News by the *Daily Mail* (through Rothermere) in the 1930s, and the more recent media empires of the Murdoch era. Topical Budget continued after Hulton's death until 1931. Its film library is now owned by the British Film Institute."

For details of Luke McKernan's book "Topical Budget" see page 215.

The world of Sam Marsh

Sam Marsh is 94. He started work in the publishing room at Withy Grove as a 14-year-old in 1924, the year after Edward Hulton sold his business. He finished there in 1975 when he retired. His father James had begun in 1895, at the age of nine, delivering the one o'clock edition of the *Evening Chronicle* to local pubs, eventually retiring in 1953. His uncle Charles started a year after his father and retired in 1955, aged 69. There was also his cousin Harry, another publishing room stalwart, who went to the Bury branch office, his youngest brother George who defied family traditions and chose the machine room to put in a life's work, and a nephew who eventually made the publishing room. Three generations of Marshes spent a combined 250 years of their lives in and around the hospitable confines of Withy Grove, principally in a publishing room where work methods and practices remained little changed throughout.

The language was domestic but the reality industrial. The publishing room (actually a warehouse space) revolved around tables, or benches, where newspapers arriving on an Igranic belt from the machine room were counted by quires, split into bundles, packed, labelled, tied and delivered to the vans waiting outside. A speed operation involving a splitter, two packers, two tiers up and a doorman working in teams. A demanding job when three or four titles were running in parallel, particularly on Saturday nights. Plenty of pressure when, often as not, production was behind schedule and van drivers impatient to dash for the newspaper trains. Today it is largely automated.

Sam Marsh says he "enjoyed every minute" of his Withy Grove life. He means it. He loved the routine, the comradeship, the sense of feeling part of a big organisation, always with something to do. The Hulton mix, embraced by Allied, involved morning and evening newspaper publication alongside weeklies, monthlies, annuals and paperback books. General publishing formed half of Withy Grove's production, unlike other newspaper offices. Sam

clocked on by nine in the morning, packing magazines and books before preparing for the day's newspaper onslaught.

"Before I started work there I used to come down from Collyhurst every Saturday dinner time to take my father's lunch. I got to like the place so much that I thought 'this is me'.

"You were so busy all day long, on our own jobs. The only 'foreigners' we packed were the Argosy and the Quiver (printed at Withy Grove for other publishers). Pins and Needles, Toy Box Annual, Cherry Tree Books were all ours. Overall, in twelve months, we were doing 57 publications including seven Christmas annuals. There was never a slack moment."

But newspapers of course took priority. "As a boy you went through the whole rigmarole of publishing. You started what they used to call opening wrappers – the waste (white) paper to wrap the Evening Chronicle in. Then you were picking labels out, labelling them onto the white wrappers, marking them for the suppliers – quires and copies – and then they were laid out for the men on the publishing tables. You got to the stage where you knew where every label was all over the country. The Evening Chronicle was Lancashire, but we were picking labels for the Sunday Chronicle and the Empire News, as well as for the dailies, apart from the Daily Telegraph which used its own staff."

The Withy Grove of 1924 was a hierarchical world of its own, with personal status won little-by-little over the years. As the son of an overseer Sam had to be prompt and courteous. He ran errands for the men, brewing their tea and going for their lunch orders. His first bit of overtime – threepence for half an hour's work – was cleaning up the pump yard after the horses each

Sam Marsh played trumpet for many years in the *Evening Chronicle* Prize Band. He is seen here fifth from right in the second row on November 11 1926, just two years after he started in the publishing room at Withy Grove aged 14

evening. He followed orders to stay away from the general printing rooms where hordes of young women worked binding thousands of Cherry Tree Books destined for the British Empire.

Like every 14-year-old who joined in the mid-1920s, Sam was sent to a commercial college in Hulme. He was given a chance to learn shorthand and typing, which might have led to a career in journalism, "but I'm afraid I didn't do very well." He was content with the routines of the publishing room, which included Saturday afternoons coping with the football editions and Thursdays preparing for the week's racing.

"Thursday was a complete day of the Handicap book. They had two teams on that, or two staffs as they were known. The books – pocket-size for practicality – were brought down from the general printing department on what we called trucks. We came in early on Thursday mornings to pack them, though some people wouldn't get them until the Saturday. The *Athletic News* was printed on a Sunday afternoon."

Sam wasn't always an exemplar. Cautioned by an overseer for being late, he was hauled before his father who promised to wake him personally each morning. Then, he admits, there was a ready supply of reading matter. "Some of the books would come down from general printing in twelves or thirteens, tied up with a thin double twine by machine. They would pull one out and send the bundle back with a note 'one short in this'.

Sam served as a fireman during the Second World War. In 1950 he was promoted to be a night overseer. He returned to day work in 1958 until the *Evening Chronicle* folded in 1963, then went back onto nights until his retirement in 1975. He was asked to stay on for a couple of years, but declined.

Since then, as his friend and former colleague Albert Hartwell points out, Sam has hardly been away from the place. He soon became a leading light in the Withy Grove Fellowship which George Dunn, then managing director of Thomson Withy Grove, started in the mid-1970s as a focus for the increasing numbers of pensioners or redundant workers. From assistant secretary and secretary he was elected chairman, and remains vice-president.

So what does Sam think of the Printworks? He answers obliquely. "Well, it rather shook me at the time because I was always given the impression that a place like that could never close down. It seemed so permanent." All the same, he's best of friends with general manager Fred Booth, who often chauffeurs him to functions.

Longevity and service has its rewards. Sam has been a member of the Lightbowne Liberal Club (now social club), where he is of course president and still enjoys a pint, for an unprecedented 74 years. He's the role model for generations of former newspaper workers coping with a much-changed world.

"I told my daughter", he says cheerfully, "you've got a bit of a record for the parson to read when I go."

The Withy Grove of 1924 was a hierarchical world of its own, with personal status won little-by-little over the years. As the son of an overseer Sam had to be prompt and courteous

A Hulton discovers his legacy

He is the scion of the Hulton dynasty. He inherited enough to be dressed in satin as a young boy, with his own Rolls-Royce, his nanny, his cook and his priest. Yet his mother had died shortly after his birth, his father had absented himself, his uncle treated him with caution, he never knew his grandfather and his pretence to a newspaper empire was long gone. He had a deprived childhood.

Sir Jocelyn Stevens, the person who 'saved' the London *Evening Standard* in 1969, the managing director of Express Newspapers who launched the *Daily Star* from Manchester, latterly rector of the Royal College of Art and chairman of English Heritage, is in the process of unearthing Manchester roots for his autobiography. Emotions ran high in May 2004 when Stevens met members of the Withy Grove Fellowship, including Sam Marsh who started work at Mark Lane in 1924 – a year after Sir Jocelyn's grandfather, Sir Edward Hulton, sold out to Beaverbrook and some eight years before Stevens himself was born.

Jocelyn Stevens, great-grandson of Edward Hulton 1, meets Sam Marsh, aged 94, at the Printworks, May 2004

Stevens is an emotional man. He doesn't deny the apocryphal story of throwing a typewriter out of an upstairs office window during his *Queen* magazine days. "Well", he says, "Hultons were always throwing things. Grandpa had this stick with a gold knob. He hit all sorts of things, including a Louis XIV clock in the French Embassy which wasn't telling the right time." Legendary actions earned Stevens the *Private Eye* sobriquet Piranha Teeth during his Express Newspapers period.

Strong-tempered, he has also a strong sense of family history. While negotiating the move of the *Evening Standard* from Shoe Lane (Hulton's London headquarters) to Fleet Street to share the composing room with the *Daily Express*, Stevens found himself pitted against an FoC whose own grandfather had negotiated with his grandfather when Hulton acquired the *Evening Standard* in 1916 as a stable-mate for the *Daily Sketch*. The FoC proudly produced a leather-bound book containing minutes of that meeting. A deal was quickly concluded and all removed to the pub.

If history hasn't been particularly kind to the Hultons, Stevens concurs with the view that some blame must be laid at the shapely ankles of his Hulton grandmother, known in the family as Pom-Pom (but to her son Edward as Mama). "Grandfather spotted her in Puss-in-Boots at the Palace Theatre, Manchester. He said 'that girl's got great legs' and decided to marry her." Pom-Pom, red-haired, Irish and a wilful social climber, set her sights on fashionable London.

"She was a wonderful woman, but enjoyed everything that Grandpa couldn't bear. He didn't like London. He hated parties. Pom-Pom took his eye off the ball." She was principally responsible for the Hulton head office transferring from Withy Grove to Shoe Lane before the First World War. By the time she appeared as Britannia at a Royal Albert Hall 1918 victory celebration in a chariot drawn by six duchesses (she had hired the hall), her husband was ailing. Stevens admits that grandfather had other interests too, particularly his passion for dog and horse-racing. He employed different trainers at his stables, and kept his name off owners' lists even when he won the Derby and the Oaks within weeks in 1916.

The third Edward Hulton, who launched *Picture Post* in 1938 and turned it into a unique illustrated

Jocelyn Stevens knew her as Pom-Pom, Edward Hulton 3 as Mama. Her stage name was Miss Lindon, her christian name Millicent. Lady Hulton before her second marriage in 1928

weekly, had a very soft spot for his nephew. He was a surrogate father. "He looked after me for my first six years and I looked after him for his last six", Stevens notes. When Jocelyn left Eton at 18 Uncle Teddy built an extra floor on the house which he shared platonically with Diana Cooper at Hyde Park Gate. Down from Cambridge in 1955 without a degree, Jocelyn was offered a £4 17s 6d job on *Lilliput* before graduating to the letters page at *Picture Post*.

"I loved my uncle. He was an extraordinary person who lived an extraordinary eccentric life." But the moment came soon all too soon in 1957 when he decided that *Picture Post* should die. He resisted offers of millions to sell it. "Maybe he was right", says Stevens. Just 25 and ambitious, he was once again – in his view – denied his heritage.

So he turned to making *Queen* magazine an icon of 1960s uppercrust chic. His involvement with Express Newspapers lasted from 1968, when he became personal assistant to Beaverbrook's son, Sir Max Aitken, until 1981 when, as managing director, he was fired by Victor Matthews in the run-up to the group's flotation. Whatever his overall contribution to the fortunes of Express Newspapers, Stevens was – unlike most top newspaper executives – no enemy of Manchester. He was the man who brought the *Scottish Daily Express* south from Glasgow to Manchester in 1974 (pages 62-63, 191-193) and the man who launched the *Daily Star* at Great Ancoats Street in 1978 (page 192). Acts of business logic or family bias?

"I felt at home in Manchester because it was in my blood. I loved it. There was a warmth and straightness quite different from London, and different again from Glasgow where the unions seemed to want something more every day. I don't think we ever had a week of clear edition runs there.

"I used to say that the staff in Manchester came to work to work, and that many in London and Glasgow came to work not to work. My days in Manchester were a joy compared with the difficulties of London." Having persuaded Matthews to launch the *Daily Star* in Manchester, Stevens took the train north. "I called the unions together and said 'This is your chance. The only place we can produce the *Star* is here' We printed the paper when London unions wouldn't touch it. We launched it from Manchester, brought it down by train and distributed it off the platforms at Euston. After about three months I called in the London unions and told them they must be looking pretty stupid. London agreed to print southern editions of the *Star* edited and prepared in Manchester. When the *Daily Star* reached a circulation of one million copies a day Express Newspapers made a profit."

Uncle Teddy, Edward the third, died in 1988, the same year Maxwell closed Withy Grove. Not long before Stevens had made a sentimental visit there with his uncle. It was, amazingly, Sir Edward's first time in the building.

At the conclusion of his informal meeting at the Printworks with the Withy Grove Fellowship, Stevens volunteered a summing up speech. He told the retired newspaper workers sitting across the table, also visibly moved, that he had enjoyed "one of the best afternoons of my life." The Hulton scion had finally come face to face with his Manchester legacy.

"I used to say that the staff in Manchester came to work to work, and that many in London and Glasgow came to work not to work. My days in Manchester were a joy compared with the difficulties of London"

Marriages of convenience

The twentieth-century dynamism of the British press was created by outsiders, men from the wrong side of the establishment tracks. Outsiders share one ideal: to be recognised on the inside. For Britain that spelled Fleet Street. Manchester was always a means, never an end. From the time around 1910 when, as we have seen, Edward Hulton transferred his headquarters to London, only the *Guardian* had a Manchester head office. But it wasn't, strictly speaking, a national newspaper in those days. It became one by osmosis, a process of gradual change which saw 'Manchester' dropped from the masthead in 1959, London printing start in 1961, the editor, Alastair Hetherington, move south in 1964, Cross Street sold off in 1970 and "live" Manchester production stopped in 1976. Hetherington and his boss Laurence Scott were Fleet Street outsiders who sought to be insiders.

The outsider trail to Fleet Street began with the extraordinary Harmsworth brothers, the future lords Northcliffe and Rothermere, born in Dublin to a dreamy English schoolmaster with a drink problem. Max Aitken, the young Canadian tycoon and political pretender, then muscled in, soon to become Sir Max and Lord Beaverbrook. The Berrys, elevated as lords Camrose and Kemsley, were from Merthyr Tydfil where their father was an estate agent and auctioneer. A second wave of investor-invaders saw Roy Thomson, another brash Canadian, attack the British market via Scotland, his ancestral home. He, in turn, was consumed by Rupert Murdoch, the ultimate Australian adventurer. Robert Maxwell, the bouncing Czech, made his own largely irrelevant but damaging interventions. Then along came Eddy Shah. Despite his North West base, Shah had little interest in the Manchester newspaper scene. His outsider sights were set higher. Conrad Black, who acquired control of the *Daily Telegraph* from the Berry family, was another Canadian outsider. The new age of low-cost, non-union operations, brought David Sullivan and Richard Desmond, porn-again publishers: outsiders to be sure.

Outsiders craved titles. Like the beer barons before them, they used the best education money could buy to open society doors for their sons and heirs. The Hultons were no different. Ned Hulton's Hulme board school allowed him to start on the ladder as a printers' apprentice; his son Edward was sent to St Bede's College, the well-established Catholic independent day school in Whalley Range; his grandson Edward went to Harrow. The Hulton ascendancy showed all the characteristics of press baronets, with one important difference: they never really made it in Fleet Street. Edward the second may have transferred his personal office to Shoe Lane but his powerbase lay in Withy Grove. He lived a double life; his business and his preferment suffered.

Manchester's involvement with the Beaverbrooks, Northcliffes, Thomsons and Maxwells of this world was a marriage of convenience, one that could and would at be broken at some later date. But the dowry looked impressive.

Edward Hulton 2 with his neighbour Beaverbrook at Cherkley Court, Beaverbrook's Surrey home, 1917

Beaverbrook, always one for hyperbole, gave his first northern edition much the same editorial plug that he had given his friend, Sir Edward Hulton, in the obituary published less than two years earlier.

"The *Daily Express*", he wrote in a front-page signed panel for the debut northern edition of March 17 1927, "makes its first appearance in Manchester and the North, in Scotland and Ireland, owing allegiance to no political party, but ready to give credit and support to every honest cause in public life.

"It will bring to the North a doctrine of individual endeavour which will be congenial to a people who may be said to have inspired it. This spirit of enterprise and effort has permeated the policy of the *Daily Express* for many years past. The newspaper has always pleaded for the freedom of opportunity which will impose no handicap on any man in the race of life – but will allow great talents to rise from the humblest beginnings to the highest positions in the state."

So on and so forth. But the claim was spelt out again, more clearly, on the leader page: "The *Daily Express* is today a national newspaper in the fullest sense of the word and looks forward to what the future has in store."

Beaverbrook had opened his Manchester office in a converted Great Ancoats Street corset warehouse. It would be more than ten years before the new building, constructed on the same site, was completed. Arthur Christiansen, despatched to Manchester by Beaverbrook in September 1932 to give northern circulation a boost, recounts in his autobiography "Headlines all my Life" how Beaverbrook was once refused admission to his own Manchester office by a sturdy Lancashire commissionaire.

"But this is Lord Beaverbrook", said his secretary.

"Oh aye", said the commissionaire, "and you can tell Lord Beaverbrook that I'm Cecil Parkin" (the celebrated Lancashire cricketer).

"Give Parkin a bonus to reward his vigilance" said Lord Beaverbrook, who had never heard of Cecil Parkin.

And so was combat joined between Beaverbrook's *Express* and Rothermere's *Mail*. It was to continue, from a northern standpoint, until the two mid-market papers retreated to London in the late 1980s. Sixty years of sparring which, from a Manchester point of view, brought mostly bonus. It sadly saw the *Mail* absorb the *Daily Dispatch* and the *News Chronicle*, at least in title, and then the *Daily Sketch*.

Kemsley seemed to be different. Kemsley inherited Withy Grove in 1937 when he assumed full control of Allied Newspapers – a swap which gave his brother Camrose control of the *Daily Telegraph* and the *Financial Times*, but left the *Sunday Times* with Kemsley. Allied was renamed Kemsley in 1943, Withy Grove became Kemsley House and Kemsley detailed his son to keep

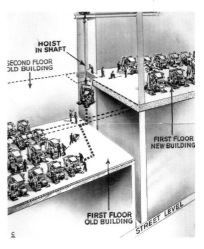

The *Daily Express*'s purpose-built northern headquarters, sister to the Black Lubyankas of Fleet Street and Glasgow and like them designed by Sir Owen Williams, opened in 1938. Contemporary illustrations show how the existing *Express* office, a former corsets warehouse, was rebuilt in stages so that nightly publishing carried on throughout the process. Linotype machines were hoisted up a floor as shown to make room for the double-storey print hall fronting Great Ancoats Street, dramatically illuminated by night (see page 55). Williams' building remains the strongest statement of newspaper publishing in Manchester

an eye on things in Manchester. Allied had already refashioned the building's Victorian frontage in 1929.

Kemsley House was the administrative centre of Kemsley's huge provincial empire stretching from Aberdeen to Cardiff. The *Sunday Times*, Kemsley's only national newspaper (apparently Camrose had wanted it, but judged that the value put on it by outside shareholders would be too high) printed in Manchester as well as London. Second World War newsprint rationing, which knocked papers down to an 8-page basic model, was partly offset by Camrose's decision to print the *Daily Telegraph* in Manchester in addition to London, starting November 1940.

Camrose, never known to set foot inside Withy Grove, nonetheless signed a leading article the day after the *Daily Telegraph* began printing there. He promised that normal service would be resumed for northern readers coping with late London editions since the war started (newspaper trains were affected by economy measures). He failed to mention the real reason: although Manchester was on Hitler's bombing list, Fleet Street was a more tempting target. It made sense to have an alternative print centre. In fact, Manchester frequently printed southern editions during the difficult war years. But once established, and with newspapers returning to a more normal size after the war, the northern editions of the *Daily Telegraph* began to take on their own life. It was an enhanced service which, as the *Manchester Guardian* started to lose interest in its home territory, offered increasing opportunities.

Kemsley treated Manchester as if it were his own. That's the verdict of living memory, people like Ken Martin, a former proof reader and NATSOPA chapel official. "I always had the impression that Kemsley was not a business person in the normal way. Kemsley did it for esteem. He was prepared to run the *Sporting Chronicle* year-in, year-out at a large loss."

Seen from the Fleet Street end, "esteem" was an expendable commodity. In 1958, when Kemsley began buying in shares to improve his personal stake and conducting negotiations behind his fellow directors' backs to sell to Roy Thomson, it hardly surprising that they were flabbergasted. Denis Hamilton, Kemsley's personal assistant from 1946-1950 and editorial director of Kemsley Newspapers until 1959, nevertheless hoped he might get a substantial payoff from his boss. Instead he was offered a photocopy of Thomson's cheque for £3.5 million, the down-payment on the deal. He got his own back. In his autobiography "Editor-in-Chief", Hamilton made this assessment:

"All the millions that Kemsley made did him no good.... From being a Lord of the press he became Lord Nobody, dying an old man, forgotten by the greater world, in a Monte Carlo hotel eight years later."

Lord Nobody, outsider to insider to outsider in one lifetime.

The first Manchester edition of the *Daily Express*, on March 17 1927 (left) carried a front-page message from Beaverbrook promising the northern half of Britain "a doctrine of individual endeavour." Scottish editions followed in the 1930s. By then, *Express* editors were using early fax machines to transmit page layouts like the one top left from London to Manchester and Glasgow

Hamilton survived a bad first meeting with Thomson to become editor-in-chief of Times Newspapers, appointing both Harry Evans to the *Sunday Times* and William Rees-Mogg to the *Times*. From the Manchester viewpoint it was downhill all the way. Withy Grove's *Sunday Times* printing contract was not renewed. Hamilton, like Thomson, had no interest in what they considered an obsolete plant. All the same, the *Sporting Chronicle* hung on until 1983.

Thomson was himself on the receiving end of Kemsley 'generosity'. Visiting the old man in his Gray's Inn Road office after the deal had been signed, Thomson undertook to look after staff and papers across the company (a hollow undertaking, it proved) then, as he recounts in his autobiography "After I was Sixty", he told Kemsley he would feel genuinely humble occupying his chair. Don't worry, Kemsley replied, it's my own chair and I'm taking it with me…

The Deansgate front entrance to Northcliffe House, home of *Daily Mail* operations in Manchester for 85 years. The original building, modernised and extended by the late 1920s in subdued art deco, was modest compared with the rival *Daily Express* headquarters

Just how hollow the promise was, and how vulnerable Manchester was becoming in the media power games of the early 1960s, is underlined by Thomson in his flippant account of the death of the *Empire News*, the Sunday paper published on a Saturday night at Withy Grove. The *Empire News* was never a Fleet Street paper, though it was a national of sorts whose circulation stood at 2.5 million in 1956 and in latter days had a South Wales edition printed in Cardiff. Thomson was concerned that the paper was losing money despite its 1.5 million circulation (what had happened to the other million copies?). So he "sold" it to Sir William Carr in exchange for a contract to print the *News of the World* at Withy Grove – "a very beneficial arrangement for us", wrote Thomson. A Sunday institution disappeared, along with the *News Chronicle* on whose presses northern editions of the *News of the World* had been printed. Ironically, the *News of the World* 25-year non-negotiable contract became a major loss-maker for the Thomson Organisation.

The death of the *News Chronicle* was not in itself a particularly bad blow for Manchester. Commitment of the Cadbury family to northern production had

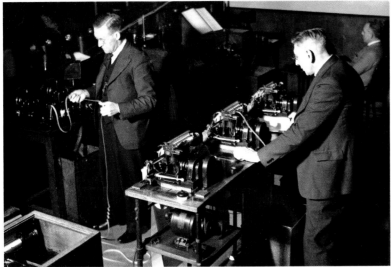

Top left: the Creed – or wire – room at the *Daily Mail* in the late 1930s. Creeds were teleprinter machines which helped assure the *Mail's* connections with London, as well as deliver wire services. In 1912 the *Mail* became the first newspaper in the world to adopt the Creed system of punching Morse code signals, making the whole nightly London edition available for simultaneous production in Manchester.
Top right: the *Mail's* art, or picture, desk in the 1930s.
Above: a Withy Grove tube room, where sheets or takes of copy were dispatched to the composing room.
Left: an early mobile darkroom, mostly used to transmit pictures of sporting events. The van had to be hitched up to a land line

been on-off. Their *Daily News* first arrived as early as 1907, the next London paper to print in Manchester after the *Daily Mail*. As a Liberal-leaning morning it should have been serious competition for the *Manchester Guardian*, but northern printing was suspended in the 1920s. By 1928 Cadbury had staged a return, setting up a plant in Derby Street off Cheetham Hill Road, helped by the *News of the World* contract. The expiry of this contract proved one of the factors in Lawrence Cadbury's decision to close the *News Chronicle* at both ends. The way he did it was devastating. Representatives of 11 unions (including the NUJ) were summoned to meetings in London and Manchester at 2pm on Monday October 17 1960. They were told: "production would start as normal in the London and Manchester case rooms, but moulds would be sent from the London and Manchester offices of the *Daily Mail* and substituted for moulds produced in the *News Chronicle* offices." What began the evening as the *News Chronicle* became the next morning's *Daily Mail*. The same thing was to happen when the *Star*, London's third evening paper, merged with the *Evening News*.

Cadbury justified his actions by saying that such secrecy helped the *Daily Mail* profit from the event and increased the sale value of the papers, at least £1.5 million of which would go to staff and pensioners. Not everyone was happy about the arrangement. H.J.Bradley, general secretary of the NUJ, wrote to Robert Willis, general secretary of the London Society of Printers, "There are numerous disturbing and,indeed, shocking aspects of the closure." True, but it happened.

Next in line came the *Daily Herald*. Supported by and linked to the union movement and the Labour Party, the paper had been the first to hit two million sales in the 1930s but, by 1960, its heyday was long past. Few read it, not even fellow newspaper workers and Labour voters. One Withy Grove chapel official suggested to a branch meeting that all members should be asked to buy the *Herald*. "You don't have to open it, just buy it" he told colleagues. Not a bad gesture for people used to getting their newspapers free.

The shenanigans over Odhams' efforts to dispose of the loss-making *Herald*; of Maxwell's failed bid; of IPC's acquisition and despairing relaunch of the title as the *Sun* in 1964; and of Murdoch's pouncing on the title – were all a London affair. Yet the net effect for Manchester was disastrous. It was agreed that the new *Sun* would not publish in the north; its editor, Larry Lamb, was headhunted by Murdoch from Manchester where he was an outstanding northern editor of the *Daily Mail*; and the new paper soon started to attack

Members of 21 Detachment B Company, 50th County of Lancs Home Guard being reviewed on parade by Lord and Lady Kemsley at Withy Grove – where they all worked – in 1944. Opposite: Queen Elizabeth viewing Blitz damage of Hulme, Manchester, in a 1941 *Daily Mail* picture passed by the censor but not published

Daily Mirror heartlands. The *Daily Telegraph* reported crocodile tears from Hugh Cudlipp "my principal regret is that (Murdoch) does not feel able to continue to employ the Sun's staff in Manchester. But I am fully aware of the economic problems with which he is faced", matched by those of R.W.Briginshaw, SOGAT joint general secretary "it is great news that the *Sun* can continue as a national newspaper, and all newspaper workers will welcome this. We are sorry that continuation of production in Manchester is not possible."

In other words, the London-led union connived at the deal, a deal which Cudlipp was to live to regret. Under Cudlipp, IPC had lost some £12.7 million on the *Sun* between 1964 and 1969 when it was sold to Murdoch for a mere £250,000. Murdoch's *Sun* was to change the face, as well as the economics, of British popular newspapers. Writing in 1973, Murdoch said: "I am constantly amazed at the ease with which I entered British newspapers."

Yet the bad days for Manchester began back in 1955 when the benign Kemsley agreed a Withy Grove deal with Mirror Group Newspapers giving the *Daily Mirror* and the *Sunday Pictorial* (as it then was) a 25-year northern print contract which effectively killed the *Daily Dispatch*, the North of England popular broadsheet founded by Edward Hulton in 1900. The *Dispatch* had a circulation of some 500,000, entirely printed at Withy Grove. It was believed the ageing presses could not cope with both the *Dispatch* and the Mirror. The *Mirror* management demanded a separate composing room, which the *Daily Telegraph* never had, and a former canteen on the floor was converted. It was a convenient excuse to do

away with the *Dispatch*, which like the *Daily Sketch*, the *Sporting Chronicle* and the *Manchester Evening Chronicle* (as well as the *Sunday Chronicle* and the *Empire News*) was said not to be profitable. Kemsley may have left them alone, even subsidised them as in the case of the *Sporting Chronicle*, but they remained vulnerable. The *Dispatch* vanished, its title incorporated into the *News Chronicle*, and then into the *Daily Mail* on the death of the *News Chronicle* in 1960. Many *Dispatch* journalists were employed by the new *Daily Mirror* operation.

Not for the last time, Manchester's fortunes were linked with Glasgow, Scotland's major publishing centre where Kemsley owned the *Daily Record*. Under a separate deal, the *Daily Record* was sold to Mirror Newspapers. The *Daily Record* became the Scottish version of the *Daily Mirror* in 1954, an issue which was to cause grief in the 1970s when the northern editor of the *Daily Mirror* launched a circulation drive in *Daily Record* territory.

On election night 1945 crowds witnessed Clement Attlee's mountaineering triumph over Winston Churchill via this State of the Parties display in a Withy Grove window (and the wall barometer shown on page 2). Cartoons were by the *Dispatch's* Butterworth

Next to go in Manchester was the *Evening Chronicle*. The Hulton evening paper, launched against the *Manchester Evening News* in 1897, retained a circulation of over 250,000, much of it in the Lancashire heartlands, and in the eyes of many was a better read than the *MEN*, but it had never managed to capture the lucrative Manchester classified ads market. Thomson, looking round the Kemsley empire after acquisition, circled the *Evening Chronicle* as a vulnerable loss-maker – apparently it was losing £100,000 a year. He called it, notoriously, the "rotten apple in the barrel" but in truth he thought the Withy Grove barrel was pretty rotten throughout. This was the time, in Spring 1960, when the *Guardian's* managing director, Laurence Scott, had joined discussion with Thomson over London printing possibilities. According to Geoffrey Taylor in "Changing Faces", the official biography of the *Guardian* covering the years from 1956-88, Thomson offered Scott Withy Grove – he wanted it all off his

hands. Scott demurred, but a new company, North News, effectively owned by the Guardian & Manchester Evening News Ltd (Thomson had 20 per cent), was created to publish the two evening papers running in competition with each other.

One can only surmise that Scott sought to kill off the competition; this he did, with much hand-wringing, in July 1963. The *Guardian* needed to maximise *Evening News* profits to cover what was proving a very expensive venture in London. But the sting in the tale for G&MEN was a 12-year contract print deal for the *Evening Chronicle* Thomson had persuaded Scott to sign. Compensation for breaking this deal amounted to £1.72 million, which haunted the *Guardian* until 1970. Not bad for a loss-making evening paper Thomson didn't want. As if this wasn't enough, he had persuaded Scott to take space at Gray's Inn Road for the *Guardian's* London office, space which proved eminently unsuitable, until 1976. Laurence joked to colleagues about playing poker with Roy; the trouble was, Roy knew how to bluff.

Beaverbrook had flirted with the idea of a Manchester evening newspaper in the late 1940s and again in the early 1960s, when Scott used it as a reason for amalgamating the interests of the *Evening News* and the *Evening Chronicle*. In the event, neither Beaverbrook nor Rothermere considered Manchester could stand a third paper, and in any case Associated Newspapers joined with G&MEN in Northprint, a company formed to print the *Manchester Evening News*, northern editions of the *Guardian* and of the *Daily Mail* on the *Mail's* presses at Deansgate when G&MEN moved from Cross Street in 1970. The company also transferred their editorial and commercial offices to a development around the *Daily Mail* building. While the *MEN* office opened onto a courtyard facing John Rylands Library, the *Guardian* had to be sought via a backstreet. Such arrangements proved transitional. Following the end of "live" publishing the *Daily Mail* building was demolished to make way for a premium office complex. The *Guardian* and *Evening News*, whose offices are also about to move again to create more development space, now print at Trafford Park; the *Daily Mail* prints at Stoke-on-Trent.

A boost for Manchester had happened in 1968 when the *Daily Mail* decided to pull back from printing its Scottish editions in Edinburgh and transfer the 95,000 print run to the Deansgate presses. However, with the closure of the *Daily Sketch*

"Welcome to the Confidence Convention! Blackpool's celebrated breezes will blow away that over-publicised jitter-bug."
—G. Lionel Berry.

Hon. G. LIONEL BERRY
President, Manchester Publicity Association

"Manchester is eagerly waiting to extend to you the hand of friendship in the Holiday-makers' Mecca."
—E. A. Paessler.

E. A. PAESSLER
Chairman, Manchester Publicity Association

Hewlett Johnson was among guests received by Kemsley at Withy Grove in 1928 despite his alleged Communist sympathies. Johnson, Dean of Manchester from 1924-31 before becoming Dean of Canterbury, was a Mancunian. Lionel Berry, Kemsley's son and heir, kept an eye on the Manchester office. He was president of the Manchester Publicity Association hosting the 15th national advertising convention at Blackpool in June 1939

in May 1971 and its amalgamation with the *Daily Mail*, some 37 Associated journalists in Manchester lost their jobs. Then, early in 1974, Scottish MPs started to get excited about reports that the *Scottish Daily Express*, "Scotland's Daily Newspaper", selling at the time over half a million copies each morning, was to be closed in Glasgow. Printing of the *SDE* would be pulled back to Manchester and the sister evening paper, the *Evening Citizen,* absorbed by Hugh Fraser's *Evening Times*. And so it came to pass, despite interventions by Peter Shore, the Trade Secretary, Shirley Williams, Minister for Prices and Consumer Protection, and the Scottish lobby.

FOR THE ATTENTION OF MR SYDNEY NUTT, PRESS DEPT. DAILY MAIL

1..CLIFF HOWARD,NEWS MANAGER ABEL HEYWOODS, M/C
2 ..A.L.SCOTT,JOINT MANAGING DIRECTOR DITTO
3.. H. MUSGRAVE,MANAGER. W.H.S. OLDHAM
4.. A.L.BARRIE,MANAGING DIRECTOR JOHN HEYWOODS, M/C
5.. MR HAMMOND
6 JACK COLLINS, G.M. DAILY MAIL ,M /C

Newspaper wholesalers lunched by the *Daily Mail* at Deansgate. The crude scrawled numbers and the caption pasted on the picture indicate that this was an identification parade, not for publication. Kemsley House became Thomson House, below, when the company was acquired by Roy Thomson in 1959

Express Newspapers' hatchet man was none other than Jocelyn Stevens, grandson of the second Edward Hulton, then managing director of Express Newspapers.

Stevens cited trading losses for the company and a cash crisis. Transfer of printing to Manchester would not solve group problems, he commented, but a failure to print in Manchester would be the end of the road for Scottish editions. He produced some interesting figures to back his case. Express Newspapers, he said, as reported in the *Daily Telegraph*, expected to return an overall loss of £22,000 for the financial year ending June 30 1974 – a loss of £1,451,000 in Fleet Street (including £220,000 by the *Evening Standard*) and a loss of £929,000 at Glasgow almost balanced by a profit of £2,358,000 in Manchester.

Such profitability, and the 1978 Manchester launch of the *Daily Star*, was not enough in the end to save Great Ancoats Street. The stories of how some 50 Scottish journalists fared when transposed to Manchester, how the *Guardian* left Manchester and how Maxwell came and went amongst a general exodus, are told in later chapters.

Above: Despite a final daily sales figure of 500,000, the north-only *Daily Dispatch* was the first Manchester-published newspaper to disappear in the post-war era. On November 26 1955, less than eight months after this promo, Kemsley "killed" it to make space at Withy Grove for producing northern editions of the *Daily Mirror*

Left: The final edition of the *Sun* published in Manchester. Murdoch's new-look *Sun* was to challenge the *Daily Mirror* from a London-only base

A culture war: Manchester v London

**"Covering Ireland was the territory of Manchester,
directed by me from the Manchester news desk.
In the late 1960s it became obvious that bad things
were happening between the Protestant and
Catholic communities in Northern Ireland.
I sent one of my top reporters, Maurice Weaver, to
make an assessment of the issues. He did the first
major interview with Ian Paisley.
It wasn't used in London: a Manchester reporter
was not supposed to write like that. When Maurice
moved to London it was a different matter"**

Trevor Bates, former *Daily Telegraph* northern news editor

**"People still think the subs here are from the
Burnley Bugle with straw in their hair.
They get a shock…"**

John Maddock, who heads the current *Daily Express/Daily Star* operation at
Broughton, near Preston

Producing a daily national newspaper live at two centres – the operation
conducted between London and Manchester over an 89-year period –
assumes a modicum of cooperation, goodwill and mutual understanding. Or
so one might have thought. In reality, the nightly struggle to meet deadlines
was exacerbated by distrust, often dislike, permeating whole organisations
from editors to messengers, via the composing room and the machine floor.
Attitudes were not much different at the *Daily Telegraph* or the *Daily Mirror*.
Because of its Manchester origins, the *Guardian* suffered more than most in
this regard. Journalists on the *Daily Express* and *Daily Mail*, competing for a
hard-to-define mid-market readership, had much more in common with each
other in Manchester than with their respective London colleagues.

Maundy Thursday was the traditional day out for newspaper workers, with
Good Friday a newspaper-free respite until Murdoch arrived on the scene,
purloining Christmas Day and New Year's Day as well. Maundy Thursday was
something special, a time for carousing on mighty communal trips to
countryside or coast, what print-workers called Wayzgoose. One such
Wayzgoose during the 1960s involved a golf society match between the
London and Manchester offices of the *Guardian* which took place

somewhere in the Midlands and was intended to encourage a sense of comradeship between fellow employees, mainly compositors, playing for the L.P. Scott Cup. The fixture had to be abandoned when Manchester took the cup five years running and London were unable to raise a team. Over lunch in the fussy golf-club environment Mancunians, awkward in their best suits, stood out from the more casually dressed Londoners. There wasn't much fraternisation. Mancunians argued about the form for Good Friday races; Londoners worried about their own race-horse consortia.

At the heart of the misunderstandings lies a cultural divide. Londoners thought (and think) that Mancunians are thick; Mancunians thought (and think) that Londoners are wide-boys. Londoners assume that nothing outside the capital – and that includes northern editions of the nationals – matters. Mancunians assume that they are in fact superior because Londoners are indolent as well as arrogant. A Mancunian living in London is teased about his accent, which he either loses or hides away among fellow northern exiles; a Londoner living in Manchester always stands out, although he is usually accepted if he conforms to local rules.

There was little love lost between the print unions at the two ends. When the good days started to turn sour Manchester knew it was on a loser, as Albert Hartwell, then night publishing manager at Withy Grove recalls: "It was always easier to chop back in Manchester. The unions in London were a lot stronger, even though we were the same union. We weren't as militant."

Frank Taylor, former night publisher for the *Daily Telegraph* in Manchester, concurs. "We always performed a lot better than London did. If there was ever an important late story here we wanted to do it. People got their fingers out in every department."

Tom Dolan, a former reader at Withy Grove, remembers with pride when, because of problems in Fleet Street, they were called on to print an extra 900,000 copies of the *Daily Telegraph*. "People were writing in from the south to say why can't we receive a northern edition of the *Telegraph* all the time, it's a far better newspaper…"

Ken Martin, also a reader and member of the NATSOPA national executive, points out that Manchester management never undertook staffing rosters, which were the duty of the chapel officials. Fleet Street was different; with lino-operators on piecework, it was every man for himself.

That was the print-workers' side. Journalists, more complicated and more devious, played different games. To begin with, most Manchester journalists were not native-born Mancunians. Manchester was split between those obviously on their way to London, those who said they would never go but eventually went, and those who had no interest at all in going even when it was their only way of staying on a national newspaper. London was split between

Londoners thought (and think) that Mancunians are thick; Mancunians thought (and think) that Londoners are wide-boys. Londoners assume that nothing outside the capital matters. Mancunians assume they are superior because Londoners are indolent as well as arrogant

those who, for managerial or story reasons, would make the occasional foray north and those who never had and never would set foot in the place.

Southern imports could have a tough time. Bob Blake is a former *Daily Express* northern news editor, alive and kicking (he still kicks his old deputy, Stanley Blenkinsop, a Geordie who took over from him as news editor and is also long retired). Blake, from Kent, came to Manchester in 1946. He had never ventured north of Birmingham before. He claims to have been nearly sacked twice in the early years simply because he was a southerner, seen as "another sacred cow wished on us from London." He resolved to stay and fight: "if the Army didn't break my heart these buggers won't." He reckons he saved his job by commandeering a Manchester Corporation bus in the 1947 bus strike, driving it to Wilmslow – "I was loth to stop after getting it into sixth gear" – and writing a story which made the centre column of page one.

There were conversions. Arthur Christiansen, who had worked his way to Fleet Street from small beginnings on the Wirral, was not exactly delighted to be ordered to Manchester in 1932 by a Beaverbrook keen to put on *Daily Express* circulation for northern editions. "Now Manchester can be a pretty awful town at any time of the week," he wrote in his autobiography "Headlines All My Life", "but that Sunday it seemed just terrible. How was I to know that within a few months I would come to admire Manchester, its ways, its people, its Great Ancoats Street, its Sam's Chop House, its West Didsbury, its Piccadilly – as well as its trains back to London." Derek Jameson had an equal number of supporters and detractors during his several forays to Manchester. In his book "Last of the Hot Metal Men" he echoes the ambivalent feelings of non-Mancunians on arrival there. "But Manchester made me and I love the place", he wrote.

Hugh Cudlipp, spring-boarded to the *Manchester Evening Chronicle* from Cardiff at the tender age of 17, wrote "in Manchester I really learned what journalism was about… I met most of the first-class operators who were later to fill the Editors' chairs on the newspapers in London: Manchester was the recruiting ground for talent for the 'nationals', a good place to be" (from "Walking on the Water").

That was the problem, from London's point of view. Manchester made too many people. It helped make Christiansen, Cudlipp and Jameson, for a start. It put Vincent Mulchrone on his way. It made Larry Lamb and Bernard Shrimsley. The *Manchester Evening News* set up Harry Evans, another northerner, and before him Sir William Haley. Manchester was the launch pad for Paul Dacre, the current *Daily Mail* editor, who Blenkinsop took direct from Leeds University where he edited the student rag. The *Daily Telegraph*'s Manchester office made Maurice Weaver, Roland Gribben and Christopher Munnion. It was hard to rubbish the place where such people came from, but London found its ways – especially among those who had started life in

Hugh Cudlipp wrote "in Manchester I really learned what journalism was about… I met most of the first-class operators who were later to fill the Editors' chairs on the newspapers in London: Manchester was… a good place to be"

Manchester. Michael Kennedy, long-serving northern editor of the *Daily Telegraph*, recalls: "I often thought it strange with people who went from the Manchester office to London. I thought, ah well, they'll be spreading the gospel but, no, they were lost in the London system. Sometimes they were even worse, like converts to a religion."

Journalists who had become famous, even notorious, in Manchester could also expect raised eyebrows in Fleet Street. This went for Henry Rose, the ebullient *Daily Express* northern football correspondent who died in the Manchester United team plane disaster at Munich. Rose, with his homburg and cigar, was an institution. As Peter Oborne recalled in a special *Daily Express* supplement published to celebrate the newspaper's centenary in 2000, such was his fame that the *Express* publicity machine would put up placards at whatever match he covered saying "Henry Rose is here today." Yet in his autobiography Arthur Christiansen noted "he was never quite right for London."

Trevor Bates, northern news editor of the *Daily Telegraph* in the 1970s and 1980s, found himself playing piggy-in-the-middle: "London felt we were incompetent. This reflected on me, and I had a lot of stress problems in trying to serve two masters. To be loyal to my own team of reporters, treating them as good professional journalists, and trying to be faithful to the *Telegraph's* requests."

Mike Cuerden was northern news editor of the *Daily Mail* from 1982. By that time, Cuerden says, London was "terminally bored" by Northern Ireland, while Manchester sent reporting teams over to the province as part of their education. But there was the problem of "selling" the story to London, the very same problem Trevor Bates had on the *Daily Telegraph*. Manchester stories always seemed a bit of a luxury to sceptical London ears. "Then, when we had a big story for once we were on our mettle to keep London out."

Cuerden notes: "it was the lack of recognition that matters of import could happen outside the South East that jarred. I always remember Stewart Steven, then the *Mail's* deputy editor, coming to Manchester to lead a drive when the *Daily Star* was launched and him telling our district men that they should treat their patch as though they were foreign correspondents – think about politics, features and so on as well as hard news. Good in theory, but difficult to sell to London in practice."

Leo White, the *Daily Mirror's* northern news editor for 20 years, is a little more sanguine. "My judgment was mine, not London's. I accepted their industrial stuff, maybe. There was rivalry because they didn't and couldn't understand the North."

Stanley Goldsmith, frontline hard news man for the *Daily Telegraph* in Manchester, recalls how the Manchester newsdesk had half a dozen reporters covering the 1985 Manchester Airport runway fire, piecing the

"London felt we were incompetent. This reflected on me, and I had a lot of stress problems in trying to serve two masters. To be loyal to my own team of reporters and trying to be faithful to the Telegraph's requests"

tragedy together. "Sometime in the afternoon a reporter from London, David Graves, arrived. 'Can you give me the story so that I can write it?' 'Fuck off.' The London editions carried his byline. He did not contribute to the story."

When he became editor, Max Hastings used to invite groups to London on a getting-to-know-you basis where they were wined and dined by the expansive young pretender. Goldsmith's group was told about the reopening of the *Daily Telegraph*'s Tokyo bureau as a very prestigious thing to do. How about reopening the Glasgow office, Goldsmith asked? That would not be half so prestigious as Tokyo. But, Goldsmith persisted, how many copies of the *Daily Telegraph* do you sell in Tokyo?

Geoffrey Mather, a former assistant editor of the *Daily Express* in Manchester, is of the opinion that London didn't care a damn about Manchester. "They cared a damn if Manchester began to challenge their authority. There has to be a top dog, and if the London editor doesn't stamp his authority the Manchester editor is going to be the top dog.

"Relations between London and Manchester could be tense depending on which editor had been sent by London. Ambitious editors naturally wanted to stamp their authority on the newspaper. London editors usually resented this and there was a friction which was not altogether bad. It had its own stimulus. If you could create your own pages, well and good. If you were running theirs, you might get a better make-up or an improved headline.

"There were occasions when we ran our own complete William Hickey pages and these could lead to furious arguments with whoever was in charge of London's Hickey. The conversation tended to be: London: 'I am in charge of William Hickey and you will run it as I run it.' Manchester: 'My instructions come from my editor. Those are the ones I will follow. If you are unhappy, talk to him.' Usual result: carry on as before."

Bill Freeman, former northern editor of the *Sunday Mirror* and long-time *Mirror* executive with many years' experience of handling London, reflects a different approach. "It depended on the personality of the Manchester editor, and also who was in London. Was the London editor willing to let them get away with doing things differently? Some did and some didn't. I remember Mike Molloy – the *Daily Mirror* editor for ten years or so – saying 'I don't care what they do in Manchester so long as they increase circulation'." Freeman also recalls that Robert Maxwell could be quite charming and rational when he rang to ask about progress on a particular edition.

Mather quotes a specific example of London blindness. "A major full leader page feature on Donald Campbell shortly before his death on Coniston was not run by London because Derek Marks, the editor, declared – I was told – that he did not want too many boats in the paper. There had been an event elsewhere; a trawler going down. Something like that. But no good reason to

"Relations between London and Manchester could be tense depending on which editor had been sent by London. Ambitious editors naturally wanted to stamp their authority on the newspaper. London editors usually resented this"

leave out Campbell beyond the usual territorial protection. In the event, they ran it all when he died. Little choice, I suppose."

And the *Guardian*? The *Guardian's* news editor from 1963, John Cole, was established in London before the editor, Alastair Hetherington, moved down in 1964. Almost all the specialists were there, too, leaving Manchester with a few leader-writers and a newsroom which, apart from Northern Ireland, had increasingly limited horizons. The reporting team of Harry Jackson, Simon Winchester and Simon Hoggart, put together as The Troubles got serious, may have been administered out of Manchester but it was closely monitored by Cole, himself a Belfast man. London made gestures: Joe Minogue, longtime deputy Manchester news editor and a solid Lancastrian, became briefly, if not altogether successfully, foreign editor.

You could say that writers attracted by the *Manchester Guardian* – Arthur Ransome, Howard Spring, Neville Cardus, Malcolm Muggeridge, Alistair Cooke, W.J.Weatherby, Michael Frayn, Geoffrey Moorhouse, Peter Lennon, Stanley Reynolds – were a more interesting bunch than the Harry Jacksons, Peter Prestons and David McKies of this world who turned the *Guardian* into a London paper. During the transition period seasoned *Manchester Guardian* journalists like John Putz and Anthony Tucker successfully reinvented themselves for London. Nesta Roberts went to London in 1961 as the first news editor before becoming Paris correspondent. Brian Redhead vacillated.

Manchester became the place for juvenilia, a stop on the way up for Preston, for Simon Hoggart, Jonathan Steele and Victor Keegan, for Michael McNay – even for Derek Malcolm, the man who brought racing coverage to the paper and became the country's best film critic. By the 1970s the Manchester newsroom was a home of lost journalist causes, never mind other lost causes.

As the end hove into sight for Manchester in the mid-1980s, lines of communication became more stretched than ever. Gerry Dempsey, *Daily Express* northern showbiz correspondent until the drop, remembers with mock despair the new generation of London features subs – "degrees in media studies, pig-ignorant of the arts."

Dempsey recalls having put a review over in the normal way when "this aggressive, bossy woman phoned.

'We haven't seen your copy this week yet, Gerry' she moaned. 'Well, I've sent it. The Admirable Crichton'.

'It says here you're doing the Admiral Crickton.' I realised I was getting nowhere. Another girl, when I had written something about a stately home, queried Capability Brown. 'Is Capability her first name?'"

Long live the cultural divide.

Gerry Dempsey, Daily Express northern showbiz correspondent until the drop, remembers with mock despair the new generation of London features subs – "degrees in media studies, pig-ignorant of the arts"

Northern editors: living with insecurity

To be northern editor of a national newspaper was only rarely a calling. Too often, the appointment was stop-gap. If the editor was no good he was sacked; if the editor proved himself he became a threat to London and was either taken there to join the team or sacked. Northern editors could find themselves in problems with the courts, particularly for Scottish-edition stories where the contempt law is different to that south of the Border (and Scottish judges ruled that Manchester was responsible for its own news pages). But these same editors were routinely humiliated by Fleet Street executives when it suited. It suited more and more as the industry ran into crisis during the 1980s. Some feel so strongly about this period that they decline to talk about it even after 20 years.

There's consensus, all the same, that the successful northern editors were the ones who stood up to Fleet Street and survived. They, and the editors put into Manchester to do a specific job. In the first category are Michael Kennedy of the *Daily Telegraph*, who's written about on pages 80-83, Larry Lamb of the *Daily Mail*, Tim Hewat and John McDonald of the *Daily Express* and Bernard Shrimsley and Derek Jameson of the *Daily Mirror*.

Having proved himself in the north and having become editor of the *Daily Express* as a consequence, Jameson was sent back to Manchester by Express Newspapers to oversee launch of the *Daily Star*, which also puts him into the second category (see the profile on pages 76-79). This category includes Kennedy Jones, entrusted by Harmsworth to set up the *Daily Mail* operation in 1900, Arthur Christiansen, ordered north by Beaverbrook in 1932 to put on sales at the *Daily Express* soon after Manchester publishing began, and Oscar Pulvermacher, sent from Fleet Street to establish the *Daily Telegraph* in 1940.

Shrimsley, from Southport, had been brought in by Percy Roberts, northern general manager of the *Daily Mirror* in the early 1960s, who was himself sent from London to improve staffing from the *Daily Dispatch* residue mainly in place. Shrimsley created the space and freedom to make northern editions almost a separate newspaper from the London ones, and to boost circulation. Cold-shouldered in the end by Hugh Cudlipp he joined Larry Lamb as deputy editor of Murdoch's *Sun*, took over from Lamb as editor in 1975, and later edited the *News of the World*.

Lamb, a miner's son from West Yorkshire, was a backbench executive on the *Daily Mirror* in Fleet Street when he was offered the northern editor's seat at the *Daily Mail*, where his news editor Ken Donlan and chief reporter Harold Pendlebury had the reputation of running the smartest operation in town. Lamb and Shrimsley were competitors who became friends, and friends who became colleagues after Shrimsley followed Lamb to the *Sun* via the *Liverpool Daily Post*. Lamb's departure was a double blow for Manchester. Not only did it lose its best editor: Murdoch's rising *Sun* started to poach circulation from the *Mirror* and other popular dailies even though it didn't attempt a northern edition at that time.

Editors at play: Ted Fenna of the *Daily Mirror* with Harry Myers of the *Daily Mail* take part in a charity dinner during the 1960s

In his autobiography "Headlines all my life" Christiansen tells his brief was to produce a daily "as unlike the London editions as human ingenuity could devise" aimed at the northern working family. He started an 8-page children's comic section which added 27,000 to Saturday sales, and a Monday racing selection which put on 35,000 sales. When he was brought back to London after a brief six-month stint it was as assistant editor, soon to depose Beverley Baxter as Beaverbrook's top man. Among his Manchester colleagues was Trevor Evans, who was to become the doyen of Fleet Street industrial correspondents.

As editor, Christiansen determined never to be usurped by a bright young thing like himself from Manchester. Geoffrey Mather, a long-time *Daily Express* assistant editor in Manchester, recalls Christiansen's stipulation that the northern editor go through the paper each morning on the phone with the great man (who would have a Manchester edition in front of him). Any deviation from style was questioned, down to the number of "shorts" on page one. Mather once used a Garamond headline typeface on a light page three lead he thought would benefit from it. The northern editor of the time, Tim Hewat, came rushing to him the next day. "Christ, what have you done? He's been on to me and he ran out of words." Blame me, said Mather. Hewat returned

Editors at play: Bill Deedes of the *Daily Telegraph* with his northern counterpart Michael Kennedy enduring another charity dinner

to his office, where Christiansen came on a further three times. But Hewat kept mum and held his ground: "never complain, never explain" was his way of dealing with his taskmaster.

Mather continues: "I rather think that Christiansen had Tim Hewat in mind as his successor. Hewat was extremely forceful and became editor in Manchester at the age of 28. He and Christiansen got on well in a semi-amused, abrasive way. When he went to London, it was in an equivalent post (assistant editor, I think) to that of David English. The classic two in opposition. But somewhere along the line Hewat decided to move to Granada where he began What the Papers Say and World in Action, and that, unfortunately, was that. He was a great journalist."

Daily Express journalists at Great Ancoats Street took their calling seriously, as Mather remembers: "Pub discussions in Manchester could be intense under ambitious editors. People developed a whole philosophy on how to change the *Daily Express* in London. When John McDonald, editor in Manchester, went south as deputy editor to Ian MacColl, a small group – no more than three or four – had discussed to the nth degree what he intended to do and which writers the new regime might buy from other newspapers. Almost his last words in Manchester were – 'I think I've got this straight but what did we agree about so-and-so? Ah. Right, I'm off then'. The next stage, of course, was to discuss it all with the new editor, who was heading south from Glasgow. They brought in a great sports writer, Hugh McIlvanney, among others, but used him on subjects which were not his normal line. To a degree he was wasted.

"It wasn't an attempt at takeover. It was a new approach. London had a lot of talented writers and that was the paper's strength. We were all committed to selling more newspapers. It wasn't a question of takeover, it was a question of expressing views on London to the betterment of the newspaper using the available talent.." The dialogue had been encouraged by Max Aitken himself, but of course it foundered on the day-to-day realities of life in Fleet Street.

The *Manchester Evening News* has its own little hall of fame: William Haley, later of the BBC and the *Times*; Harry Evans, later of the *Sunday Times* and the *Times*; and Tom Henry, the legendary evening newspaper editor who timed editions to split seconds. For the *Manchester Guardian* C.P.Scott must claim emeritus status, along with W.P.Crozier and A.P.Wadsworth who by and large carried on the Scott traditions. Alastair Hetherington, the man who took the *Guardian* to London, should be seen as a Fleet Street editor, in aspiration at least. After 1964, Manchester traditions were carried on for a time by Paddy Monkhouse, a second-generation *Guardian* man who many believed should have been made editor in 1956, and by Brian Redhead, who believed he should be editor after Hetherington.

Michael Kennedy tells a Redhead story with affection, and indeed the story must have come from Redhead himself. It was one of those rare occasions

"London had a lot of talented writers and that was the paper's strength. We were all committed to selling more newspapers. It wasn't a question of takeover, it was a question of expressing views on London to the betterment of the newspaper"

that saw Alistair Cooke back in Manchester, no doubt being honoured for something. The ceremony over, there he was in his lonely Midland Hotel room not yet ready for sleep. He rang Redhead at the office, suggesting he stroll over for a nightcap after the edition was put to bed. They met in the Midland's main lounge which at that time had a night bar service for residents, with a little staircase down to the stewards' quarters.

As they sat sipping their whiskies, Redhead was suddenly aware of a waiter at his shoulder. "Excuse me, gentlemen," the waiter said, "I overheard that famous voice. My wife would never forgive me if I failed to get the autograph." At this he proffered his autograph book. Redhead took it, signed his own name, and handed it back to the waiter while Cooke sat silently by. Some years after, following a stint as editor of the *Manchester Evening News*, Redhead indeed became a household voice on the Today programme where he put his adopted town of Macclesfield on the national agenda.

The Midland has an important place in the city's history. It was there in 1909 that *Guardian* editors (not including Scott) lunched with Arnold Bennett and it was there that the substantial Oscar Pulvermacher chose to stay and eat dinner each evening while he set up the *Daily Telegraph* at Withy Grove from the autumn of 1940. Print-workers recall him as a Hollywood mogul type; Michael Kennedy, an office-boy at the time, remembers him regularly leaving for the night at about 9pm, calling out to his chief sub Gilbert Yates as he strode off "Yates, going now and I don't want disturbing unless Hitler surrenders."

It was at the Midland that northern *Mirror* executives met to celebrate Hugh Cudlipp on his farewell tour of the country before retiring from Mirror Group. Much food was eaten and much drink consumed. Then there were a couple of worthy but dry speeches until it was Derek Jameson's turn as northern editor of the *Sunday Mirror*. He was compèring the evening, had done his homework and played the stand-up-comedian with Cudlipp's extrovert career. The audience were in tears, as was Cudlipp. Within a couple of weeks Jameson had been invited to London then sent back to Manchester as northern editor of the *Daily Mirror*, which is where he really made his name.

On return Jameson called a meeting of *Mirror* editorial staff. He gave them the usual sort of let's-get-on-with-it-chaps talk, ending up with a standard invitation: don't forget, my door is always open to you. "Yes", commented someone from the back of the room, "that's because you're never there!" Jameson was the sort of editor who you either loved or hated. Jane Fickling, a Manchester feature writer for the *Daily* and then the *Sunday Mirror*, recalls the phrase current at the time, "man of iron whim." He tended to change his mind. Bill Freeman, his assistant editor on the *Sunday Mirror*, saw him as "not much good, but good at projecting himself."

Michael Kennedy remembers Pulvermacher leaving for the night at about 9pm, calling out to his chief sub Gilbert Yates as he strode off "Yates, going now and I don't want disturbing unless Hitler surrenders"

Jameson stories are legion. When editor-in-chief of the *Daily Express* and the *Daily Star*, he was chairing the midday conference of the recently-launched *Star* in Manchester.

"Not much today, is there," said Jameson.

"I think I can get an interview with Elvis from the grave through a clairvoyant for £7,000," said features executive Nigel Blundell.

"It was only £5,000 when she spoke to me about it this morning," replied Jameson.

"How do you know?" said Blundell.

'She' was feature writer Ellen Petrie, offering the clairvoyant story, who Jameson lived with at the time and later married.

"It was a load of old rubbish then; and it's a load of old rubbish now," Jameson concluded.

Over on Deansgate at the oak-panelled *Daily Mail* office life was more formal. Into the 1960s reporters were expected to wear dark suits, white shirts and dark ties. That was until Larry Lamb came along. On his first day in Manchester he sported a pink shirt and a floral tie (very sixties). The next day many of the reporters, having jettisoned their funereal garb for something more colourful, were again thrown to find Lamb in a turtle-neck sweater. "It's OK, chaps, relax" he said. They did, and enjoyed one of the best periods in the *Mail's* long Manchester history until Lamb went south to the *Sun* in 1969. After all, this was the man who was soon to bring full frontal upper body nudity to Page 3.

In the gathering gloom of the mid-1980s, when it was evident that the consequences of Wapping were destroying any economic rationale for Manchester, northern editors became increasingly helpless. Bill Freeman, who left the *Sunday Mirror* in May 1988 when the live Manchester operation closed, believes that Manchester was always going to be badly hit because it was so much easier for London management to make people redundant 200 miles away than on their doorsteps. London looked after its own, to the point of offering very little of interest to the final round of Manchester exiles. Freeman thought at the time that a scaled-down live news and sport operation in the north would work, but that wasn't to be. When your empire is vanishing, you have no clothes.

Perhaps the fate of the northern editor is best summed up by the 86-year-old Bob Blake, a former northern news editor of the *Daily Express*: "I was at the *Express* for 36 years. I suppose I saw 15 or more editors come and go, but their names have gone too. At that time editors played god and I was doing my best to keep afloat in that wild journalistic sea where rival reporters let down your tyres, climbed through hospital ward windows and told lies to news editors – does anything change?"

In the gathering gloom of the mid-1980s, when it was evident that the consequences of Wapping were destroying any economic rationale for Manchester, northern editors became increasingly helpless

Del Boy's home from home

"As a very successful national newspaper editor I was back at Withy Grove for some leaving do or other. I'd put on weight and was wearing a suit and tie. An old comp called Len who I'd worked with on the stone for many years came up to me.

'Where've yoo bin?'

I told him I was down in London.

'Y'look lyke a fookin' rooptured dook.'

I love it. Love it."

Derek Jameson loved Manchester, and Manchester for the most part loved him. He loved the informality, the anarchy, the take-you-as-I-find-you attitudes after the "phoney baloney" of Fleet Street. "Manchester was like a breath of fresh air" he confides, savouring the warm late-October breezes on the balcony of his ninth-floor Miami Beach super-luxury condo with its million-dollar view across Miami harbour to the downtown skyline. One way or another, a lot of water has passed under Del Boy since he left Manchester for the last time in 1980, but his affection for the place remains spontaneous. After all, it made him.

Never one for self-doubt, Jameson rode his luck in becoming northern editor of the *Daily Mirror* at the very moment when Murdoch's *Sun* under Larry Lamb was beginning to challenge the *Mirror's* tabloid hegemony. But the *Sun* did not print in Manchester, which meant that it was unable to get mid-week football results, let alone match reports. Jameson, no sports specialist himself, went big on football as well as producing his own version of page three girls on page five. "Larry Lamb said that the only impediment to the *Sun's* onward progress was Derek Jameson in Manchester." Mike Molloy, the *Mirror's* editor, took the view that whatever sold papers was good for one and all, so Jameson had a licence to do as he wished.

His reputation as a circulation builder went back to 1965 when he was sent to help oversee installation of the web offset colour press in Belfast, fed by pages faxed from Manchester. He'd been picture editor of the *Sunday Mirror* in London and before that had done photo news at the *Daily Express*. By his own admission he was little more than a production sub with a flair for handling pictures, but paper qualifications never meant much to the man who clawed his way up from a Hackney waif's home. Soon, as assistant editor in charge of Irish editions, he was supervising *Sunday Mirror* growth. "I quadrupled its circulation in Ulster then moved into the Republic, where it was outselling some of the Irish papers within a year."

Successes at the *Sunday Mirror* – he became northern editor in 1972, following a stint back in London – led to his being made northern editor of the *Daily Mirror* in 1974.

Derek Jameson with (left) night editor Andy Carson and (right) assistant night editor Ian Pollock at the launch of the *Daily Star* in November 1978. Picture by Denis Thorpe for the *Guardian*

Jameson never lost Fleet Street ambitions. His achievements as northern editor could hardly pass unnoticed in Holborn Circus, "and in no time at all they made me managing editor in London, where a great many people thought I should have been editor." But that was not on the cards. Molloy, the younger man, was firmly entrenched and in any case a "good friend."

So back, by 1976, in the land of phoney baloney, "I knew it wouldn't be long before Fleet Street came knocking at the door. Sure enough the phone rang one day, and it was Charles Wintour – who offered me the editorship of the *Daily Express* on the recommendation of Harry Evans. I naturally seized the opportunity, much to the horror of the *Mirror*. I was told to leave the office immediately – I wasn't even allowed in the building to collect my mail. I used to have to stand on the pavement outside while the secretary brought my post, as *Private Eye* discovered."

At the *Express* Jameson found himself up against Jocelyn Stevens, then managing director of Express Newspapers. Their first meeting was conducted by Stevens stretched out on the floor, his feet in an armchair, asking with studied insouciance, "shall I call you Fred?" *Express* editors came and went so frequently, he observed, that it wasn't worth learning their names. Actually, Jameson says, Stevens was furious that the appointment had been made behind his back. Yet Stevens and Jameson, the patrician and the pleb, forged a strong working relationship. "He was a tremendous driving force", Jameson says, "very good at squeezing agreements out of the most difficult unions." For his part, Jameson got on with his speciality, circulation building. He claims to be the only editor in recent history to put on sales at the *Daily Express*.

Things became complicated in 1978 when Stevens and Matthews decided to launch the *Daily Star* from Manchester to take on both the *Sun* and the *Mirror*. Jameson's version of events is that he'd been doing so well circulation-wise at the *Express* that he was accused of taking the title downmarket. "The ad department and other toffee-nosed execs took the view that I was dragging the *Daily Express* into the dirt by putting on circulation. They were so unused to it they thought there was something very alien about adding readers and that this man should be regarded with the gravest suspicion." Sending him to Manchester as launch editor of the frankly downmarket *Star* would solve the dilemma.

Jameson wasn't having it. In his view he'd "done" Manchester. Eventually a compromise was reached, with Jameson given the role of editor-in-chief of the *Star*. He remained editor of the *Express* but appointed Peter Grimsditch as the *Star's* editor. Arthur Firth, a former northern editor of the *Express*, looked after the paper in London while Jameson was back north.

It was an unhappy arrangement. Jameson had little wish to be in Manchester again, Grimsditch proved to be a tearaway. Matthews, a Thatcherite even

"The ad department and other toffee-nosed execs took the view that I was dragging the Daily Express into the dirt by putting on circulation. They thought that this man should be regarded with the gravest suspicion"

before Thatcher really got going and the largest single donor to the Conservative Party, reluctantly agreed to the *Star* supporting Labour just as long as it didn't attack the Tories.

The launch edition not auspicious. "The paper was pretty awful. The lawyers killed the splash about ten minutes before we were due off stone. We had to put in a make-weight on some betting scandal. Everyone was patting me on the back saying great, wonderful, marvellous, but I wasn't happy. I went over to the Midland Hotel at one in the morning. Half of Fleet Street was there, including all my rival editors. I walked into the room where drunken revelry going on. I stood in the doorway. 'What do you think of it so far?', I shouted. 'Rubbish'. 'Now I know I'm home', I said. That was the birth of the *Daily Star*."

Between them Grimsditch and Jameson took the *Star* to over a million daily sales in a year largely via bingo, which Jameson, alerted by a circulation rep, had discovered posing as housey-housey on the Saturday children's page of the *Western Morning News.* Even if bingo wasn't strictly legal, it was trialled on Tyneside and Merseyside and looked an obvious winner. "It was fantastic, but Lord Matthews and his chums wouldn't allow me to give away more than £10,000." The *Sun* caught on, initially offering £50,000 before a battle between Murdoch and Maxwell drove top prizes up to £1 million. The *Star* got left way behind.

With the *Star* demanding so much of Jameson's time, Firth had been made *Express* editor. "I went down to London to ask for my job back. 'Oh no', they said, 'you're doing fine, you stay with the *Star* in Manchester.' Much as I loved Manchester I'd made it in London. I wanted my job back. They wouldn't give it to me, so we parted company."

Thus began an odyssey through the world of showbiz. Apart from a spell as editor of the *News of the World* he was not to work in national newspapers again. Newspapers were his life, but showbiz finally brought him fame and fortune.

Asked to sum up his feelings about Manchester, Jameson puts on his most formal voice and selects his very best syntax:

"Only those of us who were involved understand the significance of Manchester as a centre of newspaper production. The great strength of the British press is to deliver a paper to the nation from the Orkneys to the Channel Islands by breakfast time, and the only way it could achieve that was by printing in Manchester. Manchester covered five countries – Northern Ireland, the Irish Republic, North Wales, Scotland and northern England. You could never have done that from Fleet Street. So Manchester was a vital link in the chain of communication that made the British press so efficient and successful."

You could say the same about the extraordinary career of one Derek Jameson.

"Only those of us who were involved understand the significance of Manchester as a centre of newspaper production… Manchester was a vital link in the chain of communication that made the British press so efficient and successful"

The man from Paddy's Market

Michael Kennedy is a constant in the vortex of Manchester newspaper publishing. He joined the *Daily Telegraph* as a 15-year-old messenger boy in 1940, the year northern printing started. Apart from war service in the Navy (when old enough to join up) he was with the *Telegraph* in Manchester until 1986, first as a sub-editor, becoming northern editor in 1960. As a 'sideline' he was northern music critic from 1950. When the *Telegraph* transferred from Withy Grove to Trafford Park with a much-reduced editorial team, Kennedy signed off but was immediately re-employed, at Lord Hartwell's invitation, as joint music critic before moving across to the *Sunday Telegraph*, where he remains.

Kennedy never had any ambitions in Fleet Street, and still lives in Manchester, but admits these days to running a small London flat for convenience after late-night performances. Over the years he has written the official biography of Sir John Barbirolli and the history of the Hallé Orchestra as well as monographs on Vaughan Williams, Elgar, Walton, Mahler and Strauss among other composers, and editing both the Oxford Dictionary of Music and the Concise Oxford. He is, like Neville Cardus before him, a lover of cricket. Cardus was Kennedy's idol and inspiration; but Cardus never mastered a typewriter, let alone edited anybody else's copy. Kennedy has done it all.

He remembers being sent sometime in 1941 by Oscar Pulvermacher, the *Daily Telegraph's* first northern editor, to Cross Street with a message for W.P Crozier, the *Manchester Guardian* editor. "The first thing I saw was the Epstein bust of C.P.Scott glaring at me. I remember going up in the lift to find the Corridor. It was like being in the holy of holies. Returning to Withy Grove immediately after was like walking into Paddy's Market."

He stuck with Paddy's Market. The only thing that irked him about the *Guardian* (and still does) is for people who don't know Manchester to assume that he, as a Manchester-based music critic, must somehow be associated with it. He accepts – "people won't like it but it's true" – that the *Manchester Guardian's* international reputation helped attract famous musicians like Hans Richter to the city. "It was read abroad more than London papers and of course carried notices of the Hallé." But by the time Kennedy became northern editor, the *Guardian* was transferring its energies and affections to London. The quality newspaper field was wide open to the *Daily Telegraph*, not just on the arts page but for news and sport, too.

Between 1960 and 1985 the *Telegraph's* northern coverage increasingly outpointed the *Guardian's*. Kennedy had more space for general news and of course the soberly-written titillation, based on court cases, in which the paper had developed a national market. Its newsroom, understaffed compared with the *Daily Express* or *Daily Mail*, developed a reputation for

LATE NEWS

Phone 061-834 1234

Classified Advertisements
061-834 1234 Ext. 305

This edition of the Daily Telegraph is a historic example of a newspaperman's determination to ensure the continuity of the paper. It was produced single-handed by Michael Kennedy, Northern Editor when, as the result of a dispute no other member of his staff worked. This framed copy of the paper was presented to Mr Kennedy by his closest colleagues as a permanent reminder of how he kept faith with our readers.

The first of a series of *Daily Telegraph* northern editions produced single-handed by Michael Kennedy when Manchester journalists walked out in February 1974, on the eve of a General Election. As northern editor, Kennedy was not bound by NUJ chapel directives. He won praise from Manchester colleagues for keeping the title in the marketplace (see the Late News column, blown up above, in the edition presented to him)

The Daily Telegraph

LATE NORTH EDITION

No. 36941 MANCHESTER, WEDNESDAY, FEBRUARY 27, 1974 Printed in LONDON and MANCHESTER 4p

'STAND FIRM' IS HEATH'S LAST PLEA

Risk of militants next time

BY A POLITICAL CORRESPONDENT

IN his final television appeal to the nation before it goes to the polls tomorrow, the Prime Minister last night held firm to the themes which had dominated his campaign in the three weeks of this unprecedented crisis election.

He posed a stark choice between a Conservative Government both strong and moderate — and a Government which would "encourage a powerful minority, any powerful minority."

Mr Heath said: "The Government has a policy to beat inflation. It is not easy, but it's fair—it's fair for everyone. And it's working. If you vote for a Conservative Government, it will go on working. But you must decide."

"The alternative is to encourage a powerful minority, any powerful minority, to believe that they can bend the rules of the game when it suits them.

"People tell me I'm stubborn," Mr Heath said. "Well, is it stubborn to fight and fight hard to stop the country you love from tearing itself apart?

"And is it stubborn to insist that everyone in that country should have the choice and the chance to take his life and make of it what he can?

Firm and decisive

"And is it stubborn to want to see this country take back the place that history means us to have? If it is —then, yes, I'm most certainly stubborn.

"But surely 'stubborn' means not giving up when the going gets rough? And isn't 'stubborn' another way of saying 'determined'?

"We've had to be determined these last few years, for no Government in recent times has been more tested by events. And each one has been dealt with firmly and decisively.

"We shan't get on by giving up. We have never been afraid of the unknown. Dangers have never deterred us. Whatever the future holds, we must seize it. We must shape it.

"If there is fire, we shall face it. And come through it stronger, wiser and more at one with each other. We've never failed to yet."

At the start of his broadcast Mr Heath said that if we did not go on fighting inflation it would cripple us all, maybe for more than a generation.

WILSON'S HOPES RISE

THERE had been a "massive swing" back to Labour since the weekend despite what all the opinion polls showed, Mr Harold Wilson claimed last night.

He indicated to reporters in Huddersfield that he firmly believed Labour was in the same position that the Tories were in the final run-up to the 1970 General Election.

Then Mr Heath won with a dramatic last minute surge, defying pollsters' predictions. Mr Wilson's confidence was based on Labour's private surveys taken as late as this weekend.

He refused to say what the figures were, but pointed out that most of the published polls were taken before last Friday.

South London example

He quoted the South London area as an example of change. The Conservatives had a massive lead there last week, but Labour's findings showed a swing round and Socialist support was back to the level of last year's Greater London Council elections.

Mr Wilson accepted the size and effect of Liberal support, and realised that some Conservative and Labour seats would be in danger.

He went on to disclose the existence of an ultra-Left threat to the Labour vote. He said he had been told of evidence of Trotskyite shop stewards, particularly in the heavy engineering industry, telling people to vote Conservative.

Their aim was to ensure the return of a Conservative Government which would suit "Trot" policy and help them to flourish.

Mr Wilson was asked about the intervention of Mr Powell and the possibility of Labour working with him. "My Government will not be big enough for him and me," the Labour leader replied.

PENSIONS OUR PRIORITY, SAYS CROSLAND

Pensions and housing would be Labour's priorities in an "inevitably limted" public spending programme, Mr Anthony Crosland said in Grimsby last night.

"The elderly and ill-housed are the most conspicuously underprivileged groups in our society, and their relative position must be improved—rapidly improved—if we are to retain any claim to be a jsut and fair society."

This would be one result of Labour's "social compact" with the unions. The compact would also mean increased taxation of the better-off — particularly of their capital wealth, "which they will otherwise use to cushion themselves against the relative austerity that faces the rest of us over the next two years."

It had been a "mature" election, Mr Crosland said. "The voters have refused to be swayed by empty slanging strongly against them. They have, for example taken a lot of idiotic talk about extremists with a healthy pinch of salt."

£22,000 BET ON TORIES TO WIN

A £22,500 bet on the Tories at odds of 9-4 on—to win £10,000—was placed with Ladbrokes yesterday by a Midlands industrialist.

The total now invested with Ladbrokes is £750,000. The bookmakers quoted the Tories at 3-1 on, Labour at 5-2 against and Liberals 25-1.

Hills quoted 5-2 on the Conservatives, 9-4 against Labour and 25-1 against the Liberals.

Joe Coral said that after £50,000 in bets on the Conservatives the odds had shortened to 4-11. Labour eased to 5-2 and Liberals at 33-1.

DIVERS TO SEEK OTHER CARGOES

By Our New York Staff

Undeterred by their failure to salvage the treasure on board the Italian liner Andrea Doria off Nantucket Island last summer, the divers who took part in the project are returning to the area this summer to search for the cargoes of other sunken ships.

One of them, says Mr Christopher Delucchi, vice-president of a San Diego firm, is a British ship which went down a few hundred yards off the eastern shore of Cape Cod more than 100 years ago with a large cargo of tin.

Dr Kissinger, American Secretary of State, with Mr Heath outside 10, Downing Street, yesterday. Later Dr Kissinger flew to Damascus.

Powell votes Labour

MR POWELL has already voted Labour, using his postal vote, he said in an interview last night on the Thames TV programme "Today."

He said he had confronted the situation and taken the only decision he could honourably take. "I don't know what will happen next."

Mr Powell said he had for 30 years opposed most of the characteristic policies of the Labour Party. But of none of them could one say they were irreversible, in the sense that after five years membership of the Common Market, Britain's membership, if unaltered, would be "signed, sealed and delivered."

"It is a funny sort of Tory who, when he has a choice of regaining and retaining the sovereignty and independence of this country as a Parliamentary democracy, votes the other way for temporary reasons."

He said he would not be very interested in Toryism if its loyalty meant "turning when Daddy turns."

Front's denial

Any rumours that Mr Enoch Powell is about to have an affair with the National Front Movement can now be categorically denied.

The National Front if not exactly openly wooing Mr Powell to support their cause at least did make compromising gestures to him about his former seat in South West Wolverhampton.

With their respective views on the Common Market and immigration not 100 miles apart, one would have thought: here is an ideally matched couple — just name the day. But Mr Powell not only resisted these blandishments.

He did not even bother to acknowledge them. Now his new bed-fellow, the Get Britain Out campaign, has angered and infuriated the National Front more than ever.

With the petulance and fury of a spurned suitor, they rounded on Mr Powell yesterday, accusing him of being "naive." The rebuke came from Mr Martin Webster, the national activities organiser of the National Front, who is their candidate in West Bromwich East.

Mr Webster complained: "The Keep Britain Out campaign is telling people to vote Labour and we don't believe Labour will get Britain out.

"We think Mr Powell is naive if he thinks the Labour party is going to get Britain out of the Community. So, alas for the National Front, the couple have proved incompatible and no union will take place."

PREMIER IN MERRY MOOD ON TOUR

Mr Heath was in merry mood last night during a tour of five pubs in his Sidcup constituency. Beaming and clutching a half pint of bitter he chatted with saloon bar "regulars."

Told about Mr Powell's decision to vote Labour, the Prime Minister said he did not think it would affect the Conservative's position in any way.

A relaxed Mr Heath bore no signs of his hectic campaigning. At one stop his drink was interrupted when the licensee's wife served him with a Shrove Tuesday pancake.

List of PoWs for Kissinger

DR HENRY KISSINGER, United States Secretary of State, expects to be given a list of Syrian-held Israeli prisoners during his talks in Damascus with President Hafez Assad, senior United States officials said last night.

The officials, who travelled with Dr Kissinger by air yesterday from London to Damascus, said he was expected to fly to Israel tomorrow to discuss the disengagement of Israeli and Syrian forces along the Golan Heights front.

Israel has insisted on getting the list of its soldiers captured during the October war before it will negotiate with the Syrians.

Immediately after his arrival, Dr Kissinger was driven to the guest villa near the Presidential palace where he will stay the night.

It was not known whether he would start his talks with President Assad last night or later. When asked for reaction to Dr Kissinger's expectations that he would be given a list of Israeli prisoners, Syrian officials remained guarded.

They said Syria was not moving from its two conditions for handing over the list that Israel commit itself to total withdrawal from occupied Arab territory, and that as a first step the Israelis should withdraw at least to the pre-1973 war ceasefire lines. Reuter.

(Talks With Heath—Back Page)

MORTGAGES UP UNDER LABOUR, SAYS BARBER

The election of a Labour Government would mean higher mortgage rates for Britain's four million home loan borrowers, the Chancellor, Mr Barber, said last night.

The balance of payments problem meant it was essential to retain maximum confidence abroad, for a lack of confidence would lead to higher interest rates generally, and these could not be isolated from the mortgage rate.

Labour's "irresponsible policies" of taking the brakes off wages, Government spending and nationalisation would be bound to push rates up.

The Liberals holding the balance of power would also diminish confidence overseas, said Mr Barber in his constituency, Altrincham and Sale. "So let everyone buying their home with a mortageg work out what a Labour or Liberal vote would cost."

A BOOT FROM MR NADER

By Our New York Staff

Mr Ralph Nader, the consumer advocate, has accused the shoe industry of callousness in ignoring the safety and comfort of its consumers.

Addressing the Podiatry Society of New York, he referred to the "fashion tyranny" of stiletto heels and the "ultimate idiocy" of platform shoes. He urged members and doctors to bring pressure to bear on manufacturers by citing growing evidence of foot ailments, posture problems and accidents as a result of wearing improper shoes.

INDIANS SAY NO TO FREE KIDNAP FOOD

By ALEX FAULKNER in New York

REPRESENTATIVES of 13 Indian organisations in the San Francisco area announced yesterday that they would have nothing to do with the scheme to distribute free food as a condition of Patricia Hearst's release by the Symbionese Liberation Army.

Mr Adam Nordwall, chairman of the United Bay Area Council of American Indians, said: "Many Indian people in the Bay area are hungry today, but we will not accept any free food until Patricia Hearst is released. We will not be co-conspirators in extortion. This is not to condemn those who are now accepting food from People in Need, it is a matter of pride with us."

A number of Left-wing organisations have expressed similar misgivings about this kind of blackmail, but 14,000 people did receive food during the first distribution last Friday, when rioting occurred.

The organisers of PIP now say that they will not proceed with the programme until they are assured of supplies of fresh food and have organised the hand-outs in an orderly and dignified manner, but they hope to be ready for another distribution tomorrow.

As the Hearst family continued the agonising wait for some word from Miss Hearst's kidnappers, Mr Jay Bosworth, her brother-in-law, who has been acting as a spokesman for her father, Mr Randolph Hearst, said yesterday: "There is nothing to do and it is frustrating. We feel she is still alive and healthy."

LATE NEWS

Phone 061-834 1234

Classified Advertisements 061-834 1234 Ext. 305

This edition of the Daily Telegraph is a historic example of a newspaperman's determination to ensure the continuity of the paper. It was produced single-handed by Michael Kennedy, Northern Editor when, as the result of a dispute no other member of his staff worked. This framed copy of the paper was presented to Mr Kennedy by his closest colleagues as a permanent reminder of how he kept faith with our readers.

TV and Radio Programmes and Entertainment Guide —Inside Back Page

'DEAD' DONOR WAS ALIVE

A MAN who was thought by doctors to be dead was still alive when they started an operation to remove his kidneys for a transplant.

He died fifteen hours later in the intensive care unit of Birmingham Selly Oak hospital.

The Birmingham City Coroner has ordered a detailed investigation of the case. The man concerned, Mr Michael McEldowney, was injured in a road accident 11 days ago and taken to Selly Oak with brain damage.

Three days later he was declared dead and doctors prepared for the kidney operation. After the incision he was found to be breathing.

Mr McEldowney was a native of Belfast who had lived in Birmingham for more than 20 years. His relatives are all believed to live in Ulster.

A neighbour, Mr Edward Cronin, said he understood Mr McEldowney's kidneys had been used for a transplant, but later discovered this had not happened. "I was really pleased when I thought his kidneys had been used to save life because it was the sort of thing he would

Continued on Back Page, Col. 4

Today's Weather

GENERAL SITUATION: A ridge of high pressure will persist over the British Isles. It will be generally dry but rather cloudy. There will be some brighter spells here and there but in South-eastern parts of England occasional rain may occur in places. In Shetland and Orkney there will be some rain or drizzle.

Temperatures in Northern and Western areas will be near or rather above normal but in South-eastern parts of England they will be near or somewhat below normal.

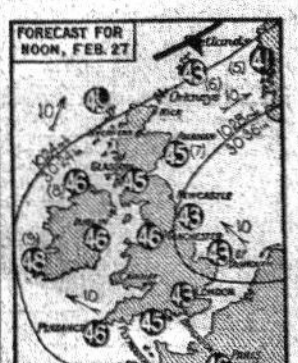

Issued at 6.30 p.m.

Black circles show temperatures expected in Fahrenheit. The equivalent temperatures in Centigrade are given alongside in brackets. Arrows indicate wind direction and speed in m p h. Pressure in millibars and inches.

LONDON, S E ENGLAND, E. ANGLIA, C. S. ENGLAND, E. MIDLANDS: Cloudy, perhaps occasional rain in places. Wind easterly, light or moderate. Temps near normal. Max. 6C (43F).

E. ENGLAND, W. MIDLANDS, N W ENGLAND, CEN. N ENGLAND, N E ENGLAND: Rather cloudy, mainly dry. Wind S E, light. Temps near normal. Max. 7C (45F).

CHANNEL ISLANDS, S W ENGLAND, S WALES AND MON., N WALES: Rather cloudy, mainly dry, some bright periods. Winds S E light or mod. Max. 8-9C (46-48F).

LAKE DISTRICT, ISLE OF MAN, BORDERS: Rather cloudy, some bright or sunny intervals. Wind variable, light. Max. 8C (45F).

CAITHNESS, ORKNEY, SHETLAND: Cloudy, perhaps a little rain in places. Wind S W mod. Mild Max. 7C (45F).

OUTLOOK: Cloudy but mostly dry.

Talks today in effort to end Press dispute

JOURNALISTS on *The Daily Telegraph* began a 24-hour strike yesterday in the pay dispute which has hit Britain's national daily newspapers. The decision was taken at a "fairly heated" meeting of the newspapers' National Union of Journalists' chapel (office branch). Voting was 119 to 52 in favour of the one-day strike. A similar decision was taken in Manchester.

There were talks between staff and management and union meetings at other Fleet Street newspapers, but at the *Daily Express* there were also hopes of an "historic solution to the dispute."

A special meeting of the Council of the Newspaper Publishers Association has been called for this morning to consider peace proposals in the dispute.

The meeting was requested by Sir Max Aitken, chairman of Beaverbrook Newspapers, which publish the *Daily Express*, the *Sunday Express* and the *London Evening Standard*.

Yesterday the Beaverbrook management and journalists on its papers in London, Manchester and Glasgow held talks lasting four hours. As a result the Beaverbrook management is expected to submit proposals to solve the dispute to today's NPA council meeting.

5 hours of talks

At the *Daily Express*, the management after nearly five hours of talks, issued a statement saying that it would strongly recommend to an emergency meeting of the NPA council tomorrow morning "the principles of a highly responsible proposal presented this evening by the NUJ chapel."

This was that there would be an agreement to increase the wages of NUJ members within the limits of Phase Three when a further increase in the cover price of the *Daily Express* could be implemented or in the light of other relevant factors. But it would not be before July 1

The journalists' leader at the *Daily Express*, Mr Bruce Kemble, said that the NPA chairman and the management had described the proposal as historic. It provided a possible basis for a wage settlement for the whole industry.

Developments on other papers were as follows:

Evening News: Journalists are prepared to pursue the claim now—it is within Phase III, from July 1—backing it with industrial action. But the chapel does not support strike action.

Evening Standard: By 59 votes to 20, journalists decided to postpone their claim for two months.

The Observer: The Chapel

Continued on Back Page, Col. 6

The Daily Telegraph

The Daily Telegraph apologises to its readers for the reduced size of today's issue and for any shortcomings which may be found in its contents. Members of the National Union of Journalists refused to work yesterday on today's issue of the paper which has, therefore, been produced by a small number of editorial executives and other members of the staff who are not members of the NUJ.

WILSON PLEA 'DON'T LET IT SPREAD'

MR WILSON last night intervened in the newspaper dispute, appealing to journalists not to let it spread further.

Speaking at an election meeting at Brighouse, Yorkshire, he said he was sorry to hear of the decisions taken by a number of journalists, and that one national newspaper might not be printed today.

He had said at his London Press conference yesterday morning that it was essential in a democracy that the public should have the fullest information and news of an election.

In making his appeal to journalists he added: "I very much regret this action has been taken and I hope it will not be followed by others."

Mr Wilson said he hoped the particular national newspaper involved would soon be back in print.

NEW AIR LINK

A new weekday air link between Manchester and Dusseldorf will be opened by Lufthansa German airlines on April 1.

speed and accuracy (helped by an influx of talent when the *Manchester Evening Chronicle* folded in 1963). On the sports side it became the paper of record for then-amateur games like rugby union. At its height there were 70 or 80 journalists in the Manchester office, an operation which had drive and bustle. It was a far cry from the carbon copy of the London edition planned by Camrose when the paper first printed in the north.

Kennedy is the first to admit that editing the northern editions was never like being editor of the paper as a whole. In any case it was complicated by the *Telegraph's* internal hierarchy which made Lord Hartwell (Michael Berry) editor-in-chief, with Colin Coote, succeeded by Maurice Green and then Bill Deedes technically editors under him but increasingly threatened by the rise and rise of a man called Peter Eastwood. Eastwood became managing editor in charge of newsgathering and the news pages from 1970. His abrasive style is attested by Deedes in his autobiography "Dear Bill" and by Duff Hart-Davis in "The House the Berrys Built." But what was a problem for London, where the editor was at least in charge of policy areas like the leader page, became all-but impossible for Manchester.

Kennedy is uncharacteristically outspoken in his loathing of Eastwood, a Mancunian brought up in Yorkshire. "He's the only person in my whole career I've hated. He was a bastard. He tried to destroy Manchester. He really did." Eastwood's assumption of power coincided with advances of newspaper production technology, particularly page facsimile which the *Guardian* introduced from London to Manchester in August 1976. The *Guardian* had been preparing for that day for years; the *Daily Telegraph*, in the throes of coping with traditional Fleet Street practices and tied in by contract to print at Withy Grove, was in no position to make such a switch but Eastwood turned up in Manchester when it was publicly announced in 1974 that most jobs would go within a couple of years.

This led to unprecedented go-slows by normally cooperative Manchester sub-editors. Frequently, Kennedy – who as northern editor was considered management and not bound by NUJ instructions – produced northern editions on his own, or with his deputy Ken Loran. He remembers Bill Deedes dictating all three leaders to him by phone from London one evening while Eastwood sat by in Manchester scowling. Eastwood had offered to help, but kept asking for London headings on stories. Loran said to Kennedy: "this bugger's getting in the way. Can't you persuade him to go to the Midland for dinner and come back later when we've got the paper away?"

To make matters worse, Eastwood had tempted some of the best Manchester office reporters to London, people like Roland Gribben who became City editor and Chris Munnion, the paper's South Africa correspondent, insisting that they be replaced by non-staff casuals. He did his best to prevent northern-based reporters handle big stories like Northern

Kennedy is the first to admit that editing the northern editions was never like being editor of the paper as a whole. In any case it was complicated by the Telegraph's internal hierarchy which made Lord Hartwell editor-in-chief

Ireland. Things got worse. "From then on production of the paper became a very dicey thing" says Kennedy. "We had NGA troubles, NATSOPA troubles, NUJ troubles. The ridiculous thing was that the papers were getting bigger all the time. Eastwood's idea was to deplete regular staff by gradual wastage. But as the paper's size increased, and edition times had to be met, we were forced to start a regime of casual sub-editors. Dozens of casuals, some of whom were good and some awful. They didn't have the same kind of feeling for the paper. Naturally. Why should they?"

Kennedy adds wryly that he was told by Andrew Hutchinson, the London night editor at the time, that Eastwood was terrified Kennedy would transfer to the London office and be given his job (Eastwood had made many enemies in Fleet Street, too). "I said he could have asked me because I've never wanted to go to London, never had any ambitions in that line at all."

Open warfare apart, Kennedy has affectionate memories even of the bad days. "I loved working on the stone. You remember that business about sub-editors never touching anything there? Well, they'd known me since I was a boy. Sometimes when I was waiting for a substitute headline from the random I'd be over there and a chap would wrap the headline in a bit of paper and hand it to me. I'd then take it back myself to the stone. They all knew it went on and they didn't mind. I couldn't have produced those editions on my own were it not for the printers. It would not be possible now because computers would simply be shut off."

Long before the Eastwood troubles Kennedy had established a routine based around nightly production. "My happiest times were on the stone. I suppose you could say I was northern editor cum night editor. I used to go into the office around 4pm and move onto the stone about 8.30. I didn't do the front page. I worked on the inside pages and the social page, just where I felt like it and whichever one was lagging behind. On the days when I was reviewing a concert I would go in earlier then walk across to the Free Trade Hall. After the concert I'd return to the office, write my notice while I had my supper – they'd set it off my handwriting – then I'd go up and cut it in on the stone."

Editing northern editions of the *Daily Telegraph* had little cachet, the office space occupied in Withy Grove had no character, the carefully-assembled editorial team was under fire, production was contracted to a Thomson Organisation whose machinery was ever-more outdated. And yet. The Paddy's Market Kennedy had sensed as a young office-boy had been transformed, with care and affection, into a very efficient operation. Kennedy was not the sort of editor to slap backs in the pub. It wasn't his style and he didn't have time. When the *Daily Telegraph* finally left Withy Grove, a decade and more after Eastwood's cry of doom, it was with sorrow and respect all round.

"I loved working on the stone…I couldn't have produced those editions on my own were it not for the printers. It would not be possible now because computers would simply be shut off"

Definitions of Fellowship: printworkers talk

Members of the Withy Grove Fellowship, the association of former workers at the print centre, discuss the comings and goings of newspapers, managements and trade union relations:

Tom Dolan   Reading dept, Fellowship chairman
Albert Hartwell Night publishing manager
Barry Lord   Administration (Mirror)
Sam Marsh   Publishing
Ken Martin   Reading dept and NATSOPA official
Bob McGee   Chief engineer
Barry Peirson   Circulation

Diana Dors, an 18-year-old starlet set to become the Blonde Bombshell of the 1950s, on a tour of Withy Grove in 1949 with Peter Hammond, who played alongside her in the Huggett Family series

Ken: This office was unique. In the early 1950s, workers at Waterlows who published the *Radio Times* went on strike. They had seven plants spread across the British Isles. It was an unofficial strike and the union office in London asked if we could print it. We were the only office capable of printing nine million copies of the *Radio Times*. We were all on double money, working any hours we cared to. It ran for nine weeks. I made a fortune. In the composing room it was continuous production because we were still keeping the papers going around the job. People working through their breaks, working their nights in. We thought that if we did well the *Radio Times* contract could finish up here. We were the only printing establishment in Europe who could set, run off and handle nine million copies. Only one edition, though. The talk at the time was that if we got the contract, newspapers would be swept out and then we would be able to editionalise. But of course it all went back to Waterlows.

Barry P: When Thomson came in he did not want to print his own papers. He didn't want editorial staff. When he first arrived he was claimed to have said that the *Evening Chronicle* was "the rotten apple in the barrel", then straight away the *Empire News* went. The *Evening Chronicle* merged with the *MEN,* which meant that Thomson was left with the *Sporting Chronicle* and contract printing of the *Daily Telegraph* and the *Daily Mirror*.

Q: So it was Thomson who killed off the Withy Grove empire?

All: Yes.

Ken: Thomson's idea was contract printing. The only reason the *Sporting Chronicle* was kept on was for Mr Burnett-Stuart, a racing man, a horse-breeder who we knew as Burnt Out Stuart, but he came here to start the carving up, the cutting out…

I recollect Thomson only coming here twice. One time I was talking to John Blakey, the FoC in the machine room. Thomson came into the room with his bottle glasses on. I was standing there being introduced when this bloke walked by, his sole flapping. Thomson says "young man." The lad comes over. Thomson reaches into his back pocket and pulls out the biggest wad of notes I've ever seen in my life. He had an elastic band on the wad which

he took off, with the bloke thinking "I'll get a new pair of shoes." Thomson handed him the elastic band and said "put that round your sole." It's a true story. He had a wonderful sense of humour.

Q: At the same time Thomson was not a good thing for Withy Grove?

All: No.

Barry P: Kemsley seemed to be the kings of printing. Throughout the North, down into Wales and up to the Lake District they had branch offices, one of whose tasks was to update the editions of the *Evening Chronicle*. The home edition would be out by just before midday but the branch offices would have extra quires which they put through the Bush machine to print all the latest cricket scores and racing results. All through the Lancashire towns.

Ken: Kemsley papers were part of the community. The *Daily Dispatch* was a true northern paper.

Bob: When Thomson arrived all papers became part of Thomson Regional Newspapers and Withy Grove became a company of its own (Thomson Withy Grove Ltd) isolated, in many ways, from the Thomson Organisation.

Q: So whereas with Kemsley all the regional papers had been coordinated here, under Thomson that role went?

Ken: It was a sort of asset-stripping.

Bob: For two 25-year printing contracts. The *Daily Mirror* and the *News of the World*.

Barry P: The demise of the *Empire News* was engineered; within a week of its ceasing publication the *News of the World* contract was signed. So Thomson had got rid of all the editorial, advertising etc, the whole thing. All he had to do then was print the paper. We know that it was making a profit for about ten years then things started to go downhill. By the early 1980s they were losing a lot of money on the *News of the World* contract, because it couldn't be renegotiated.

Ken: When the *News of the World* first came here the NGA insisted that 25 per cent of any newspaper printed here had to be set here. There was a daft situation where London was sending proofs up for pages to be set off the proofs. The NGA thought if the *News of the World* was allowed to get away with just printing, the other papers would follow suit. They probably would have done. Some people thought we might lose the contract at one stage.

Machine room control console at Withy Grove, 1964.
Right: Extracting a page stereo plate, ready to go on press, from the stereo caster. A staged picture; the plate's edges would normally be trimmed after the stereo casting process. Pages 88-89: The machine room at Withy Grove in 1959. A third line of Crabtree presses later filled the foreground space

Q: Was the Empire News printed in London too?

Sam: No. That was the reason why it could be sold on a Saturday evening, because it wasn't printed in London.

Ken: The *Empire News* was printed in Manchester and Cardiff. The Welsh edition was sent down for printing there. Half the leader page was in Welsh. We had to read proofs between us spelling the Welsh out letter by letter. There was one Welsh chap on the lino machine. We'd send the proof back to him and he'd read it through for grammar.

Albert: *The Sunday Chronicle* and the *Empire News* were principally northern papers. The London edition of the *Empire News* was on the 8.25pm train.

Sam: They tried many times to scratch the Saturday night edition, but they never succeeded.

Ken: The Saturday after the *Empire News* was closed we had the *News of the World* here, and the *Evening Chronicle* printed a broadsheet called the *Saturday Night Special* – it was a similar publication to the *Empire News*,

which they sold outside pubs. Its main selling point was football reports (Ken Wolstenholme, tv's first real football commentator, worked on the *Empire News* in the late 1950s). It lasted only for a few weeks.

Albert: A strange but true story. It was never announced that the *Dispatch* was going to close. The last edition, a Saturday morning, was its highest ever print order.

Sam: The same thing happened with the *Evening Chronicle*. The first we got to know about it was one Friday afternoon, the tv cameras came in, and the FoC asks him are you doing some kind of show? Oh, no, he says. This is the last publication.

Q: I still don't quite understand why the Dispatch had to close when the centre here had huge capacity. Surely there would have been capacity to print them both?

Albert: We could have printed the *Daily Dispatch* and the *Daily Mirror* at that time but the *Mirror* was on a rolling contract and looking to the future. There wasn't the potential to increase pagination with the *Dispatch* around. It was purely economics. The *Mirror* wouldn't come here alongside the *Daily Dispatch*. That's the key to it.

Ken: The *Mirror* had made certain demands. One was that they had their own composing room and proofreading department. There was a canteen on the lino floor. We didn't know but they'd already earmarked that canteen for their composing room. They had their own lino machines.

Bob: The *Mirror* paid to maintain their own machines. They were not for anyone else. So we suddenly found ourselves in a very large machine room with a limited capacity because of the restrictions enforced by certain customers. Even though it was the largest in Europe.

Q: Would the log jam have been in printing?

Bob: Yes, because they could only run at a certain speed. At that time it had a fairly big circulation and we were increasing the size of the papers from 32 to 48 pages.

Q: We haven't touched on the whole area of unions...

Albert: Have you got a couple of days?

Q: How was demarcation managed?

Albert: With difficulty.

Ken: In this place there were two main print unions – NATSOPA and NGA. The cost of protecting the NGA's 12.5 pc wage differential and the grey area of whose job it was created more problems for this unique office than any other printing plant in the country. It was always complex and it depended on the FoC of the night. Management was like the nut in the middle of the nutcracker. They were doing deals which they thought were secret and somebody leaked them.

That's another reason why the costs in this office exploded. We knew that we had the Thomson management over a barrel because they were dealing with a customer and were trying to keep the customer happy. Fred Bale, the production manager, had the devil of a job. As FoC of the reading room I felt sorry for him at times. I'm giving him a good hiding but feel sorry for him because the problem was insurmountable.

Checking papers off Withy Grove presses before they left for the publishing room via the Igranic belt. Another posed picture

Bob: I think one of the main problems was differentials, because you had two sections of the unions – the people directly related to the publication and the people not directly related. You might say well, you're an engineer you've nothing to do with printing so you can't be accepted as part of the printing crews, you don't get the same rates of pay. You say, hang on a minute, we don't get that and you don't run that press. This scenario went on for years and years. The only time it changed, I'm sorry to say, is when our wonderful friend Mr Maxwell came in and all of a sudden demarcations disappeared because the people who were left would do anything. You could do it yourself if you wished. Nobody stopped you.

Q: How much did union greed contribute to the end of production here?

Barry L: Most would say it was bad management. Managers had to produce their paper at all costs. They had to have their paper on the streets the next day when the competition had theirs. I believe their management style was very weak. When they should have been saying no and meaning no they said no, then go into negotiation. Management was lily-livered.

Ken: I think you're partly correct, Barry. Probably weak management, but we weren't working in a button factory. We were working with a perishable product. The main problems, I have to say, were the restrictive practices of the NGA, demarcation issues between NGA/NATSOPA, and joint production problems. Towards the end there were stoppages for all manner of reasons.

Q: Was the atmosphere here different from Fleet Street?

Ken: Yes (muted).

Q: More cooperative here?

Ken: Yes. NATSOPA was a centralised union, run by a general secretary. If he decided there was going to be a strike in London he would instruct the Manchester branch secretary to stop the job even though there was no dispute here in Manchester. That happened several times to our frustration.

Barry L: But it certainly wouldn't work the other way round.

Ken: What was unique to Manchester was that management never did the staffing lines on a job. FoCs did all the staffing. It was like a mini labour exchange.

Tom: Fleet Street staffing had nothing in comparison to Manchester. Lino operators there worked on piece rate. They wouldn't allow anyone in to that system.

Albert: Casuals in London were controlled by FoCs and not by the branches – paid the same night.

Bob: We tend to forget that technology was changing a long time ago and going into other parts of the printing industry even if not to the nationals. We fought against it because of jobs.

Q: Was Maxwell a mixed blessing?

Ken: When the *Mirror* was put up for sale, 12 months before he took over at Withy Grove, I was at a council meeting where Bill Keys, the general secretary, was saying "I don't want a predator. We've got to ensure the *Mirror* does not fall into the wrong hands." Teddy O'Brien, a national officer, was sworn to secrecy so it was only months before the *Mirror* takeover that we realised who he was referring to. There were so many writs flying about that people were very careful what they said. Suddenly somebody said Maxwell. He wasn't a blessing but an absolute nightmare.

Bob: In one fell swoop he wiped away all the demarcations here.

Albert: From the day he arrived at Withy Grove we knew we were in for it. He influenced *Mirror* staff immediately.

Bob: He was charismatic but you couldn't trust him.

Tom: Maxwell called a meeting at the Co-op building, arrived half an hour late, made a statement, took no questions and went off to a football match.

Barry P: They were delicate questions to which he made no answer and he just got up and left..

Tom: The heart of this building was the people who worked here. I'm not talking about management. There was real expertise here. We did more editions that they ever could in London.

The same heart of this, if I may say so, is reflected in our Fellowship now. It was a whole culture here. People worked and played as families, part of the building. The Fellowship is presently increasing in numbers even with people dying off. We have 360 members now. Many much younger than ourselves here are joining the Fellowship. We have 130 people at our Christmas lunch, 80 or 90 at each lunch meeting. People contribute to allow the less well off to come free – on the trip to Southport or wherever. We will collect them if necessary, we also send get well cards, condolences and so on. The Fellowship has been involved in the Printworks since it was a building site.

Ken: I used to spend a lot of time with the national council down south. As I came back late at night, getting off at Piccadilly Station, I would look for the newspaper wagons on the station approaches, then walk past the *Daily Express* and see the presses rolling. I used to think 'marvellous'.

Hot metal, on and off the stone

A conversation with Sid Downing and Eric Saltmarsh

One of the givens of the final decades in national newspaper hot metal publishing was that the hot metal men, the linotype operatives, their compositor colleagues on the stone who made up the pages, and those proof-readers, or readers, who also sported NGA cards between them held the industry to ransom. It is certainly true that NGA members earned top wages in a sector hardly underpaid by national standards and that they were not loth to use the industrial muscle they enjoyed.

Fleet Street was one scene, Manchester another. NGA members at Withy Grove had a 12.5 per cent wage differential over NATSOPA/SOGAT members at the same plant, but their take-home pay was perhaps half that of Fleet Street NGA men, who were often paid piece-work rates. If Manchester was a jungle, London was a snake-pit.

Eric Saltmarsh remembers visits to Fleet Street as a northern NGA rep. "On the surface we had quite a good relationship with the London chapels. But London FoCs had far more muscle than Manchester FoCs and if they didn't produce a paper then we normally couldn't, whereas if we did the same kind of thing they could still produce.

"We were once at a national paper in London negotiating a bonus. We got to the point where management said 'no way'. In the end we came out and told them 'management has said no'. We had chapel members shouting 'get back in there and do your f-ing job'. 'The management has said no.' They wouldn't have it, so the national officer turned round and said 'if you want to go on the cobbles (down tools) we'll take you on the cobbles." That was one of the situations you had down there. I remember an FoC in London who had had gold nuggets on his fingers. Not just gold rings. He wore expensive suits to work. He offered you drinks from a bar in his chapel office. We didn't have that in Manchester.

"There was a lad down there. A nice guy called Eric Gregory. He was Imperial Father of the *Daily Telegraph* chapels. He looked a bit like Peter Ustinov. He was a wine connoisseur and his family were restaurateurs. One day he went with a manager from one of the nationals to a top restaurant for lunch, where they had an excellent meal. A fortnight later the manager returned to the same restaurant with a companion. He asked for the wine he'd had before. 'Sorry, sir, but we don't offer that wine' he was told. 'But I had it here only a fortnight ago.' 'You can't have had.' 'Yes I did, with Mr Gregory.' 'Oh, Mr Gregory – that's his private stock.'"

Eric Saltmarsh and Sid Downing are both members of the Withy Grove Fellowship but it is indicative that they did not join the roundtable discussion recorded on pages 84-92. A decade and more into retirement – with the NGA, NATSOPA and other print unions long amalgamated – the cultural

differences remain, similar to those between engine drivers (ASLEF) and railway workers (NUR). The seven-year apprenticeship served by NGA operatives and compositors made them, in their eyes at least, craftsmen, while NATSOPA or SOGAT members who had not served time were, however experienced, simply workers.

Eric, a linotype operator and Sid, a compositor, insist that they often shared a pint with non-NGA men. But when Sid says "we were like one big happy family" he is talking primarily about a composing room where everyone had a nickname, names he lists in a memoir of Withy Grove he's currently writing. George Kirwan, head printer, was Cod's Head, Dave Nolan was Monkey, Jack Lomax was Jack the Hat, Fred Dodd was Dead Frog, Pete Sweeny was Sweet Peony and so on. Sid himself was known as Health & Safety because of responsibilities on the composing room floor.

Apprenticeship was the key, and apprenticeships were usually served in jobbing houses. "There's a complete difference in work and quality between jobbing printing and newspapers. Almost all NGA people were time-served in jobbing. Jobbing is printing; newspapers are ink staining paper," Eric claims.

His own apprenticeship started in 1952 at the small Manchester printing house of Harry Bolts. He finished his time at the *Warrington Guardian,* with night school four evenings a week and study at technical college to learn linotype operation. He was at a Linotype exhibition in the Deansgate Hotel in 1960, trying out the new Electron machines, when he was approached by

Above: Operators on the Withy Grove linotype machines, claimed to be the longest sequence in Europe.
This photograph shows "Ruby Alley", where small ads and City prices were set.
Right: Stone-hands putting the *Evening Chronicle* to bed

Ronny Hall, head printer at the *News Chronicle*, and offered a job. He duly started there but before he could be 'kept on' the *News Chron* folded. After a few years 'in the sticks' he was offered a job as composing room overseer with Argos Printers, Ndola, Zambia, but decided not to go because of the Congo troubles. He then worked for three more Manchester jobbing houses before being offered holiday relief work at Cross Street.

Eric takes up the story: "Just before the 1964 holiday season was due to end they started the *Sun* on Oxford Road. I got a job there. When I went for interview the head printer, Fred Etchells, said 'we work with all fingers here you know' – you used to get some who would be like journalists typing. 'Oh, I can do that, I'm college-trained.' We had a great time; you could leave your wage packet on the machine for a week and nobody would touch it. It was that kind of place." However, Eric, who was deputy FoC, fell out with his own union about overtime working. "The dispute was over one word 'will'. Whether you had to work overtime, or not. We were also in dispute with management at the time and we said we're not working our nights in.

The union told us 'you will'. We said two fingers to that. The court case carried on after the *Sun* had gone. I stayed in the union. Then I got a job at Withy Grove – I was one of 22 lino hands who went there on holiday relief and we were all offered jobs at the end of the season."

Headlines being hand-set, then cast, on the Ludlow machines at Withy Grove in the early post-war period

Sid's journey to Withy Grove was less tortuous. He served his time at the *Salford City Reporter* before National Service in the RAF, then did general jobbing with the Addressograph Multigraph company where for three years he set sensitive technical data on an Atomic Energy Authority job. In 1959 he secured a five-month holiday relief contract at Withy Grove, leading to a fulltime job which lasted 27 years.

Their stories reflect composing room life.

Sid: Do you remember the time when a party from Russia were over here in Brezhnev days? They came round with top management. Bill Duffy, our FoC, accompanied them. All the management had been given red stars – red enamel set in gold. Bill played bloody hell. How come they've got stars and I haven't? A red star was found for him PDQ. A couple of the lads on the stone were sipping mugs of tea. One of the Russians asked Bill why they were drinking tea and the others weren't. "Oh", he said, "they're from the League of Communists."

Eric: If things were late it was usually editorial's fault. Quite often the (head) printer would say "right, what's holding this page up – page one – OK, get a filler," and they'd bang the filler in. Lock it up. Away it went. The page sub-editor would protest – "but, I've not finished…" "Hard luck, it's gone."

Sid: One of the main shifts started at 5.30pm. The break for that shift was 10-10.30pm, but – human nature being what it is – we took five minutes washing-off time, plus ten minutes pinched. So people would knock-off at a quarter to ten. That quarter of an hour before 10pm was the busiest time of the night, with x number of bodies down.

Eric: One night page one fell on the floor at press time (the metal scattering into thousands of pieces). It was nobody's fault – a trolley collapsed. Luckily they had a page proof. It was quickly cut up, pushed out to all the operators. The page was back reset and reassembled in about ten minutes.

Sid: One of our jobs was to polish the standing obituaries. We would slide them out of the shelves, update them, reproof them and send the new proofs down to editorial. One time I was earmarked to do the updating of the Queen's obituary. I reached the stage where I proofed the front page. I had it on the spike ready to go downstairs to editorial when a party of visitors came round. They all stopped in horror before the banner headline 'QUEEN DIES'.

Eric: Editorial failed to realise with copy flow that a lull of five or ten minutes at crucial moments would snowball to 25 or 30 minutes by the time it was printed because, of course, you couldn't start to run the machines until the stereo department had made the plates, and they couldn't all be made at once. London was often the guilty party in sending late copy. It wasn't a problem for them because their press times were later. They didn't have to distribute to Ireland and Scotland. And there was very little communication between chapels in Fleet Street and Withy Grove. They wouldn't inform us of production problems unless the problems went to management.

Q: So what do they both think of today's computerised setting, with journalists editing copy onscreen, the whole thing going to plate with nary a compositor, reader or stone-hand in sight?

Eric: Modern setting is atrocious. Hyphenation is particularly obtrusive. I've set a book since I retired without a single hyphen in it except for compound words. It's quite easy to do. It's just time-consuming.

Sid: When we served our time if you had more than one hyphenation in the story you received a right bollocking. If there were rivers of space running down a column you had to reset it. But you'll always get 'someone shitting over the bar' rather than shooting over it, the literals.

Q: Was the endgame worse in Manchester because Withy Grove and other newspaper presses were obviously so vulnerable to new technology and the turmoil in Fleet Street?

Eric: I don't think so. All we ever wanted here was a policy of natural wastage but in the end everybody in the craft unions lost out.

Quire boys

A conversation with Albert Hartwell and Frank Taylor

Albert Hartwell and Frank Taylor were, along with Ken Brooks of the *Daily* and *Sunday Mirror*, responsible for packing and dispatching titles from Withy Grove, Europe's largest newspaper print centre. Albert was employed by Thomson as night publishing manager, responsible for staff across all the titles. Frank was the *Daily Telegraph*'s publisher. Both worked at Withy Grove all their lives, though Frank went to Trafford Park Printers with the *Daily Telegraph* for a few years before he retired. Albert started in 1941, Frank in 1938, moving across to the *Daily Telegraph* when it arrived in 1940.

Handling smaller volumes but embracing a much wider circulation area than Fleet Street, Withy Grove publishers had to cope with up to 13 editions of the Sunday papers and a nightly routine that included Scotland and Ireland as well as England north of the Trent and North Wales. Late editions – an increasing fact of life in the 1970s and 1980s – demanded on-the-spot negotiation with British Rail's newspaper train department, or if the train was missed provision of vans to deliver bulk supplies to Scotland or the North East. Dublin editions were increasingly flown from Ringway, Belfast from Speke. When newspapers arrived at a distribution centre like Kilmarnock they would be met by agents who ensured, one way or another, that the bundles reached the correct newsagents in country areas.

Albert and Frank talked about the perils and satisfactions of night life in the publishing room over the years.

Q: Did the times change much over the years?

Frank: They weren't a great deal different. You've got to remember it's speed that counted. You had to go as direct as you possibly could, whether by road or rail.

Albert: Some rail services were packed on the train. Stoke was one, Leeds and Hull others. It was vital to catch those trains. If you didn't and had to send papers by road to the agent, you had extra cost because his staff had to be put on overtime to pack.

Q: So you're always in the hands of what's coming off the press?

Frank: The editorial department. I used to wait for them coming past my office on the way home. They had to pass the publisher unless they decided to find a different way out.

Q: As production difficulties came in – print unions and journalists – it must have made your life absolute hell?

Frank: I've got diaries at home with huge parts missing because the London people didn't print at all. From time to time we handled some of the London print here when the NGA was striking in Fleet Street.

Albert: It was particularly difficult on a Saturday night because of the number of editions. The *Sunday Pictorial* had 10 editions, the *News of the World* had 13 when it first came here in 1960, starting with a special edition for Malta – they did that from the satellite plant at Harthill Street – which was only about 2-3,000 copies. The Maltese customs wouldn't allow the Irish edition in – it had to be cleaned up specially. The Irish edition had no sex at all, or very little. Malta was even stricter. Of course London didn't want to be bothered with a little thing like that so it was done here, first off the press and flown from Ringway. That would go at about 7.30pm.

Copies of the *Sporting Chronicle* destined for London and the South East were flown from Ringway by Northern Executive Aviation to Luton or

Pre-war action in the publishing room at Withy Grove, where working practices were largely unchanged for 50 years

Heathrow, though Luton was preferred because landing charges there were much lower. We had to check flying conditions at both airports before making the decision. Van drivers phoned us by 10.30pm to know which airport to collect from, and since this was before mobile phones there was no way we could divert them once they'd set off.

Frank: The *Daily Telegraph*, on Friday nights, used a direct flight to New York at 11pm from Ringway. Not a special edition – two or three quires, that's all.

Albert: We would send a Scottish edition parcel of Sunday papers to Corby in Northants for the thousands of Scottish steelworkers. We could do it but London couldn't. We used to pack the parcels of the Scots editions for Kettering around eight or nine pm on the Saturday night, then hold them for the train some time after midnight. If you were running late you still had to send the South Yorkshire edition to South Yorkshire. It was no use sending them the North Yorkshire edition, so you're propping and cocking all the night.

Q: That was part of the interest of the job, wasn't it?

Albert: Yes. In the days of the *Empire News* we had a London edition and a Scottish edition. We started with London; as we were getting through the edition we changed the machines over to Scottish, with the two editions running together. The London train deadline was 8.25pm. One night we were running late. Henry Sargent my boss and I were together. At the end of the run you have to give a lift order for the papers to go. It was already 8.25 and we still needed eight quires for London. In the end we said 'Bugger that, we'll pass the Scottish in, nobody will know'. So we packed a parcel of Scots. You wouldn't believe it possible that Eric Cheadle's newsagent managed to deliver him a Scottish edition to his London home (Cheadle was managing director of Kemsley's northern operation). Our chief publisher, then, was C.H.Womack. Cheadle phoned Womack on the Monday morning and played bloody hell with him. Womack said "Don't you blame my staff, it's those minders in the machine room (minders used to take a couple of copies out to check papers as they came off the press, then replace them). They don't care." But what an amazing coincidence!

On a Saturday night there was no way you dared get your Eire and Ulster editions mixed up. For the *News of the World* we decided to split the edition. We printed the Ulster edition at Harthill Street to prevent the parcels getting mixed.

Top: two titles from the Kemsley era on a 1951 van. Above: *Evening Chronicle*s wrapped in *Daily Telegraph*s being loaded from the publishing room at Withy Grove. Right: South East editions of the *Sporting Chronicle* were flown nightly by light aircraft from Manchester Airport. This picture is from 1972

Frank: I used to get through to railway control at nights to beg for another five or ten minutes… Railway control were very cooperative – a lot of cash came in for them.

Albert: Trains were the responsibility of the circulation managers' committee of the NPA. If Frank wanted ten minutes he could get it. But you couldn't delay ordinary passenger trains. The *Sporting Chronicle* used to catch the 10.20pm from Victoria for Holyhead, the boat train for Ireland. We weren't due to start delivering until 10pm. It was only a small order, in small parcels. One particular night the first van made it just as the train was due to depart. Charlie Tomlin drove down the platform alongside the train guards van, opened the van doors so that they locked with the guards van, threw his parcel in, and somehow couldn't get his van going again. His gear lever had mysteriously stuck. He didn't free that gear lever until the last *Sporting Chronicle* parcel arrived. They'd been coming down in dribs and drabs.

Frank: I remember Norman Hodgkiss breaking his arm, doing an *Evening Chronicle* pinch-run – pinching for time to get to the station. They were throwing parcels from the middle publishing room into the back of these little Morris 1000s. Womack said jump in so that you can help at the station. Norman Hodgkiss dived in and broke his arm!

Albert: The Bradford train used to go from the Rathole. At Victoria Station No 11 platform ran through to No 1 platform of Exchange Station, said to be the world's longest platform at one mile long. The 10.20pm to Holyhead was also 10.20pm at Exchange. It was via a little side passage, just like a rathole, near Exchange Station that you drove up to the platform.

Frank: One of my first jobs in the *Daily Telegraph* circulation department was every Monday morning for H.D.Weaver, the circulation manager. He would give me 5s (two half crowns) and say – just slip down and see Joe. Joe was a big knock-kneed policeman who directed traffic at the junction of Withy Grove and Corporation Street. I used to wait in fear and trepidation as a young kid for a gap in the traffic. Joe would swiftly pocket the cash as he carried on waving cars through. Joe allowed Weaver to park his car on Withy Grove. He was there for years and years, an institution. He must have made a lot of money.

Albert: There was always the culture of the black economy. Swag. Stolen copies. Management tried to cut down on it every now and then. I told them you can stop it altogether if you're prepared to take the consequences. What consequences? When you go home tonight there will be no papers for you. No *Express*, no *Mail*. Oh.

Frank Taylor's presentation sheet for showing visitors round Withy Grove, 1948

THE WORLD'S LARGEST NEWSPAPER OFFICE

At
KEMSLEY HOUSE
MANCHESTER
are produced
11,000,000
NEWSPAPERS EACH WEEK
out of the
25,000,000
COPIES PRINTED WEEKLY BY
KEMSLEY NEWSPAPERS LIMITED

POINTS FOR YOUR TOUR

COMMUNICATIONS

Telephone Room Over 150 Post Office lines and 27 multiphones. Private lines to Kemsley Houses in London, Glasgow, Newcastle, Sheffield, Middlesbrough, Aberdeen, York, Blackburn and Stockport.

Telegraph Room Can receive from London and Kemsley Group offices 42,000 words at rate of 700 words a minute each hour of day and night. Telephone and Telegraph channels cover 3,000 miles.

Photo Telegraphy Links Manchester to London and Glasgow. Service is supplemented by mobile Telephone Vans.

EDITORIAL Reporters, sub-editors and associated staffs on editorial floors produce FOUR Sunday, FOUR Daily Newspapers and ONE Evening Newspaper in addition to sporting and topical periodicals.

MACHINERY HALL Giant printing presses set out in three lines of 24, 25 and 30 units, and yet to be completed, now produce 11,000,000 copies each week.

Ink —Six tons are used each week. Paper —Sufficient used each Saturday alone to lay a five-foot wide carpet over 3,000 miles.

LINOTYPE Battery comprises 100 Linotype machines, 4 Ludlow machines, and up-to-date auxiliary plant, which each play their part in producing that clean-looking, easily-read page which is the hallmark of the modern newspaper.

PUBLISHING Over 34,000 newsagents are supplied by this Department, which also serves Kemsley Branch Offices in 50 cities and towns. Four copies for a village shop or two thousand and four for a big wholesaler—the Publishing Department deals with them all.

AUTOPLATE Produces each Saturday nearly 2,000 plates in 12 hours. Before wartime restrictions this Department produced each week 20,000 plates, using 500 tons of metal.

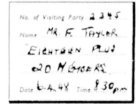

No. of Visiting Party 2345
Name MR. F. TAYLOR
EIGHTEEN PLUS
20 MEMBERS
Date 6.4.48 Time 8.30pm

Drivers going to the stations always had a few copies to give out on the way. There was a nightly car for Nottingham with the *Sporting Chronicle*. My job when the car left Withy Grove was to phone Hazel Grove Police Station to tell them the approximate time it would be coming through.

On the 4.45am bus to Heaton Park, the 62, they always gave the guard a paper or two. I happened to be on days at the time and was coming in early. I got the 62 on its return journey at 5.15am. When we passed the Jewish bakery near Derby Street the guard got off with his pile of papers and came out with a bag of bagels.

A vehicle went every morning to Lancashire Hygienic Dairies, one went to the Senior Service cigarette factory, one went to an abattoir near Stockport.

Kemsley used branch offices in places like Salford, where I worked for a time, as a move to cut out the newspaper wholesalers. The drivers would drop off a load, we'd make them up and drop bundles off at the newsagents. But Kemsley's drivers were also doing foreigners for the wholesalers. We had a Reliant van at the Salford office. One Sunday morning at about 4.45am we broke down on Eccles New Road with a lot of papers on board. Who comes up but Arthur Heywood, delivering to Eccles. He stops.

"Arthur!"

"What's the trouble?"

"Broke down. Give us a tow."

"Oh, I'll have to come back. Can't do it now."

"What d'you mean you can't do it now?"

"I can't do it now, I've got to get to…"

He had his foreigner to do! They all did it. One time there was a railway strike. Billy Barlow, a driver who had a foreigner on Sunday mornings, was sent to Oxford on the Saturday night to deliver the *Empire News* which usually went by rail.

"Who's doing your job (foreigner) on Sunday morning?"

"I am."

"You'll never be back."

"I will."

He got back. I can remember him in the yard. He was sitting there, he couldn't get out of the cab having driven all the way to Oxford and back, long before motorways, by 5am. Then he had his foreigner to do. They all did it. It suited the wholesalers because they got reliable, trained people and paid them cash in hand.

Q: What did you think about moonlighting?

Albert: It didn't bother me at all. Early in the year several drivers would come to the Salford branch office for a little meeting so they could make sure that their holidays didn't interfere with their foreigners.

Too many left-footers?

The Hultons were Catholics. Manchester is a strongly-Catholic city. So it is not surprising that there was a Roman Catholic bias to employment at Withy Grove. It is, however, surprising that Catholic employment traditions survived 35 years of the Berry brothers, lords Camrose and Kemsley, who came from a Welsh non-conformist chapel background. Sid Downing, a compositor, claims that when he started as a holiday relief in 1959 "if you weren't RC, or if they found out you weren't, you hadn't much chance of being kept on. The staff at Withy Grove was probably about 85 per cent Catholic."

Sid's initial duties were in the classified ad section where he was introduced to the number two overseer, Bernard Goulding, by the overseer Fred Lawton.

"You look well! Have you been on holiday?" Goulding asked.

"Yes", Sid said, "I've just come back off my honeymoon."

"Oh, what church did you get married in, then, and did you have a nuptial mass?" inquired Goulding.

"We were married at St Mark's Church, Bolton, and it wasn't convenient to have a nuptial mass" Sid replied quickly.

Later, Lawton had a quiet word with him. "I couldn't help overhearing your conversation, and had to smile because St Mark's is my church" – it was Church of England – "there are too many left-footers in this company, anyway. Don't worry, son, your secret's safe with me."

Each year the tradition of Whit Walks – church parades through Manchester and other North West centres – divided Catholic from Protestant, as it still does in a less charged way today. Catholics walked on Whit Friday, Protestants on Whit Monday. Sam Marsh, a Protestant, recalls how, as a trumpeter with the *Evening Chronicle* Prize Band he was among those hired to lead the St Patrick's contingent to Albert Square. He, and his fellow trumpeter Bill Callaghan had a rose in their caps for the occasion. When they arrived at Reather Street to march to Livesey Street they were told to remove the roses. "Well, we're not carrying on if you make us do that – we're going." After a few hard words they were allowed to proceed.

Albert Hartwell tells the story of two Withy Grove workers standing in Corporation Street watching the Catholic walks one Whit Friday. When the young women of the Children of Mary, in their white blouses and green sashes, filed past, one (who Albert declines to name) remarked quite loudly "I've stuffed most of these." The other, who worked with him, turned round and thumped him. It seemed that his sister was a Child of Mary.

Linotype in Manchester

Len Brenner writes: In 1890 Ottmar Merganthaler, the German-born American inventor of the Linotype typesetting machine, chose to site his European manufacturing base beside the Bridgewater Canal at Altrincham, just south of Manchester – in the same year that he established his Brooklyn plant. This placed his facility within easy reach not only of what was to become one of Europe's great centres for newspaper production, but where engineering expertise was among the best in the world at the time.

Throughout the 100 years or so that hot metal typesetting dominated newspaper production the machine – called by none other than Thomas Edison 'the eighth wonder of the world' – changed in detail but not in principle. It held fonts in interchangeable magazines in the form of a brass matrix – or mould – for each letter, and the spacebar on the machine placed a space-band consisting of two tapered steel pieces which justified the line to column measure. The later machines held up to four magazines enabling font and typesize changes from the keyboard which, incidentally, was not the QWERTY format we're all used to. Once assembled, the line of matrices and spacebars acted as a mould from which the machine produced its 'line'o'type' as a metal slug which dropped into a galley. The matrices, through an ingenious system, were then automatically distributed back to their magazines.

In the early 1960s the company was experimenting with computerised typesetting using primitive 6-level tape to transfer instructions to remote machines, and later even producing the Linotron machine that used a system of photosensitized paper to produce type for lithographic printing, but there was no way Linotype could compete with the new technology.

An early Linotype machine at the Museum of Science and Industry in Manchester

Munich and the Manchester Eight

"I'm sitting in the office on a Thursday afternoon, what one would call a slow news day. I thought 'Archie will be on shortly with his follow-up to the match. That'll fill the back page.' And then of course came the flash. Aircraft crashed at Munich. I was dispatched immediately to Old Trafford – what good I could do there I don't know – and already the press were gathering.

"Jimmy Murphy, Matt Busby's assistant, who would have been on the plane but for the fact that he was in charge of the Welsh international team the day before, came out and told us all that he knew, which wasn't very much at the time. He spotted me. I was the familiar one in the small crowd. He said 'Derek, come inside'. So I went inside and he sat me down. He sat down himself and burst into tears. 'They're dead, they're all dead, I know it.' They weren't, of course. There were some survivors who played again. He poured me a large whisky. Frank Taylor of the *News Chronicle* was thought to be dead. One of the few people who has ever read his own obituary."

Derek Wallis, the *Daily Mirror*'s chief football writer in Manchester for many years, might have been on the plane bringing the Manchester United team back from a successful European Cup fixture in Belgrade himself except that, in February 1958, he was second string to Archie Ledbrooke, who had moved across from the *Daily Dispatch* when the *Daily Mirror* arrived in 1955. Ledbrooke was one of eight Manchester-based journalists to die in the crash: Alf Clarke of the *Manchester Evening Chronicle*, H.D. Davies of the *Manchester Guardian*, George Follows of the *Daily Herald*, Tom Jackson of the *Manchester Evening News*, Ledbrooke, Henry Rose of the *Daily Express*, Eric Thompson of the *Daily Mail* and Frank Swift, the legendary Manchester City goal-keeper by then writing for the *News of the World*. Frank Taylor was badly injured but eventually returned to work. He died in July 2002. The photographer and wire room man on the plane, Peter Howard and Ted Ellyard of the *Daily Mail*, also survived.

David Meek, who covered Manchester United for the *Evening News* from the time of the crash until he retired in 1995, had been immediately switched from his job as political leader-writer by Tom Henry, the *MEN* editor.

"My initial brief was to do the job for a few weeks. Then I went to ask the editor whether I should carry on. He replied that they were on a cup run so I should stay with them for the moment. That took us until the end of the season of course, playing Bolton at Wembley. I had another meeting with the editor when he asked me what I wanted to do. I said career-wise I'd be better to go back to leader writing. He said 'well, some of us haven't done too badly who've come up by the sports desk' – meaning himself. I had to acknowledge that. He asked me to stay with football, saying 'more people read what you write about United than will ever read your leaders'. So I said – 'well, yes'. Then he produced his clinching argument and offered me a rise. I meant to do it for two or three years, but then the thing gathered momentum again."

"Jimmy Murphy spotted me. I was the familiar one in the small crowd. He said 'Derek, come inside'. So I went inside and he sat me down. He sat down himself and burst into tears. 'They're dead, they're all dead, I know it'"

United star may never play again—Tragic families fly out

ABOVE: Those who died   RIGHT: Some of those who escaped

MATT 50-50: EDWARDS 'GRAVE': BERRY COMA

50 doctors battle to save their lives

FIVE German surgeons fought desperately to-day to save the life of MATT BUSBY, Manchester United's famous manager critically injured in the disastrous Elizabethan air crash at Munich. First dramatic message from the Rechts Der Isar Hospital said: "He is lying between life and death." Then came brighter news—"He is somewhat improved," but to-night it was still "touch and go."

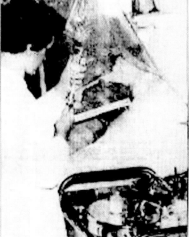

MORALE AT ITS HIGHEST

HOSPITAL STAFF WONDERFUL

FLYING FROM BELFAST

TURN TO BACK PAGE

More might have died . . .

To-night's bulletins

INJURED IN HOSPITAL

THE DEAD

UNACCOUNTED FOR

OUT OF HOSPITAL

'Barrel of death' hunt

Disaster fund

More miners in pay strike

Coping with the aftermath of a crash in which over half of the celebrated Busby Babes team had died as well as so many journalists proved a difficult time for all. "It was two-fold", says Meek, "because everybody obviously knew about all the players who were killed, eight in the crash with Duncan Edwards to die later. Naturally that overshadowed the loss to journalism, but the journalists were top men."

Football journalism ran in Meek's family – his father covered York City for the *Yorkshire Evening Press* for 45 years – but he himself had only visited Old Trafford on a couple of occasions, as a fan. "It took me and others a long time to get close to Matt Busby because every time he saw us I suppose it reminded him, just as the new players reminded him, of the ones who had gone. He saw the dead journalists. They had been very close. It was an era of success before Munich with the Busby Babes. Journalists like Henry Rose had been part of the bandwagon. Apart from 1948 when they were in the Cup Final this was the first time United had made it big – the Busby Babes concept caught the imagination. It was really taking off. All the journalists in on that got quite close to the management and in particular to Busby, who was a shrewd publicist, so it took us a long time to establish our relationships."

The makeshift United team was removed from Old Trafford. "I always associated those weeks after Munich with the smell of swimming bath chlorine because Jimmy Murphy, who took over, got the players out of the way by removing them all to Blackpool. They stayed at the Norbreck Hydro. They'd go training, then they would come back for a swim and a massage. That was the emergency headquarters after the crash. Murphy would give his press conference after the morning training session, often in the area of the baths. We'd either drive over every day or maybe stay a couple of nights. Jimmy didn't want you in the hotel – he was trying to distance his new team from the tragedy."

Henry Rose (left) was more than just a sportswriter – he was a supreme showman whose death in the Munich air crash was mourned by many. **Peter Oborne** takes an affectionate look at his life

'Henry Rose is here today.' Those five words said it all. It meant that the game in question was the biggest, most glamorous and most important of the afternoon. The fans were duly appreciative

Henry Rose, the *Daily Express* football writer killed in the Munich crash, was singled out for special treatment in the *Express's* centenary commemorative issue, 1900-2000

Keith Dewhurst was detailed by the *Manchester Evening Chronicle*'s sports editor, Jack Smith, to replace Alf Clarke. Dewhurst had been with the *Chronicle* for four years, had survived the Kemsley training scheme, and was enjoying himself as a sports journalist. He had no intention of staying in newspapers. He was already developing contacts for a writing career in television and theatre. But, as a United supporter and a Mancunian, he could hardly say "no." He stayed in the job for 18 months. He remembers Smith as leading the best team he was ever lucky enough to be part of, including the time when he was a scriptwriter in early 'Z Cars' days.

Dewhurst also was to get to know Norbreck Hydro well in the weeks following the crash. Soon enough he too had struck up a bond with Jimmy Murphy. "Murphy was the greatest coach in 50 years", says Dewhurst. His opinion of Matt Busby is less clearcut: "Busby was the ultimate spin doctor. Everybody believed in the myth of the team." But it was a delicate one because Busby wrote an *Evening Chronicle* column (ghosted by Ted Coghill) in which he elaborated theories like the English league should be reduced to two divisions (because of lack of players) as well as the need for professional referees. Later, Dewhurst was himself to ghost *Evening Chronicle* columns for Jimmy Murphy and Bobby Charlton. After the *Chronicle* died in 1963, the sports staff held a lunch in its honour at the Cromford Club. Dewhurst was invited back and sat in between Busby and Murphy.

Meek recalls working with Dewhurst in the weeks after the tragedy, and they have remained friends ever since. "Keith and I were the youngest. Yes, there was a bond. After the crash the club didn't fly. They were still in Europe. I remember going with the team to Milan for the semi-final of the European Cup, the next European fixture. We went by train and boat to Paris then got the trans-Europe express to Milan. Most of the other journalists flew because of time constraints though Keith and I travelled on the train. That way we were closer to the players and the management – Jimmy Murphy, Jack Crompton the trainer. It was a very volatile atmosphere in Milan and they were well beaten – too many new players in the team."

Meek's brief was to write about the new team – how it was coping, what sort of transfers were going on and its likely future composition, as well as to report the games themselves. The *MEN* news desk looked after stories about the survivors, the funerals and the inevitable recriminations. Wallis, too, was among regular visitors to Norbreck Hydro, where he believes Murphy did a "wonderful job." But he was also covering funerals and more. He started to get sick of the perhaps understandable media obsession with the crash.

"I took myself off one afternoon to Rotherham, I think it was to watch Rotherham v Cardiff. It started to snow on the way over the Pennines – I'd bought a new car, only had it a week or two. The match was abandoned because of snow at half time, so I had to make my way back. It proved

"After the crash the club didn't fly. They were still in Europe. I remember going with the team to Milan for the semi-final of the European Cup, the next European fixture. We went by train and boat to Paris then got the trans-Europe express"

impossible that day. I came to a halt in snow somewhere on the Woodhead Pass behind lorries which had slued across the road. Fortunately I was right beside a transport café, the Robin Hood Café. I spent the night there. All they had to offer was bacon and eggs of course – and warmth. There wasn't a pub nearby. I queued to phone the office and to phone home – I always got my priorities right. I put over the story of a baby who was with her mother way back in the line of halted cars in the snow. The mother had a bottle of milk in a baby's feeder with a teat which was passed from driver to driver all the way down to the café to warm it up, then passed back. I thought the news desk would be interested. In fact, they spiked the story. That didn't worry me too much. It was a time for reflection."

A time of opportunity, too, for those lucky enough not to be on that plane. "Right after the Munich air crash the *Express* came on for me", recalls Wallis. "I turned them down eventually. Ted Fenna, the *Mirror* editor, called me in. 'I knew this was going to happen, sit down there. What are the *Express* going to pay you? I told him, and also that I would be covering matches on a Saturday for the *Sunday Express*. He wrote down a figure and showed it to me. 'If I can get that, will you stay?' 'Yes.' 'Right, I'll have the bloody chairman out of bed if necessary.' Somebody thinks something of me, I thought."

There remained a very awkward question about the crash – though it did not receive a great many column inches at the time, for obvious reasons – whether the ill-fated BEA charter Elizabethan twin-engined turbo-prop should ever have attempted take-off from the ice-bound Munich runway. The pilot had already tried twice, but a technical fault called 'boost surging', over-rich fuel causing the engines to fluctuate when power was applied for take-off, had prevented it. The longsuffering passengers were twice sent back to the departure lounge while checks were made. Why was it third time unlucky?

Meek has his own views, 46 years on:

"I'm sure that the unspoken pressure was to get back for the league game on the Saturday. United had defied the authorities to take part in the tournament. One of the reasons the Football League didn't want an English team to compete in European football was because travel was very uncertain in those days and they could see it wrecking the domestic programme. That was the main reason for influencing Chelsea to turn down the invitation. They tried to pressure United into turning down the invitation but Busby and his chairman Harold Hardman agreed that they would defy the authorities and would enter. So, having done that, it was in everybody's mind in the administration and certainly in Busby's mind that 'we mustn't mess up the league programme, we must be back in time'. It was a midweek game on the Wednesday; nowadays they fly back straightaway.

The first goal scored at Old Trafford by Manchester United after the Munich tragedy. *Daily Mail* picture by Denis Thorpe

But they stayed over and the return journey was on the Thursday. Well, if they'd aborted the flight they would have been coming back on the Friday, a day before the next league game. Then the issue would have been could they repair the plane, or could they put a new plane out even by Friday? They might have missed the game on the Saturday so there was pressure to get back. That had very little attention because you can't prove it and I suppose it was pointing a finger at Busby, but I'm sure that must have been a factor."

It is an issue on which Wallis, who retired in 1986, is still not prepared to speculate. "How Matt Busby survived I'll never know", he says, and leaves it at that.

From today's perspective Dewhurst feels that the football writers who died at Munich left a void which was never really filled. People like the *Manchester Guardian*'s H.D.Davies, "a fantastic writer, the Cardus of football"; Eric Thompson of the *Daily Mail*, who used to draw cartoon illustrations showing tactical moves which fitted into the columns alongside his copy; and of course Henry Rose, Mr Personality, who once remarked when he announced himself 'Henry Rose, *Daily Express*' to an officious gateman at Belle Vue "I don't know why I bother to say *Daily Express*."

Between them and the other five there was, Dewhurst notes, a living memory which went back to the 1920s. Their replacements didn't have the same depth of knowledge of the game. And, in the faster-moving 1960s scene, there was increasing emphasis on off-the-field antics. Ironically, it was the crash as front-page news which also helped change the typical news editor's view that sport was not news and the typical sportswriter's view that news was no concern of his.

Dewhurst was later commissioned to write a film about Munich, but the film never happened: "I don't suppose we will ever know the full truth about the crash", he says. He is much more sure about Manchester's ability to recreate itself, in life as in football. "Manchester is a special place. City have the same love for the game as United, except that their boardroom has had less vision. Manchester can recreate and rebuild; Liverpool seems just not able to."

Journalists and stories: Where's Mr Pendlebury?

Harold Pendlebury was, by common consent, the best reporter of them all. He never went to Fleet Street. That was entirely his choice, of course. A Lancastrian from Horwich, Pendlebury joined the *Daily Mail*'s Manchester office in 1936 and became chief reporter there for 25 tears before retiring in 1976. Roy Greenslade, the former *Daily Mirror* editor turned media commentator, worked in the Manchester office as news sub during the late 1960s. He remembers Pendlebury as "one in a million" who "compared with the best in Fleet Street." Ken Donlan, Pendlebury's news editor before joining Larry Lamb at the *Sun* in

London, wrote on Pendlebury's retirement "His interviewing technique was masterly, even on the cruellest doorstep. A marvellous Mailman." Harry Whewell, the *Guardian's* northern news editor, added "Harold was the greatest telephone user of all time."

Some colleagues claimed even more. In a spoof issue published by the Manchester office to mark his retirement, he was cast favourably alongside the legendary Vincent Mulchrone. The piece, headed 'Mr Pendlebury? What a lovely man – he kept all those nasty reporters away' began:

'GOOD MORNING, Mrs Braithwaite. My name is Mulchrone. I'm from the *Daily Mail*.'

'Oh, yes? Where's Mr Pendlebury?'

'Well, it's his day off, you see, so they sent me to ask how your sextuplets are getting on…'

'Is he all right? I mean, he's not ill or anything is he?'

'No, Mrs Braithwaite, he's fine…'

'Well, if you're a friend of his…'

'Oh I am, Mrs Braithwaite, me and Harold are like that…'

'You'd better come in then. I hope you're as good as he was at keeping them nasty reporters at bay. Mr Pendlebury spoke to them very quietly through the letterbox and they all buggered off down to the White Swan.'

'Well, I'll try, Mrs Braithwaite. Now could you tell me anything that Harold – I mean Mr Pendlebury – didn't cover yesterday. I mean, well anything?'

'Such a luvly man. Had the kettle on before I could turn round. And their

bottles warming. Told me all that I had to do was relax. A luvly man…'

'Yes, Mrs Braithwaite. Good old Harold. Now, if I could just ask you a few questions about…'

'Ooh, you've got your notebook out. Mr Pendlebury didn't do that. He said only nasty reporters did that. You're not going to put anything in your column, are you? Mr Pendlebury just sort of chatted while he was changing their nappies, mostly about railway engines it was…'

'Sorry, Mrs Braithwaite. I've put my book away. Quite right. Just a chat. Like Harold. I mean, Mr Pendlebury…'

And so on. Behind the running gag lie the old Manchester-London tensions. But Mulchrone, a Yorkshireman who had passed through Deansgate on his way to Fleet Street, had no such hang-ups himself. Mulchrone once wrote: "My telephone manner is a straight lift from the best reporter in Britain, a man called Harold Pendlebury."

Among numerous Pendlebury stories still circulating in Manchester journalist circles are his admission that he was saved from being beaten to a story by a *Daily Express* rival when he found the story in question left carelessly behind in a telephone box the *Express* man had just used to phone his copy over. And advice to a young reporter: if you are asked for just two paragraphs make sure they are the finest in the paper.

You're not nominated for best reporter in Britain if you're employed by the *Burnley Bugle*. You have to be working with the top stories of the day. Manchester reporters, Pendlebury leading the pack, did just that. The list of stories is headed by two of the greatest murder sagas of the twentieth century – the Moors Murders and the Yorkshire Ripper – both of which happened on Manchester's doorstep. It embraces the dreadful years of Northern Ireland Troubles from the late 1960s and, well before that, the 1916 Easter Rising, civil war and creation of the Irish Free State.

It encapsulates the Icelandic Cod Wars, Sputnik-tracking at Jodrell Bank, Albert Pierpoint, the last hangman, the Poulson/Pottinger scandals, the Great Escape of John 'Muscleman' McVicar and Walter 'Angel Face' Probyn from Durham Jail, the Winter Hill air crash of 1958, the Stockport air crash of 1967 and the Manchester Airport runway disaster of 1985, the Abbeydale methane explosion. It includes the murder of Blackpool police superintendent Gerald Richardson by the Sewell gang, the so-called Black Panther murders, the disappearance of Lord Lambton and the Vicar of Woodford who faked his own death, the Mountbatten assassination in Sligo, the Liverpool 8 and Moss Side riots of 1981, the Miners' Strike of 1984, the York Minster fire.

Amongst sporting tragedies, Heysel and the Bradford rugby league stadium fire stand out (for the Manchester United Munich disaster see pages 106-112). Donald Campbell's death on Coniston Water was a Manchester story, as

Harold Pendlebury in the Manchester newsroom of the *Daily Mail*, shortly before he retired in 1976. Picture by Denis Thorpe

were sundry potholing tragedies in the Peak district and the Yorkshire Dales. The Beatles phenomenon was first picked up by northern reporters (see page 136). Coronation Street became a national obsession via The other Fleet Street, which also tracked Louise Brown, the world's first test tube baby, born in Oldham.

Of course these stories did not halt when the nationals decided to drop live Manchester production. Think of the Lockerbie tragedy, Hillsborough, the Strangeways Prison siege, of the IRA murders in Warrington, the Jamie Bulger abduction and the IRA

explosion in Manchester city centre. As a grisly reminder of dread events in North East Cheshire, the recently-completed Shipman Inquiry at Manchester Town Hall investigated the doings of the country's most profligate mass murderer ever. Mike Cuerden, northern news editor of the *Daily Mail* until 1987, ran the prime stage of public relations for the Shipman Inquiry. Interestingly, Cuerden believes that Manchester-based news editors like himself would have handled the inquiry in much the same way as London-based ones did. In other words, they would have cherry-picked from the evidence while leaving day-to-day coverage to agencies. He commends *Manchester Evening News* enterprise in arriving at a close estimate of the overall number of victims via data available on the internet.

The long hunt for Peter Sutcliffe, the Yorkshire Ripper, whose victims were prostitutes in West and South Yorkshire as well as in Greater Manchester – the Leeds/Bradford, Sheffield and Manchester conurbations – saw journalists

Top left and above: Agency pictures used by the *Daily Mail* taken outside the Dewsbury court where Peter Sutcliffe, the Yorkshire Ripper, was first charged with murder. Top right: Peter and Sonia Sutcliffe on their wedding day. A "pick-up" by the *Daily Mail*

in competition or conflict not just with each other (and their respective London offices) but with the West Yorkshire Police and the might of the cheque book. From the viewpoint of Manchester news editors, the Ripper was the most important story they were likely to handle. They were determined not to be outshone. Stanley Blenkinsop, news editor of the *Daily Express* at Great Ancoats Street, recounts his reactions:

> The Yorkshire Ripper murders were one of the biggest-ever and longest running national crime stories. For five years Peter William Sutcliffe terrorised women and girls throughout the North. He killed 13 of them – and attacked several others – before his arrest in January 1981. As the fears of millions increased, I suggested that the paper should mount a national campaign urging more government action.
>
> I wrote to Derek Jameson and Ted Dickinson, the respective *Express* editors in London and Manchester: 'If this was happening in the Greater London area surely the Government would be demanding that more be done in the way of more police and more advanced scientific and forensic techniques.'
>
> Both editors were considering how to launch such an *Express* campaign when Sutcliffe was arrested in Sheffield, almost certainly minutes before killing his fourteenth victim. News broke late on a Sunday afternoon. Blenkinsop, on a day off, raced into Manchester to take charge. I had lived with this story for years and I was not going to sit at home at this stage.
>
> All that West Yorkshire police would say was that a man had been detained and was helping police with their inquiries into 'the so-called Yorkshire Ripper murders'. There was no indication of his identity, where he had been arrested, or where he was held. The police insisted there would be no further announcement until the following morning.
>
> In such a massive crime story, the earliest possible identification of the central figure is invaluable to journalists. Even if it cannot be immediately published, say for legal reasons, it enables reporters and photographers to start foraging for collected pictures and background. Being minutes ahead of your opposition can make a massive difference.
>
> Among the calls from frustrated reporters vainly seeking details of the arrested man, I took one from an *Express* reader in Garden Lane, Bradford.
>
> **Reader:** 'I've just seen the TV news. They say a man has been arrested for the Yorkshire Ripper murders. I think it might be one of my neighbours.'
>
> **Blenkinsop:** 'Has he got a Geordie accent?'
>
> **Reader:** 'Oh no – broad Yorkshire.'
>
> At this stage I thought immediately that the neighbour could not be the Ripper. For years Yorkshire police had insisted the killer had a Geordie accent

— they had released a tape recording of their prime suspect. His message, taunting police in Geordie tones for their failure to catch him, was played repeatedly on national TV and radio channels. West Yorkshire's Chief Constable was so convinced that the accent was the vital identity clue that three times Sutcliffe was detained for routine questioning – and was released because he did not speak that way.

But I persevered. Why did the reader think a neighbour was the Ripper?

'Because lots of policemen have been there all day. From the noise of hammering and banging they seem to be taking up some of the floor boards. And one or two have been digging about in the garden.'

I asked the neighbour's name and address.

'Peter Sutcliffe, 6 Garden Lane, Bradford.'

His job?

'Lorry driver.'

'On the phone?'

'Yes.'

'Could you look up the number for me please?'

The reader dictated it.

Taking the reader's name and address, thanking him for his help and promising that the *Express* would send him a cheque for his help, I hung up.

No, no Geordie accent – can't be him, I thought.

But worth a try?

So, on a direct line, I rang the Sutcliffe number.

'West Yorkshire Police' came the crisp male reply.

Blenkinsop (with assumed authoritative tone): 'What weapons have you found so far?'

Police officer: 'Three hammers, four chisels, three knives, one a carver, very sharp…'

Blenkinsop: 'Fingerprints?'

Police officer: 'Being fingerprinted now sir. May I have your name, sir, please?'

Blenkinsop: 'My name is Blenkinsop.'

Police officer: 'Rank and division, sir – please.'

Blenkinsop: 'News Editor, *Daily Express*, Manchester.'

Police officer: 'Fuck me!'

Phone slams down.

I dial back immediately.

'Blenkinsop here', I announce as the phone is picked up

Different voice at the other end: 'No comment to make, no comment at all.'

Phone slams down.

But it was enough.

An *Express* reporter was in Garden Lane, Bradford, within half an hour and minutes later was filing back a word picture of Sutcliffe built up from people living nearby.

Within four hours Expressmen had collected photos of him, including one of the mass killer working happily at his previous occupation. He had been a grave digger and the exclusive snapshot showed him busily shovelling out earth from a newly-excavated grave – smiling broadly. After exclusive use in the *Express* it was syndicated round the world.

I organised a massive background investigation in the following months as Sutcliffe awaited his Old Bailey trial. When the material was typed out in booklet form I took it to London where I briefed Jameson and senior editorial executives, sitting at Jameson's request in the London editor's seat.

During the Ripper trial I and my northern reporters went to London to cover it directly, with the aid of London staff.

It was our show from the very start. We were the Ripper experts and we were allowed to get on with it. **"**

Brian Crowther, the *Daily Mirror*'s crime reporter in Manchester, remembers the specific problems created for police forces by serial killings which crossed police authority borders. "On the Yorkshire Ripper case each squad had a different method. HOLMES was the standardised, computerised system developed but there was so much paperwork with the Ripper that they had to reinforce police stations to take the weight! They used a reader in some forces – like a copytaster on a newspaper – who read everything coming in. Some had exceptional memories, down to recognising every criminal record."

The West Yorkshire Police didn't exactly cover themselves in glory during the hunt for Sutcliffe, but Crowther remembers a point scored during one of the routine press conferences:

"Why haven't you called Scotland Yard in?", the police spokesman was asked

"Well, they haven't caught their Ripper yet!" came the reply.

The relationship between crime reporters and police has always been controversially close, and few were closer than Jim Stansfield, the *Daily Mail*'s northern crime man. "Gentleman Jim", as he was known, lived (and still lives) on the Fylde near Blackpool, an area synonymous for crime as Essex is to

Londoners. Stansfield was a very good friend of Joe Mounsey, the former assistant chief constable of Lancashire, whose own close colleague Gerald Richardson, Blackpool's police superintendent, was gunned down by Frederick Joseph Sewell during his escape from a botched Blackpool jewellery raid in August 1971.

Stansfield was in Bournemouth on holiday when he heard about Sewell's arrest. He immediately rang Blackpool police station.

"I'd like to speak to Joe Mounsey."

"Mr Mounsey is not available."

"Tell him it's Jim Stansfield from the *Daily Mail*'."

Moments later, the head of Blackpool CID came on the line. Mounsey was interviewing Sewell, who he had personally arrested in London, but his colleague gave Stansfield the inside story. Nobody else had it that night.

The *Daily Mirror*'s Johnnie Walker catches the despair of Ann West, mother of Lesley Ann Downey, the ten-year-old victim of Moors Murderers Ian Brady and Myra Hindley

The *Daily Telegraph* may not have had the contacts, but it considered the Sewell story big enough to "detach" Trevor Bates for as long as needed to collect the background on the case and to cover court proceedings. When committal hearings opened at Blackpool magistrates court on November 29 1971 reporters were frustrated by the ruling that reporting restrictions applied. However, Bates stayed in court. His patience was rewarded when, four days later, Lord Widgery overruled the reporting ban in the High Court, and Bates could write a summary of three days' committal proceedings from his shorthand notes. The following February and March, Bates covered Sewell's trial at Manchester Crown Court.

Stansfield was close to the police but able – he stresses – to resist pressure not to write stories embarrassing to the force. He recalls how Frank Williamson, when Chief Constable of Cumbria, came on asking him not to follow up the story of a copper who had been got rid of after the two-year probationary period, Stansfield transferred him to his editor, Harry Myers.

Then Stan Parr, a Blackpool chief constable, was investigated for offences including improper use of his chauffeur-driven police car, falsification of police records and misuse of powers for personal favours. The abuses came to light after Parr had issued a shotgun licence to a Blackpool acquaintance who had been refused one in the normal channels by a detective constable. That constable reported the incident to the next HMI police inspector doing his rounds. An inquiry conducted by Hampshire police found Parr guilty. "I was there before the inquiry" says Stansfield, "when Bill Palfrey, chief constable of Lancashire, told him 'put your ticket in, Stan, you've got your time in'. But he wouldn't hear sense. He was sacked. I think it shook him. It was a very big story at the time. But he didn't lose his pension."

Crowther remembers Ernie Lewis, his predecessor, as "All contacts. He knew everyone. You had to live with the cops, and had no chance unless they accepted you. You needed recommendations, then you had to earn trust. I had a fair number of police contacts. If I was really stuck after Ernie retired I rang him. He was famous for not revealing his sources. He was charged under the Official Secrets Act and fined £5 back in 1930. Later, much later, Hugh Cudlipp gave him his £5 back when celebrating the *Mirror's* 5 million readers."

One reporter, bizarrely, was accused of the very crime he was covering. When Arthur "The Fox" Hutchinson came across a marquee outside a house in the wealthy Sheffield suburb of Dore he murdered the bride's parents and brother, and raped the bride. At his trial his defence was that he'd been visited by a *Sunday Mirror* reporter and pointed at him in court – "he did it!"

Sometimes newspapers got caught by using agency copy. Stanley Goldsmith, the *Daily Telegraph*'s top hard news man, recalls the 1977 case of the Billy Hughes murders near Chesterfield, committed after he escaped

First picture of police operations on Saddleworth Moor which uncovered the remains of children murdered by Ian Brady and Myra Hindley. Denis Thorpe, who took the scoop for the *Daily Mail*, was told to charter a light plane and to stay in airspace until dusk to prevent other newspapers getting a similar image (police were keeping reporters and photographers well clear of the digging on the moor). The picture, internationally syndicated, made page 8 of London editions

Top left: Andersonstown women marching to protest Belfast intercommunal violence, August 1976. A *Daily Mail* wired picture. Markings show the portions used/excluded from printed picture. Bottom left: Londonderry riots. *Daily Mirror* picture by Johnnie Walker. Bottom centre: INLA volunteers give a masked send-off to a comrade who died by hunger-striking. An unpublished freelance submission to the *Daily Mail*. Above: British soldiers patrol the Divis flats, Belfast, 1980. Denis Thorpe for the *Guardian*. Left: Londonderry Orange parade, 1985. Picture by Denis Thorpe for the *Guardian*

from police custody. Hughes took refuge in a cottage, murdering four of the Moran family before fleeing in a vehicle with Mrs Gill Moran. Hughes was caught attacking her with an axe at Rainow near Macclesfield and shot dead by police.

The story from Raymonds News Agency, which Goldsmith incorporated into his piece, stating that DCS Alf Horobin, head of Derbyshire CID, led the hunt, was written several months later when Horobin was transferred to uniformed duties. Horobin sued Goldsmith and the *Telegraph* for libel on the basis that a uniformed officer had in fact led the hunt. "He claimed that whoever wrote the 'transfer' story 'had dipped his pen in vitriol'. I showed off the pen for years on the strength of that!" The *Telegraph* was ordered to pay £4,000 damages plus £9,000 costs. Goldsmith adds, ruefully: "All the witnesses (for the case at the Royal Courts of Justice) were put up in the Savoy except me, stuck in some kennel near Kings Cross. Bill Deedes gave me keys to his drinks cabinet saying that if the deputy chief constable of Derbyshire, a key witness for us, arrived when he was in conference why not offer him a whisky?"

By the 1960s, chequebook journalism was on the march, particularly for the biggest stories. "I was the first reporter to do an in-depth interview with David Smith, the 17-year-old husband of Maureen Hindley, Myra Hindley's sister" says Crowther (Smith and his wife tipped off the police to Brady and Hindley). "Smith had witnessed the killing of Edward Evans. He used a very vivid phrase like 'crumpled to the ground'. He became in the pay of the *News of the World*. Smith said it could have been the *Daily Mirror* – I'd bought him drinks in the Swan; but Bill Freeman, my news editor, was against paying for stuff because that can go very wrong. He was correct."

Sometimes, however, the story came simply through reaction to a particular scenario and the way it was described. On the day of the Stockport air disaster in 1967 when a plane crashed on approach to Manchester Airport killing 36 holidaymakers returning from the Costa Brava, Stansfield was sent to Colne by Ken Donlan, to pick up the passenger list from the office of Lyons Tours, organisers of the Perpignan flight. James Preston, the tour firm owner, was himself in France at the time. Stansfield arrived to find Paul Dacre, now the *Daily Mail* editor but then a Manchester-based reporter on the *Daily Express*, already installed. The two sat around watching as Patricia Newton, the firm's 26-year-old office manager, dealt with a flood of telephone calls, coping with the tragedy.

"The story almost wrote itself," comments Stansfield. "I'm a bit chuffed now to think that I had the centre spread in the *Mail* next day, while Paul was given only five or six inches in the *Express*." It was a case of picking up on the sensitive and sympathetic efforts this "slip of a Lancashire lass", as Stansfield called her, made to inform distraught callers.

Turf wars

We know that the *Daily Mail* was editionalising as early as 1912 (see pages 28-29). It is not surprising, given their fixed-cost Manchester investment, that newspapers sought to maximise a northern presence through creating reader loyalty in places as different, and as remote from each other, as Liverpool and Newcastle-upon-Tyne. This meant opening offices in the big centres usually staffed by a two or three reporters and a photographer, and ensuring that the Leeds edition went to Leeds, not Sheffield or York. As competition got more fierce with the arrival of the *Daily Mirror* in 1955, regional offices vied for exclusives and engaged in circulation battles via slip editions produced in Manchester.

Scottish editions were handled from north of the Border – apart from the *Daily Telegraph* and the *Guardian* – until the *Daily Mail* and then the *Daily Express* decided to pull back to Manchester in the late 1960s and early 1970s. The *Daily Mirror* for the most part left Scotland to its sister paper, the *Daily Record*, except for a period in the 1970s when *Mirror* northern executives launched a circulation drive in Scotland, much to the annoyance of the *Record* and the confusion of readers.

Ireland was always Manchester's domain. In the case of the *Daily Mirror* the Irish editor sat in his office in Withy Grove deciding what he would take from the northern (or London) editions and what he led on from his Dublin and Belfast staff. Editions for the Republic and for Northern Ireland became more separate as the Troubles of the late 1960s developed. Manchester-produced editions were, of course, competing with strong Dublin and Belfast newspapers as well as other UK titles.

In 1965 the *Daily Mirror* opened an offset colour printing plant in Belfast, printing pages faxed from Manchester. This was the first UK use of the page-faxing technology which would eventually finish off Manchester as a publishing centre, and the first stage of a plan by Cecil King to set up regional printing plants around the country which never happened. The Belfast press had a 130,000 print run but the operation lost money (although it put on a lot of Irish sales) and was not reinstated after a well-placed IRA bomb disabled the plant in 1970.

Turf wars fought over more conventional issues like sales and circulation could make life difficult for the regional morning papers whose patch they were "invading." Ian Hamilton Fazey, who was to become northern correspondent of the *Financial Times*, remembers the days in 1969 when, as night editor of the *Liverpool Daily Post*, he was suddenly faced with a Merseyside circulation war between the *Daily Mail* and the *Daily Express*.

"We felt duty bound to produce a later front page than theirs, which carried 4am slugs. We changed everything we could. We were helped by Merseyside's

Ireland was always Manchester's domain. Editions for the Republic and for Northern Ireland became more separate as the Troubles developed. Manchester editions were, of course, competing with strong Dublin and Belfast newspapers

The most galling thing to Manchester sub-editors would be a London editor's insistence that third or fourth edition page changes were made to incorporate London stories not available earlier

Daily Mail news subs filmed by BBC-TV cameras, 1963

love of chess and the world championship being fought out between Fischer and Spassky in Buenos Aires. We carried bills like '5am: Fischer's sensational opening gambit'. We achieved a 20% circulation increase, beating them on the street every morning, but it probably cost us because we had to keep a dozen or so people on overtime each night."

Stanley Blenkinsop was with the *Express* on Tyneside in the late 1950s and worked for the *Sunday Express* on Saturdays. He used to delight in following up 'exclusives' in the *Empire News* available to any punter at Manchester's Victoria Station by six pm on a Saturday evening when the *Empire News* went on sale, and which the Manchester newsdesk duly alerted him to. He would then have time to phone around and dictate a story which still got into the North East edition of the *Sunday Express* and sometimes improved on the original.

London editors who rang Manchester colleagues suggesting someone pop up to Carlisle, or over to Grimsby to follow up something – it was all "north", wasn't it? – would receive incredulous responses, particularly since Fleet Street reporters had the reputation of never leaving London if they could possibly help it.

The most galling thing to Manchester sub-editors would be a London editor's insistence that third or fourth edition page changes were made to incorporate London stories not available earlier. Much of the resistance of *Mirror* Boys Behaving Badly (see pages 142-147) to returning from the evening break came from their dislike at jettisoning their own handiwork in favour of – in their opinion – an inferior London product.

Women in a men's world

If the world of newspaper production was almost entirely, throughout the age of hot metal, peopled by men, newsrooms and sub-editors' tables were not much better. Women journalists had rarity value on the nationals, though often star quality. Was it that news editors and night editors did not wish to be responsible for lone women going home late at night, were they jealous of the effect they might have on younger male journalists, or was it simple misogyny? A bit of all three, probably.

There were exceptions. Mary Stott, the *Guardian* women's editor from 1957-1972, was offered her first real break in journalism by John Beavan as a sub-editor on the *Manchester Evening News* in 1945. Five years later she was disposed of because, it seems, she was uncomfortably close to becoming chief sub. But in 1957 Alastair Hetherington invited her back to Cross Street to create the women's page, or Mainly for Women as it was christened. She stayed put in Manchester, where her husband Ken was an executive with the *News Chronicle* and the *Daily Mail*, while many around her were moving to London, and it was from Manchester that the *Guardian* fostered a revolution in women's journalism symbolised by writers like Marghanita Laski, Margaret Drabble and Jill Tweedie. Mainly for Women brought urgent women's issues of the day to the national agenda in a way that tied them into society as a whole, and ran several successful campaigns. Mary Stott was joined in 1964 by Fiona MacCarthy, known later for her writing on design and architecture.

Mary Stott, who revolutionised women's page journalism from Manchester between 1957-1972, portrayed in later life by Jane Bown

Much at the time Mary Stott started to make her mark, Nesta Roberts was quietly ascending *Manchester Guardian* newsroom ranks so that, by the time London printing started in 1961 she had national experience of social services reporting and was dispatched as news editor to Gray's Inn Road. She ended her *Guardian* career as Paris correspondent and became an author of guides to regions of France.

Shelley Rohde, of the *Daily Mail*, was a successful author while still filing front-line news features. She made the most of her friendship with the artist to write her 1979 biography "A Private View of L.S.Lowry", which remains the standard work on a reclusive figure. She moved across to television as did Esther Rose, her opposite on the *Daily Express* (and niece of Henry Rose, the football correspondent killed in the Munich crash, as well as being the wife of the *Guardian's* Harry Whewell). Rose is remembered by former colleagues for her descriptive powers. Writing about the 1958 Winter Hill air crash of a flight from Douglas to Manchester she described the Isle of Man "dangling like a jagged teardrop in the Irish Sea." She became a Coronation Street scriptwriter.

This Manchester home industry increasingly dominated the pop paper features agenda. At the *Daily Mirror* Jane Fickling (married to Brian Wood, also of the *Mirror*) found herself playing reluctant chaperone to the Street's Julie Goodyear on a weekend in Paris with Goodyear's then fiancé which for some reason the *Mirror* was sponsoring.

Manchester was the start point for the *Daily Mail*'s opinionated columnist, Ann Leslie. She was wished on the *Daily Express* news editor Bob Blake, not known for his love of women journalists or graduates. The story goes that Blake asked her to write a 1,000-word feature on something suitably abstract for her first day in Manchester. She rushed into his office the next morning in high dudgeon. Why hadn't they used her feature? But they had, replied Blake. But it's not in the paper, countered Leslie. Have you read the Irish edition? No, of course not. If you'd got in earlier you might have had time, said the implacable Blake. At that, he recalls with nostalgia, "she stomped her pretty little feet and stormed off."

It was a two-way game. Charm offensives lurked around every corner. Were you offered jobs on merit, or for other reasons? Some opted for caution. Angela Neustatter, later to be fashion editor of the *Guardian* and to write a history of feminism amongst other books on social issues, acquired the name Angela Nonstarter when, as a young reporter for the broadsheet *Sun* in the 1960s, she made a practice of rejecting the advances of male colleagues, including that ageing Lothario Hugh Cudlipp.

Secretaries were more evident in the Kemsley House newsrooms than women reporters

The colourful and eclectic Bridget Taylor became a sub at the *Guardian* in the early 1970s, when she was already over 40. A former professional violinist and member of Ivy Benson's Band, she modestly put down her appointment to the fact she had mentioned in passing at her interview that she had toured Latin America with the Hallé. After the *Guardian* halted live Manchester production in the summer of 1976, Bridget Taylor moved to the *Daily Mirror*. She died tragically young.

Sue Bromley joined the *Daily Mail*'s Manchester news subs' desk in late 1975 – the year the Sex Discrimination Bill became law. She occupied the *Mail's* splash sub slot before moving to the *Daily Mirror* in 1978, and believes she may have been the first woman 'splasher' on the nationals. Ironically, the only rivals for the title – despite Page 3 duties – would have been on the *Sun* in

London. Murdoch, who had successfully employed senior women journalists in Australia, was to appoint Fleet Street's first women editors.

"It was the best of times and the worst of times," Sue Bromley suggests. "Those of us who arrived first felt excited and privileged to be there. We derived a certain kudos from our novelty value. Many male colleagues welcomed us and treated us with friendship and fairness. But it was early days and life wasn't always easy.

"Professionally speaking, you had to be one and a half times better than the average bloke to survive. A stiff upper lip was also vital. Old School boys who'd opposed the recruitment of women waited to pounce on any hint that you 'couldn't take the pressure'.

While at the *Mail* Sue turned up at a colleague's fancy dress party as a dragon. "I'd found a wonderful, green, hairy outfit at the theatrical costumier in Moss Side and thought it would raise a giggle," says Sue. "It did – with most people. But one of my bosses had a face like thunder. Dressed as Superman, with his knickers over his tights, he summoned me to a quiet corner where he admonished me for not being feminine enough – in and out of the office. Pointing to his partner, dressed as the obligatory schoolgirl in gymslip and black stockings, he berated me: 'Just look at my wife. Isn't she pretty? Why can't you be like that?' Useless to protest that, at such a stage of history, 'schoolgirl/subs' desk/survival' would have been an incompatible combination."

But when she moved on to the *Mirror* things were distinctly worse. "In my first week I was approached, separately, by two editorial executives each claiming that the chief sub had been dead against employing a woman and it was all down to him that I had the job .... so 'when are we having the night out?' After I declined the invitations, neither of them gave me anything more than a filler again and made a point of complaining about how I'd subbed those."

When the newly-launched *Daily Star* offered Bromley a staff job in 1978, she was delighted to leave the Mirror. Both the launch editor, Peter Grimsditch, and his chief successor, Lloyd Turner, welcomed women recruits. By the time United Newspapers bought the Express group from Trafalgar House in the mid-1980s, Trish Foster and then Annie Riddle had joined Bromley on the news subs' desk.

"Trish appeared for a late shift one hot summer evening in jeans and a very revealing top, with no bra. It caused a minor sensation on the stone, but brought no adverse repercussions for her. It was a sign that nationals were finally catching up." But the *Daily Express* proved to be the last bastion of male supremacy. Its failure to hire women was eventually challenged under discrimination legislation.

"When the Manchester news subs desk finally fell," Sue Bromley concludes, "it was to Eugenie Verney, who drove to the office on a motorbike and wore black leathers. What would Superman have made of that?"

"Trish appeared one hot summer evening in jeans and a very revealing top, with no bra. It caused a minor sensation on the stone, but brought no adverse repercussions for her. It was a sign that nationals were finally catching up"

Blenkinsop's Ancoats

Stanley Blenkinsop writes: Arthur Christiansen once commented in his legendary daily bulletin for staff:

"A high-spirited staff produces a high-spirited newspaper. The *Daily Express* is a high-spirited newspaper"

In the Golden Years of Ancoats the dictum was embraced with particular enthusiasm by the news desk, who worked beneath self-written posters proclaiming: "Every day is a fun day."

During my 17 years as news editor (an Express Newspapers record), I always answered the phone with the jubilant cry: "This is the news desk of the World's Greatest Newspaper!"

In the Blenkinsop years there was a Christmas tradition that immediately after the final editorial conference before the holiday, the entire news and picture desk staff moved their seats on top of the desk as if aboard a stage coach.

I took the part of the coachman with make-believe reins fashioned from the twine used to wrap up newspaper parcels. All aboard drummed their feet loudly on the metal table tops to match the beat of horses' hooves.

And the climax came as one deskman played "The Posthorn Gallop" on a four foot length of piping (borrowed from the plumbers' shop below) to loud applause.

****

After the Great Divide of November 1978 the *Express* Ancoats staff was split down the middle – one half to form the new downmarket girlie *Daily Star*, the others staying beneath the Crusader banner.

Express Newspapers' proprietor Victor (later Lord) Matthews – Fingers to *Private Eye* – and managing director Jocelyn Stevens – he of the Piranha teeth – travelled north from Fleet Street for the official birth of the *Star*. Or as the *Eye* put it: "A Star is Porn!"

Blenkinsop and picture editor John Knill were determined that their paper should not be overlooked in the festivities. So they borrowed full Crusader outfits from the Royal Shakespeare Company at Stratford and gatecrashed the *Star's* switch-on to the amazement of the dinner-suited "Fingers" and

Stanley Blenkinsop, *Daily Express* northern news editor, and John Knill, *Express* northern picture editor, kitted out as crusaders at the 1978 launch of the *Daily Star* to remind bigwigs of the Beaverbrook heritage

"Piranha Teeth." Both burst into laughter while Blenkinsop and Knill stamped around in their chain mail, flourishing their swords and shields at the VIP guests. As the *Guardian* reported on page one next morning: "It was the Crusading Couple who drew the loudest cheers of the night."

Although printed in the same building, the *Express* and *Star* were in competition with each other just as much as with the *Daily Mail* or *Daily Mirror*. The staffs, separate in every way, were divided on the vast editorial floor by a high partition, the "Berlin Wall." The division meant that the *Express* sub-editors were cut off from the wire room where copy arrived from London. So management installed an overhead wire for a spring-charged device to fly back and forth high above the heads of the *Star* subs. *Express* deskmen decorated it with RAF roundels and christened it the Flying Shite-hawk.

Once, as a leg-pull, a fake *Express* exclusive was loaded so loosely that it fell out half way to the wire room – to flutter down among the *Star* subs. Efforts made to substantiate the story by the Star Matters team were about to get out of hand when the *Express* admitted the hoax to save red-faces all round. But *Star* subs hit back – buying a catapult in Tib Street and attempting to shoot down the Shite-hawk as it flashed back and forth in its RAF insignia.

****

Expenses were a key item in Ancoats life. Stories about them were legion – and sometimes true.

Bob Blake, former *Express* news editor and Poet-Laureate-manqué, wrote a much-sung ditty on the subject. Verses include:

Put it on your exes	*Put it on your exes*	*Put it on your exes*
What a lot of wealth	*Everybody smiles*	*Make the taxman howl*
Get another round in	*Manchester to Salford*	*Don't just tear the arse out*
And one for yourself	*Is ninety-nine miles*	*Simply disembowel…*

****

On his retirement in 1982 Bob was awarded the MBE for services to journalism. When he received it from the Queen, on a summer's day, she commented: "It's warm today." Bob, slightly deaf in one ear, thought she said: "What did you do in the war?" To which he replied: "Tank driver, Ma'am!" At which HM gave him a somewhat surprised look.

Bob, a veteran of the Western Desert campaign against the German Afrika Korps, had a healthy respect for General Rommel.

For his retirement celebration colleagues arranged a personal message from Rommel's son, then Burgomaster of a German town, wishing Bob many happy years.

*****

In the Blenkinsop years there was a Christmas tradition that immediately after the final editorial conference before the holiday, the entire news and picture desk staff moved their seats on top of the desk as if aboard a stage coach

The *Express* news desk had a green cash box for expenses advances – known as "green pounds." There was also a second cash box for subscribers to "Kippers from Craister" which were delivered monthly.

One month the kippers arrived but when the appropriate tin was opened, it was empty except for a note: "I owe the kipper box £25. Signed Tom Campbell" (then news editor).

He had found the official expenses box exhausted so was forced to the next best tin.

*****

Daily Express photographer Jack Kay had a pet duck which he took to the Crown & Kettle next door, calling for a pint of beer for himself and a large ash tray full of water for the duck.

Back in the office he kept it cool floating in a developer tray in the darkroom. One day John McDonald, as northern editor, was showing major advertisers round the editorial floor to celebrate the paper's first full page in colour.

He was in the midst of telling them "This is the most modern newspaper darkroom in the country" when the duck was heard quacking happily as it floated in the tray…

The quotes of Bob Blake

From a book presented to Bob by his colleagues when he retired as the *Daily Express*'s northern news editor:

"…I'm getting them all today. Why me? That's the third call from a nutter I've had this morning. Why do barmy people ring up the *Daily Express* I wonder? It baffles me. What can the *Daily Express* do for them? It's not our fault they're barmy. I mean, why do they ring us up? Do you think they sit at home and suddenly think to themselves 'Ah, I'm barmy, I think I'll ring up the *Daily Express*'? It baffles me. Still, I suppose it's better than them coming to the front lodge… If wonder if the *Daily Mirror* get calls from barmy people. I expect they do…"

*****

"…Unfortunately I've only had three opportunities to use it in the whole of my journalistic career…the answer to "No comment" I mean. If you say to this chap "would you tell me what time you're flying to America with the vicar's wife" and he says "I have no comment to make", you say "I didn't ask for comment, I'm not interested in comment. I asked what time you were flying to America with the vicar's wife. I'm asking for facts, not comment…"

*****

"…I'm getting them all today. Why me? That's the third call from a nutter I've had this morning. Why do barmy people ring up the Daily Express I wonder? It baffles me. What can the Daily Express do for them?"

ASST.NEWS EDITOR: (unable to raise Brady) Where do they drink in Belfast on a Sunday lunchtime?

RB: Lunchtime? It's bloody quarter past four.

Brady is tracked down in a bar

RB: What's happening then?

BRADY: Sorry Bob, I can't talk to you at the moment – there's a riot going on… (holds phone towards window – sound of bombs, explosions, bullets)

RB: Would you describe that as spasmodic or desultory?

*****

TONY BROOKS: (About to depart with a contingent of relief reporters to the Herrema siege in the wilds of Ireland where restaurants are few) What do you eat out there, Bob?

RB: I'll tell you what you eat…those things you've got in your wallet. I seem to be wiring somebody a hundred quid every bleedin' morning'…

*****

On the arrival of the Scottish contingent following the Glasgow closure of the *Scottish Daily Express* "…When I was five they called it musical chairs. Now it's called readjustment of executive and minority production units."

*****

RB: Don Mackay is there – because Sewell has been brought to the court under armed guard and may at some later time be shown to the jury, as it were. That'll be nice for him, won't it. A sort of day out.

P.WHITTELL: Yes – will he charge meals for the day d'you think, Bob?

RB: No, he'll have the unexpired portion of his day's jail rations I expect.

*****

RB: Where's Harry Pugh…Is he on holiday?

Reporter: He's in London negotiating the new House Agreement.

RB: He seems to be turnin' it into a cottage industry.

*****

You could use this schedule as an examination paper for trainee journalists…

Q1. How many of these stories are true?

Q2. How many will stand close examination after 2pm?

On the arrival of the Scottish contingent following the Glasgow closure of the Scottish Daily Express:
"…When I was five they called it musical chairs. Now it's called readjustment of executive and minority production units"

Showbiz or art?

"I lived in Chorlton when Buddy Flint, the *Daily Mail* photographer, drank at the Royal Oak. I knew he was there because he sat in the corner at a seat marked Room for One Only and he was always alone."

Gerry Dempsey, former showbiz correspondent of the *Daily Express*, is in earnest conversation with his old friend and rival John Stevenson, who did the same job at the *Daily Mail* during the 1960s.

"Press photographers were a strange race. Full of misfits. Are they still like that?" John asks.

Sir John Barbirolli understood the value of having the national press on tap. This picture by Johnnie Walker captures the Barbirollis in composed domestic mode at their Rusholme apartment

"They got fashionable about 30 years ago. Went up in the world, shagging their models. They never looked back. But the old ones were different. I knew exactly what our film critic Ian Christie meant when he was talking to me about a jazz concert and said 'You see Gerry, drummers are the photographers of the jazz world'.

"It was a wonderful in for pulling birds, having a camera and saying 'You could make a fortune as a model', John reflects. "Why didn't we think of such things?"

Gerry was the *Daily Express*'s Manchester showbiz writer and television critic from 1960 until he retired in 1985. He had arrived at Great Ancoats Street from the *News Chronicle* as a general reporter "but since I could spell Scarlatti they started sending me to the Hallé."

Before that he'd tried the *Guardian* "because I could read and write in three syllable words." He saw Harry Whewell (the news editor), "who I knew a bit and he knew me."

"He said, 'I've got nothing really, but do you fancy subbing?'

"I thought, 'Dear god no, I'll do that when I'm about 70'.

"Harry said 'We take on two categories of reporter: those who'll get the engine-driver's name and those who can write'.

"I said 'I can get the engine-driver's name and still spell Scarlatti'.

"'Well', he said, 'I'll put that down.'

"'You do', I said, and buggered off to the *Express* where I tasted expenses far beyond anything I'd known before.

"Harry, god bless him, rang me up there and said 'I've got a job for you' – it was because I'd answered him back. I said 'No, thanks, I've found the golden goose'."

Gerry had tasted gold already. Soon after the Second World War he went to see a Kemsley editor at Withy Grove, tempted across from his native Liverpool. "The editor said 'Sure Gerry, you can come to work here but there's just one thing: we're very strict on expenses'. He saw my little face fall. 'We're very strict – if you don't go on a story you only charge once'."

John Stevenson knows a thing or two about expenses himself.

"There was an art in claiming when you never left the office. We once had a discussion about this, Gerry, and you said the art lay in describing briefly a story that the accounts department believed you might have been sent on but which wouldn't quite make the paper. Stories like 'No pony for Daphne' or 'Washday Blues makes Council see Red'."

"We had a couple in Liverpool that people put in every two or three weeks", Gerry adds – 'Bootle Bakery Blaze' and 'Ice Cream Man's Chimes Start Ding Dong Row'."

John quit the *Daily Mail* in 1969 to become a freelance drama script-writer for Granada Television. He had already begun to lay his golden eggs inside the

Denis Thorpe of the Guardian caught Rudolph Nureyev angrily prowling the corridors of Manchester's Palace Theatre after Paddy O'Neill of the *Daily Mail* had dared suggest during a press conference that Nureyev was too old to make a return to the stage at 40

coop. For year or so he doubled as showbiz writer and scriptwriter without the *Mail* seeming to mind because, maybe, access to TV studios was getting him stories. Then he was summoned to the Granada penthouse by the great Sidney Bernstein himself. "'Now then', he said, 'you're a very good reporter and a very good scriptwriter, but you can't be both. What's it to be?' I'd been thinking of leaving the *Mail* anyway. It was bloody hard work…"

"You mean, some nights you had to go out after 6pm," suggests Gerry.

John and Gerry are sitting there, reunited after 18 years believe it or not, over a pint or three in the Briton's Protection near the Bridgewater Hall. They are discussing old times. Old times like the terrible treatment Manchester hacks gave to Rudolf Nureyev and Margot Fonteyn.

Gerry: We were trying to find out whether Rudolf was at it with Margot, but all we discovered was that they spent a lot of time in the New Cinema together holding hands. It was rather touching.

John: I remember you giving me a bollocking because I twice got in the paper a story 'I am not retiring, Fonteyn declares'. You said, there was no question of that – and there wasn't.

Gerry: It was Paddy O'Neill (a *Daily Mail* reporter) who accused Nureyev of being too old at 40 at a press conference to announce one of his comebacks. Nureyev was magnificent in his scorn. 'Stand up', he says, 'how old are you? Look at you and look at me.' Then he swept off.

When Gerry joined the Daily Express he found himself working side by side with the late Derek Taylor, the man who became the Beatles' press officer. Taylor did the showbiz job on the Sunday Express.

John: I remember meeting Derek Taylor in 1963 when I was still on the *Oldham Chronicle*. Among my chores I'd to go down to the BBC in Piccadilly once a week and get material for a radio column. I'd seen the barriers outside the Gaumont (or Gormont as it was called). 'What's happening?' I asked Derek. 'Oh, the Beatles were there last night.' 'Who the hell are the Beatles?'

Gerry: Taylor spotted them. He was ruthless. He went to the Piccadilly Hotel to meet the Beatles and thought the press officer didn't have much clue. He came back to the *Express* and told me he'd found his next job – press officer to the Beatles. Derek got the other chap out in no time, then acquired a Beatles suit with no lapels. He appeared with them and became one of them. They lent him cash to buy something like Thetford Mill in Norfolk.

As showbiz "rivals", John and Gerry had slightly different beats. The Daily Mail's demanding news editor, Ken Donlan, expected John to come up with personality stories as well as cover theatre around the north. Gerry had a more relaxed time at the Daily Express. He stayed with Scarlatti and Mahler. He did occasionally stumble into a story, though.

"I remember you giving me a bollocking because I twice got in the paper a story 'I am not retiring, Fonteyn declares'. You said, there was no question of that – and there wasn't"

Gerry: One night I wandered into the New Theatre pub and found half the Coronation Street cast drowning their sorrows. I started talking to them. What was going on? 'We've downed tools – walked off the set.' I rang the office and told them. Are you pissed? No. I got a good show in the next day's paper. Donlan rang me the same day, furious at getting nicked on his own patch (the New Theatre was close to the *Daily Mail* office).

John: I was sent to cover the Kinks at the Gaumont early in 1965. It was a nothing concert. The next day the *Express* carried a headline 'Riot at Gaumont, Girls Scream and Froth at the Knickers as Kinks drive Crowds to Frenzy'. Old Jimmy Lewthwaite, the night news editor, asks me – 'Why haven't we got that story?' 'It never happened, Jimmy.' 'But it's in the *Express*.' There was no answer to that.

Theatre was the thing. In retrospect the 1960s was a theatrical golden age for the north, what with Howard & Wyndham and Moss Empires still putting on West End previews, the Royal Shakespeare Company and the National Theatre still touring with full casts, and repertory companies like Liverpool Everyman and the Victoria Theatre, Stoke-on-Trent, coming up with new writers and concepts.

Dame Margot Fonteyn takes a curtain call in one of her final appearances at the Manchester Opera House. *Daily Mail* picture by Denis Thorpe

John: Do you remember Tony Perrin's play at Stoke called 'Get Out in the Green Fields'? It was the plot of 'Juno & the Paycock'. The guy became a Coronation Street writer and a good friend of mine. Years later he said to me, 'You know, you were the only critic who spotted that'.

Gerry: You and I saw 'Juno & the Paycock' at the Dublin Theatre Festival…

John: It was 1966, the fiftieth anniversary of the Easter Rising…

Gerry: And afterwards you kept quoting things from it to me like 'No man can do enough for Ireland', it grabbed you in your Lancashire way and me with my Celtic Liverpool background said 'No, John, it's not like that'.

A Manchester industry, Granada's "Coronation Street", became more and more important to the tabloids as the Mirror took on Murdoch's *Sun* in the 1970s. Johnnie Walker's Christmas shot of Ena Sharples (Violet Carson) and co for the *Daily Mirror*

One high point was the pre-West End premier of Alan Bennett's 'Forty Years On' with John Gielgud at Manchester's Palace Theatre in 1968.

Gerry: I loved it. There was a Bulldog Drummond sketch. 'What sort of man was he, sergeant?' 'Sir, a cripple of the worst sort'. I fell into the aisles and Peter Eckersley (of Granada) who was sitting behind me remarked out loud 'I've never seen anyone actually rolling in the aisles before'.

John: It was as much John Buchan as Bulldog Drummond. Lines like 'Sane? He's the second sanest man in Europe'. It also had an Oscar Wilde pastiche. 'Are you really planning to marry her? Her legs leave something to be desired.' 'All legs leave something to be desired. That is half of their function and all of their charm'. But it was one of those reviews when you didn't have time to think (deadlines were about 10.30pm, often leaving less than half an hour to write and phone copy over).

Then there was the drink. Pubs, bars and cocktail receptions were unavoidable. The art was not to let them take over your life, if at all possible.

John: Gerry used to like a drink, but I've never known him too pissed to file. I used to admire his ability to go to the pub and dress stuff up. If there was nothing much to say about the show he got the word 'wrought' into the review. Badly-wrought or well-wrought.

Gerry: I remember John and Ken Tossell, the *Mirror* showbiz man, on either side of me in the Oxford bar across the road from the Palace Theatre one night after a show. I had been down at the Hallé that morning and got the appointment of Skrowaceski to myself. Malt whiskies at 11.30 in the morning – I can't take whisky anyway – then off to a piss-up at the BBC. By the time I got to the theatre that night I was reeling all over the place, chuntering. I can't remember the show. I was forced to give copy talking absolute drivel. You two realised it, and said 'put the phone down, ring off'. I didn't. The next day the editor asked me what this was, pointing at my review. 'Read it again. Not a verb in it.' Fancy them letting it go through…

John: Most of the subs on the *Mail* or the *Express* didn't give a bugger what was in a review. Sitting in the Oxford bar after the disastrous first night of Lionel Bart's 'Twang' you said to me – 'John, you know what this means, don't you. This is such a good story they can't fire us for at least a year.' You were a bit insecure at the time. The *Express* was overstaffed, but a firing paper, whereas the *Mail* was understaffed but they couldn't fire you.

It wasn't only writers who occasionally got the worse for wear.

Gerry: We had a copytaker who was a drunk, an illiterate drunk. Once I'd been to the Hallé on a Sunday night and started to phone my copy over. He was at the other end of the line. That copytaker was bad. If you complained you didn't want him it caused union trouble. So I said, it's the Hallé review. 'Fire away, boy, fire away'. It's Shostakovich's Concertante in F. Now, I'd broken the rules because I was phoning from the office pub (the Crown & Kettle). If you phoned from the office pub you were in trouble because it was deemed too close. If you phoned from Yates' Wine Lodge across the road you were OK. He said 'Hold on, there's a problem with the machine.' I held on, and on. Then, all of a sudden, the same copytaker appeared in the bar for a quick pint. He didn't seem to see me. I couldn't get mad at him because I shouldn't have been phoning from the office pub. I later told the story to Robin Thornber (the *Guardian* theatre critic). He thought about it and said 'I reckon that copytaker knew you were there'. Maybe he was right.

There were occasional compensations for having to work after 6pm at the Daily Mail.

John: When the going got tough Ken Donlan and Harry Myers would send us off to Ireland to recuperate. It took me a while to tumble to this. If they thought you were looking a bit twitchy they packed you off with instructions to go west, mooch around a bit, find a line or two. I was at Burtonport in County Donegal where I came across what I thought was a great story about a monster in the local loch to rival Loch Ness. Then I found a guy who said 'It's all codology. It was Murphy's donkey. He went into the loch drunk one night and the donkey was drunk too'. I wrote the feature and phoned it over. It never made the paper. They assumed I was pissed. But before you left for home the office would order seven sides of smoked salmon. You had to bring a lot of salmon back for Harry Myers.

"If you phoned from the office pub (the Crown & Kettle) you were in trouble because it was deemed too close. If you phoned from Yates' Wine Lodge across the road you were OK"

Gerry: Plus cigarette lighters which cost three shillings there and about fifteen quid here…

Talk of Ireland sets Gerry going about a former colleague, who once handled the northern end of the William Hickey column.

Gerry: Dan Lees was on the track of the Countess of Ross, you know, Snowdon's mother. He landed in Dublin where he was met by our photographer, Charlie Fennell, a little guy with a big shaven head. Legend had it that he wasn't Irish at all but had arrived by midget submarine at the end of the war. Dan says to him, what's the crack? Fennell replies 'It's a very formal occasion, have you brought your morning suit?' 'Shit, no,' says Lees. So he hired his tails and drove off to the countryside in search of her estate. When he finally arrived they were in the usual country garb for aristocrats – tweeds and headscarves.

John: There he is like Lord Snooty…

Gerry: Poor sod. The countess was in the news at the time, probably because of something to do with Margaret and Snowdon. So Dan in all his togs went across to her and said: 'Hello, ma'am, I'm Dan Lees of the *Daily Express*'. The countess replied: 'Fuck off, Dan Lees of the *Daily Express*'. That's all he got.

Sir Laurence Olivier with Vivienne Leigh as Anthony and Cleopatra in an *Evening Chronicle* portrait by Johnnie Walker

John: It was a good quote. You could use it now, but you couldn't then. Do you remember Arthur Brooks of the *Daily Mirror*?

Gerry: Arthur worked with me at Kemsleys.

John: Well, he wasn't really a sports writer but he had connections. He came into the Film Exchange (the Granada club) one day saying he'd just finished a book on Ron Yates, the Liverpool centre-half.

'I've ghosted it for him. Would you like to hear the intro?'

'Certainly, Arthur, certainly'.

Arthur took a deep breath. 'From the abattoir at Aberdeen to the amphitheatre that is Anfield dash that is the success story of the former slaughterman's apprentice Ron Yates comma the genial giant of the Kop full point. What do you think of that?'

Gerry: Do you recall Peter Thomas, the sports writer, a nice guy who drank heavily as many did then but few do now. He phoned over this report on Newcastle United, saying that one player was marvellous, dominating the pitch. 'The ubiquitous Palmer saved the day'. He rang in later to check all was OK. The sports sub said 'That's fine, Peter, just the right length. Only one thing I'm not happy about. What does ubiquitous mean?' Peter says, it's from the Latin ubique meaning everywhere. 'Oh, that's fine.' The next day he opened the paper and read 'Palmer was all over the place'.

John: After five years as a theatre reviewer I began to get guilt feelings about having to knock shows that weren't much good despite the talent and effort that had gone into them. I was glad to stop.

Gerry: I always felt bad about knocking a show put on with a lot of effort. I'd look for something else to say. But you were ruthless. Weren't you called The Butcher?

John: No, you invented that. But I liked it. I was called The Butcher because I knew about tripe. I once went to the old ABC TV studios in East Didsbury where they were recording a Ken Dodd show. I had a wonderful scoop because they wanted to do a clog-dancing act on tripe and UCP, the tripe merchants, who had been asked for three tons of the stuff, refused to supply it when they learnt what it was for. Bad for the image of tripe, apparently. But they found a butcher with no conscience who agreed to sell them the tripe and the show went on. They danced on tripe. A true yarn.

Every newspaper had its "home" pub. The Victoria, just behind the *Daily Mail* on Hardman Street, was as associated with the newspaper as the Thatched House was with the *Guardian* and *Evening News* or the Crown & Kettle with the *Daily Express*. Demolition of the Vic to make way for an office development (including a soulless New Vic) was a traumatic event meriting a slip edition of the *Mail* for local consumption

Mirror Boys Behaving Badly

Bob Gray is a prince of storytellers among Manchester journalists. A Glaswegian who came to Manchester in 1966, aged 25, having already worked on the *Daily Record* in Glasgow and the *Daily Mirror* in London then been a very young acting night editor of the *Scottish Daily Express* back in Glasgow, Gray was recruited by Derek Webster to join the northern *Daily Mirror* subs team. He was promoted to chief sub in 1969 but moved across to Great Ancoats Street in 1976, where he became night editor of the *Scottish Daily Express* (production had been switched from Glasgow in 1973 – see page 191). He was chief sub for the launch of the *Daily Star* in Manchester before opting out of national newspapers for a time. Today he is one of the stalwarts of the Broughton-based Express Newspapers operation and lives on the Fylde.

Lamb to the slaughter

"The first guy I ever got drunk with was Larry Lamb. It was 1960 and I was just 20. I was on trial at the *Daily Mirror* in Fleet Street from the *Daily Record* and Larry was chief sub for the week. He took me to the press club and because I was a Scot – I didn't drink much in those days – insisted that I drank Scotch, plus weasel's piss, the press club beer. I was staying at the Waverley Hotel in Southampton Row, a temperance hotel. Larry poured huge amounts of whisky down me. He had a beat-up Rover in which he drove me to the Waverley at four in the morning. The hotel was locked tight. He leaned on the door-bell. The night porter was very upset and wouldn't put the lift on for me. I had to crawl up on my hands and knees. It was absolutely dreadful."

Bob was Mirror chief sub (in charge of the subs' table) when northern circulation was rising fast and staff felt they had the right to play hard as well as work hard. He takes up the story:

'We're in Oldham'

"Evening breaks at the *Mirror* got longer and longer, starting with Bernard Clarke having discovered that there was a topless barmaid at the Salford Arms, quite a walk away. This would be in 1974. He came back to the office with his stories and he was quite right. They had two topless barmaids. Of course, there was a complete exodus from the Swan with Two Necks, The Wellington, Fawlty Towers (the Castle & Falcon) and so on. Fawlty Towers had taken over as the prime spot because Peter McGregor had gone there with his pay-off and table football was the big attraction.

"As breaks got longer the lads became more difficult to control because of the amount of drink they had. I used to make the odd raid. Things would calm down for a few days, then liven up again. They realised that they could have more drinking time if they stayed around Withy Grove, but then they would break out again for Salford. An hour and a half became the norm. There was a reason they stayed out. One star (the third edition) was an absolute gut out, a tick-up job, but nobody wanted to do it because of all the hard work you'd put into the three star (the first edition). It was policy at the time, you had to tick-up London copy regardless of quality.

"This particular night, there was no sign of the lads. The whole desk had disappeared. I'd get earache from Bob Sands, the night editor. 'You're too bloody lenient. Where are they?' I'm subbing the whole damn paper myself.

"Then I get a call. Roy Milner, who was very quiet but also liked a good drink, quite deep and certainly not the type you would shout and rage at, had been elected to phone me.

I get this call.

'Don't shoot the messenger'

'Where the fuck are you all?'

'Well, we're late'

'I know you're bloody late. Get your arses back here. What's happened?'

'Well', he said, 'we decided to go a bit further out'

'Yeah, but where are you?'

'Well, we've missed the train'

'Jesus Christ, where are you?'

'We're in Oldham'

"They got back eventually. I banned long breaks again. But, you know, the circulation of the *Mirror* had gone through the roof, particularly in the North. It had been three million as a London-only print which went up to five and a half million. I believe there was a certain amount of jealousy and fear in London that Manchester might overtake it, but the paper was ultra successful, and we were all young men. So the repercussions weren't fierce because they were probably the best subs table I've ever known. They included Roger Wood, David Banks, David Montgomery, Malcolm Hall, Louis Yaffe, Dick Wilson, Geoff Kuhillow and Crawford McAfee."

Singing for the job

Ted Fenna was a legendary Northern editor of the Daily Mirror in earlier times, legendary as much for his activities as his editing prowess. Bob retails a story of Ted, one of the many, via his friend Larry McDermott.

"Larry McDermott had been invited for interview. Fenna had been at the

"Better grab a glass—there's always a chance he'll split one open!"

Daily Mirror

"Oh, look—daddy's brought a bottle home for you in SPITE of your rotten racing tips!"

Daily Mirror

lunchtime conference, which tended to go on a bit. A few drinks would be had. Larry's sitting waiting for his interview. All he can hear from the editor's office is raucous singing. Fenna's secretary is getting more and more irate because Larry has been waiting over an hour, until she storms into the editor's office.

'Mr Fenna, this young man has been waiting hours for his interview…'

'Interview, what's he doing here?'

'You arranged to meet him'

'Oh, send him in'.

The editor's office had a bench-type layout so you all faced the editor. Fenna was at his desk.

'On the desk, lad. Can you sing?'

As a matter of fact, Larry had a good tenor voice and could sing very well.

'Can you sing?'

'Yes, I can'

'Up on the desk, then, lad'.

He sings, to repeated cheers of more, more. This goes on for an hour or so until he's ushered down by Fenna himself.

'Brilliant, lad, brilliant'

'But, Mr Fenna, what about the job?'

'Job, what job?'

'Well, I came for interview'

'Oh, that's all right. You've got the job.'"

No-one leave the room

"George Harrop, the night picture editor, was a great character, and - like many - a big drinker. During the strike of 1973 the *Daily Mirror* chapels had broken away from the NUJ in negotiating house deals. I was chosen by the chapel to be a negotiator because as chief sub I refused to take union office. We're all in the Wellington on a Sunday afternoon at about 4pm hammering out an agreement with management to go back to work. But the chapel, for reasons best known to itself, voted not to return to work until all members were present, including the strike breakers. We went back to negotiate with the strike breakers – 10 or 12 of them – to participate in the vote. John Grewcock, the FoC, stood up and announced that the chapel had taken a decision – 'Bob and I will go back and negotiate a return to work. No-one must leave the room.' Harrop says 'No-one leave the room? Here we are, 4pm on a Sunday, a pint in each hand, leave the room, you must be fucking mad!'"

Wiggy and the young reporter

"A Maurice Wigglesworth story, again with George Harrop. I wasn't there. A young reporter had just joined the *Mirror* staff. It was the time of the evening when people started drifting off for a drink. Those down first were usually first back. It was getting to around 9.35pm. Nobody had returned. Wiggy says: 'the buggers aren't coming back, I think we'll bugger off for a pint.' George was off like a rocket. The young reporter says to Wiggy: 'Mr Wigglesworth, you're not going to leave me in the office on my own are you, I've only just started.' 'Eeh, lad,' he said, 'It's all right. We'll leave lights on.'"

Rochez and ricochet

"Mike Terry was another northern editor who liked a drink. He'd got a glass eye. Terry Stringer, a reporter at the time, went to the loo and saw this pill box on the shelf, opened it and found the glass eye. Mike and Paul Rochez, the managing editor, would come back in the mid-afternoon having sunk a few, and one or the other of them would be bouncing against the corridor walls of Withy Grove. George Harrop sat there watching them. 'There they go', he remarked famously, 'Rochez and ricochet'."

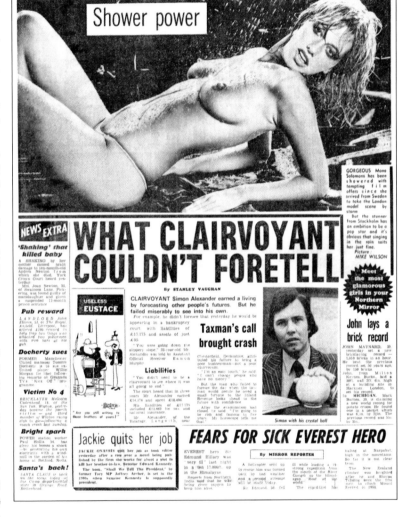

The stripper, the drunks and the dogs

"One Christmas Party at the Mitre Hotel near the cathedral proved to be outrageous. We'd had a stripper, that was compulsory, and she'd done her stint. They had a whip round because she wondered if they wanted her to do a special – she was quite an attractive woman. We never got as far as that because the drink had got to the lads by then. They chose more booze rather than pay for the special. They were well filled and not in good humour. I went back to the paper at about 3.30pm because there was work to do…

"The party would have started at lunchtime. The Mitre was the only place in Manchester that would have us for Xmas parties, which took place at least a week before Christmas itself. The boys who stayed were totally arseholed, falling down stairs…

"The manager was getting increasingly alarmed not only because they were frightening the customers downstairs – we were in a private room – but because he was afraid that somebody would get injured. A picture that came out of that session showed Crawford McAfee stretched on the table out cold; someone had stuck an orange in his mouth. Someone else fell over the Christmas tree and destroyed all the lights. That kind of thing.

"Then I got a call from a police officer, who fortunately wanted to keep it low key.

'Mr Gray', said the police caller, 'your staff are outside the Mitre. They're causing quite a disturbance and they're refusing to go back to work unless you come and lead them back.'

'My staff are a pain in the bloody arse,' I said, 'I'm trying to get the paper out here. Tell them to come back, or be sacked.'

'Well, it would be better if you could come down. I'm sure they will come back with you.'

'Bloody arrest the lot of them.'

'We don't want to do that, Mr Gray. But we were called by the manager. We've had to bring the dogs.'

'Set the dogs on them.'

'We have done, Mr Gray. Your staff are on their hands and knees barking at the dogs.'

'Oh, I'd better come down then.'"

The Indoor Olympics

"I used to work over Christmas because we didn't have a family. We had a big house in Swinton with a bar in the cellar which the *Mirror* lads frequented. Audrie, my late wife, would cook for them. Around Christmas I would get all the booze left over for the year from our cellar, take it into Withy Grove and set up a bar in the Irish editor's office. It was a good atmosphere, but of course when they'd had a few drinks a singsong suddenly wasn't enough.

"Around one or two o'clock in the morning, with the edition gone, we'd already had one or two attempts at jumping on the desk so we decided to invent the Indoor Olympics. We had things like Leap of the Year contests up onto the desks. I came off and ripped my shins apart. Then someone discovered the ski sticks. These were the cleaners' mops. Desk tops at the *Mirror* were of removable Formica which we propped up against the wall then climbed on the newspaper files to ski down. The great race was the Chariot Race. We had huge basket skips for rubbish. We raced down the long corridors at Thomson House. I was a jockey and so was Brian Sutherland because we were the smallest. One of the chariot-pullers was David Hay, now up at Carlisle, a big guardsman. The *Mirror* offices led off a corridor so all these heads looking out, from the back lift to front lift. There were great cheers and many bets."

Bob Gray ends where he began, with a London story:

The earthquake

"Harry King, a good reporter and FoC of the *Mirror* at the time, Neil McKay, who wrote the serial on the Ripper and I were down in London as chapel officials in the Heath strike year, 1973. Of course there were blackouts. It was a Friday and there were no trains to get home on. We scouted around for hotels. All we could find was a room at the Kennedy which had three single beds in a line. Fine. Harry had suspected heart problems. It must have been some sort of virus because it certainly wasn't a heart attack; he'd been off for some weeks and I'd insisted he take brandy just in case. We arrived fairly well oiled back at the Kennedy, in darkness. We decided to have a game of cards by cigarette lighter – which led to burned fingers and much cursing. We managed to purloin a bottle of scotch from somebody. This was seeing us through the long dark night. None of us had the sense to leave a switch on so that we would know when the lights came back on. The beds had undulating facilities which involved putting 10p in a box at the bedside. We got to bed finally, and the other two were soon snoring their heads off. I thought I'd never get to sleep, so I decided to make the bed rock me. I fiddled around to put in the 10p. The next thing Harry jumped out of bed 'Jesus Christ, it's an earthquake'. I'd put the money in his machine."

Postscript: Every now and then the *Daily Mirror* devoted special issues to burning social topics. In the early hours of the day the *Mirror* launched a front-page exposé on VIOLENCE, Albert Hartwell, night publishing manager at Withy Grove, was walking down Corporation Street after moving his car. He could not help noticing two *Daily Mirror* sub-editors fighting in the middle of the road.

Master of the one-liner

Revel Barker writes: George Harrop, former northern night picture editor of the *Daily Mirror*, renowned wit and master of great one-line jokes, died the day after his eightieth birthday. A World War Two Burma veteran, George began his journalistic career on the picture desk of the *Daily Express* in the early 1950s. He was invited to join the *Express* team by the formidable, sharp-tongued 'Strangler' Lewis, then northern editor.

The Strangler's sharp tongue was no match for George. Once Strangler roared "George, get off the bloody phone." "Have to go", said George in a voice everybody in the newsroom heard, "the editor wants permission to change a crosshead."

When the *Mirror* began printing in the North in 1955 George joined the editorial team as night picture editor, a post he held for nearly 30 years. At the *Mirror* he further honed his wit and keen observation of colleagues.

His description of two reporters, one a hypochondriac and the other always yawning, as SICK and TIRED, was typical.

George Harrop salutes The Douglas under demolition in 1986. The Douglas, facing Withy Grove across Corporation Street, was the sort of pub where you wiped your feet on the way out. Hacks called its two bars Hiroshima and Nagasaki

The *Mirror's* defence correspondent was boasting of his coverage of the Falklands War. George asked, "How long were you there?"

"Three weeks."

"I've had longer lunch-breaks," said George.

One *Mirror* northern editor, Mike Taylor, told George he was the worst night picture editor he'd known – because he was never there. To which George quipped, "How do you know when I'm never there?"

During his final illness the doctor treating him said, "George, by the state of your liver I take it that you're a whisky drinker – a bottle a week perhaps? George, indignantly: "Dear Boy – I spill more than that!"

The origins of Andy Capp

Andy Capp, the celebrated loafer created by Reg Smythe from Hartlepool, was first published in northern editions of the *Daily Mirror* in August 1957. Smythe told Revel Barker, a *Mirror* North East reporter at the time, that the character had been inspired by a visit with his father to the terraces of Hartlepool FC when he was a boy. When it started to rain the man standing next to Smythe took off his flat cap and stowed it safely under his raincoat. Young Reg was astounded. "Mister", he asked, "why have you just taken your cap OFF in the rain?" The bloke looked at the lad as if he was very stupid. "You don't think", he replied, "that I'm gonna sit in the house all night in a wet cap."

Andy Capp went national 18 months' after trialling in northern editions of the *Mirror* and was soon to be world-famous. Regional development boards have been trying to play down this image of the English working class hero ever since.

Cardus's white elephant

Giving copy over the phone was not Neville Cardus's favourite pastime. The celebrated and increasingly venerable music critic's normal modus operandum was to attend rehearsals, write his notice in longhand then add a few final flourishes after the concert before dispatching his driver to deliver the copy to the *Guardian's* London office. But, away from base, life got tougher. In 1965, and at what was to be his final visit to the Edinburgh Festival, Cardus wrote about a close friend in concert. "Elisabeth Schwarzkopf", he ventured, "was the quite eloquent singer." A Cross Street copytaker – it had, after all, been a long time since Cardus lived in Manchester – heard him as saying "white elephant." The arts page sub of the night, Ian Breach, saw nothing unusual in this, so "white elephant" appeared in the following morning's edition. Cardus fled Edinburgh in despair, but eventually managed to mend relations with the diva. He was not thought to have telephoned over copy to Manchester again.

Sir Neville Cardus with Brian Redhead when northern editor of the *Guardian*

English 1, Yorkshire 0

Revel Barker writes: Jack Crossley offered me a job on the *Daily Mail*. I was covering the Poulson corruption trial at the time against a *Mail* team that included Harry Longmuir, George Gordon, John Dale, some others and, of course, Jack himself. I was the *Mirror's* Poulson team. The *Daily Express* had six people, the *Sunday Times* had four, the *Daily Telegraph* three, and so on. So Jack invited me down to Fleet Strasse for lunch and said that he had been impressed by my "taking on and beating entire teams from Fleet Street." Wow. He had told this to David English and he wanted me on his investigations team, and I could think of no greater honour. We had the usual four-hour lunch, and he went to see English and I went to the *Mirror* office in Holborn. We had agreed to meet shortly after, at opening time in the Witness Box pub.

Calamity! A very shame-faced Jack said all had gone well until he got to the bit that I worked out of *Mirror's* Newcastle office but came from Leeds and the *Yorkshire Evening Post*. English said: "Not now, Jack. I think we have quite enough of your ee-bah-gum buggers on the London staff for the time being."

It was the sort of place you went for a quiet pint, a snack and a game of snooker. But at 3am one autumn morning in 1967, the press club was raided, some say by police who had been drinking there the night before

Pre-dawn raid on Manchester Press Club

As the Swinging Sixties wore on, Manchester swung. Its vibrant night life proved a paradise for newspaper workers finishing shifts around midnight with cash in their pockets. Clubs of all shapes and sizes catered for all tastes. By far the most sedate was the Manchester Press Club, which claims to be the world's oldest such institution, located upstairs in Memorial Hall off Albert Square, almost opposite Bootle Street police station. It was the sort of place you went for a quiet pint, a snack and a game of snooker after a hard night on the stone. But at 3am one autumn morning in 1967, the Manchester Press Club was raided, some say by police who had been drinking there the night before.

Doubtless the club, which had never bothered to obtain a late licence, was breaking the law. It's claimed that some mornings journalists would stagger out at 6am. But there was no rowdiness or other cause for complaint. Members did damage only to themselves. The press club was victim of a purge on all drinking haunts by Chief Constable W.J.Richards, who had determined to clean up the Manchester scene.

Cyril Ritson, a *Guardian* sub and club president at the time, happened to leave that morning at 2.40am. He puts that down to Divine Intervention. In any case he landed in court alongside punters arrested with pints in their hands. A fighting fund, endorsed by the irreproachable Paddy Monkhouse, included £20 personally delivered by an old member, Wilfrid Burke, Assistant Postmaster General in the Attlee government.

At the Minshull Street court, in front of Stipendiary Bancroft Turner, the journalists were solemnly warned – and fined £2 each apart from John Grewcock, a *Daily Mirror* sub who said he was only there because it was his birthday. He was fined £1. The club secretary, Denis Trainer, a devout Catholic, declined to swear on the King James Bible and was asked by the court usher whether he preferred the Koran.

The Manchester Press Club, albeit fined £200, survived. Not long afterwards it transferred to a basement address in Queen Street, discreetly away from police gaze.

Manchester's nationals produced Splash, a charity occasion, each year by rotation - offering journalists a chance to parody their own publication. 1978 was the *Daily Telegraph*'s year

The Daily Splash

AT LEAST 10p

FEBRUARY, 1978   Printed in MANCHESTER

Unique coupling in Cabinet

CON-LAB RULES OK!

Snatcher and Sailor in shotgun wedding

By CHOPPER McHAGGIS, Westminster Correspondent, at the Bar of the Swan

THE Graham Sutherland portrait of Winston Churchill rose phoenix like, last night, to become Prime Minister, in a Con-Lab pact designed to keep Britain's two major parties in office for ever.

Despite reports in the more irresponsible Press, we can state with categoric uncertainty that Churchill and his Clemmie loved the daub and gave it to Aneurin Bevan (Churchill called him "Rats") affectionately) a close friend.

It was recovered from the bottom of a Rhonda coal mine where Bevan had hung it to inspire greater productivity by the Welsh miners he conned into keeping him in a soft number at Westminster, for donkeys.

The portrait was the compromise choice as Premier in the entirely predictable Lab-Con pact, which surprised no one. The dafter than usual idea was dreamed up by Mrs Snatcher, the Tory leader, and Sailor Jim, the Labour skipper, to ensure that they would remain rolling in it and enjoying the free loading for the rest of their naturals.

Said Mrs Snatcher: "Only the greatest Tory in history can lead the country out of the mess that b----- Sailor and his crew of Lefties have dropped us in." Said Sailor: "Ho, ho, ho, she's a right one that Snatcher. We all know the old warrior dropped more clangers than my mate Harold and I put together.

LET IT ALL HANG OUT

'Now go and get this behind you...'

By BIGGLES BEN REILLY
Birching and Officer Cadets Correspondent

THE Hon Bertram "Cuddles" Flooster-Frendergast, 27, was cleared at Catterol Crown Court yesterday of murder, armed robbery, grievous bodily harm, wounding, rape, grand larceny, gross indecency, embezzlement, assault, driving while unfit through drink and exceeding the speed limit. A charge of living off immoral earnings was left on the file.

Flooster-Frendergast, of The Broonerie, Biddlesham on Cruneh, an Old Etonian and former Grenadier Guards officer, was said by his defence counsel to have suffered an acute emotional crisis at the time of the offences. This had been caused by losing more than £50,000 in one afternoon at Royal Ascot.

"The accused has no recollection of the offences of which he is charged," his counsel told Mr Justice O'Flunderberry who...

OXO WAR TOO HOT TO HANDLE
By Our Noughts and Crosses Correspondent

Threat to organ you can thrust

"The Splash Editor said he was looking for something thirty-six inches across two. Do you think this will do or will it bust?" "Well, darling, my only worry would be if he put it in upside down !"

Storm over 'up the Pole' Welshman

QUESTIONS are to be asked in the Commons next week as to why an amateur brain surgeon from Tonypandy was engaged as an official interpreter for Mr Callaghan's recent tour of the Indian sub-Continent.

Embarrassment was caused by some of the free translations made of Mr Callaghan's speeches and Tory Front Benchers are to protest that such incidents have seriously damaged Britain's standing among its Asian allies.

A Downing Street spokesman admitted yesterday: "We should have realised something was wrong when audiences started laughing at the Prime Minister's jokes. That's never happened before."

The interpreter Mr Gwilym ap Normal was replaced by a Scotland-second hand car dealer halfway through the tour after Indian Press reports had ridiculed statements and declarations attributed to Mr Callaghan.

Goodbye cheeks

A Foreign Office spokesman confirmed that Mr ap Normal's translations were often very loose indeed.

"When Mr Callaghan began a speech with 'Dear Friends,' for instance this was interpreted as 'Hullo, Darlings.' And all references to a special relationship were translated into a completely different context. They only made sense if you were familiar with certain temple carvings."

Mr ap Normal said last night that his interest in Indian languages was aroused when he first visited a local curry restaurant.

"I couldn't make head nor tail of the menu and just had to point to what I wanted. I learned later I'd ordered the manager. However, this made me determined to master those strange foreign and I darned sight cleverer at the Pontypridd Miners' Welfare Institute.

Chicken Madras please

He said he had applied for the post of interpreter because he "fancied the trip."

He claims that he has a considerable reputation as a linguist and was made an honorary member of the Gorwydd (Bardic Circle) for translating into Welsh the complete works of Rabi Jansen.

But he admitted that until...

Withy Grove:
Behind
closed doors

SPLASHGATE: the investigation which rocked Presobiz. The secrets of the stars, what makes them tick. The private lives of the infamous denizens of Thomson House.

'Splashgate,' the revelation which made Richard Nixon say: " Thank Heavens, they can't pin any of this on me." It'll more than ever before about the way the sparkling facade of the bright lights hides a world of unspeakable jealousies and passions of a suspected but never before laid bare until " Splashgate."

What happened when Zebedee spring got caught up in the silk curtain around Flip Enrica's long-ero four-poster.

Why does the Gora-Gomes love a doppersuppe at Flossie Bear on the wall of a bus. Who was caught with whom in the editorial office airing cupboard after the "Operatic Downstairs" Trouserwear party.

How do Grabsby and Clutch manage to retire ten-a-day per diem of the Telegraph, slush between them? And of what and whom are they spending on ?

The answer to these questions and more, more will be revealed in "Splashgate." Every worth waiting for date of our next proposed instalment just as soon as we have sued and the law out is...

AMIN FOR ALL

The image makers

Newspaper photographers are a freemasonry within a profession, by tradition outcasts from the newsroom, envied for the alchemy of their trade: a scoop in a single click. When early twentieth-century technology allowed stereo plates of photographic prints to be created in matters of minutes, news photography became a reality, in Manchester no less than Fleet Street, and photographs slowly replaced engravings. Newspaper hierarchies were already well established by then, so photographers had a fight on their hands for anything like equal rights. At the *Daily Mail* on Deansgate the picture desk was known as the "art room" into the late 1950s; a 1930s photograph of this art room – see page 57 – depicts a spartan space with barely a telephone, let alone a light box.

In 1908 Walter Doughty was employed as the first staff photographer for the *Manchester Guardian* (he also doubled for the *Manchester Evening News*). Doughty's images of the 1922 Irish Civil War, recently discovered by *Guardian* photographer Don McPhee and lovingly reconstituted by him from the original glass plates, are graphic testaments to the power of the news picture. They give the lie to the claim that the *Manchester Guardian* was not strong on hard news. But only recently, with the establishment of the Newsroom gallery and archive opposite the newspaper's office in Farringdon Road, London, have they been properly celebrated. Doughty and his successor Tom Stuttard, who retired in 1971 – between them they put in 87 years for the company –

Walter Doughty, the *Manchester Guardian*'s first staff photographer, joined the newspaper in 1908 and retired in 1949. His 1922 images of the Irish Civil War are classics of their period. The original glass plates lay forgotten in darkrooms until recently rediscovered and restored by photographer Don McPhee

Tom Stuttard, *Manchester Guardian* photographer from 1925-1971, covered a national beat from the North. His iconic image of Chamberlain returning from Munich bearing Hitler's pledge contrasts with a majestic Churchill at Manchester Town Hall, having been made a freeman of the city in 1947

rate only a single mention each in the *Guardian's* official biographies. Photographers were seen but not heard.

Yet photography was to play an key role in the development of the popular press. Hulton's *Daily Sketch*, launched 1909 in Manchester and London, was among the new titles taking full advantage of evolving technology. The *Sketch's* coverage of the 1912 Titanic disaster, using pictures gleaned from survivors and eye-witnesses on other liners, as well as staff photographers in port, established the *Sketch's* credentials as a serious rival to the *Daily Graphic*.

"Yep! No doubt about it: a clear case o' strained trigger-finger."

Daily Express photographers from London, Glasgow and Manchester assemble for a 1960 demonstration of the paper's picture power. In fact, the three groups were taken separately and stitched together; Manchester's 16 are on the right. Dave Cooksey of the *Daily Express* (bottom left) became a role model for successful Manchester photographers. Johnnie Walker, of the *Evening Chronicle* and the *Daily Mirror*, enjoyed playing to stereotypes. Left: The 1947 inaugural meeting of the Manchester Press Photographers' Club, formed to protect and promote the interests of photographers. The group includes (left to right, starting on back row) Wilf Cross (*Daily Mail*), Leo Carter (*Daily Express*), Clifford 'Raggy' Ashton (freelance), Dave Cooksey (*Daily Express*), Bob Bremner (freelance and Kemsley) Horace Tonge (Kemsley), Harry Bedford (Kemsley), Jack Haskell (freelance) and Bert Eastwood (*News Chronicle*). The NUJ representative, a Mr Senior, carries the briefcase

By the late 1930s, and with all the popular dailies apart from the *Mirror* publishing in the north, photonews agencies like Keystone and Fox found it worth their while to open in Manchester.

Geoff Hallawell, now 87, remembers as a 12-year-old watching passengers disembark at Barton Airport (then Manchester's principal aerodrome) and picking out a fashionable photographer in plus fours and a red camera, with exotic labels on his luggage. Hallawell's boyhood dream was to be a commercial airline pilot, but he decided there and then to become a photographer. At the age of 16 he was freelancing with Arthur Crompton in Salford, submitting pictures to motoring and sports magazines, specialising in the Castle Irwell racecourse meets.

A parallel training as an engineer saw him working with Gardners in the run

Photographers had to be resilient. Above: Clive Cooksey of the *Manchester Evening News*, together with his colleague Eric Graham, encamped outside Chester courthouse awaiting developments in the trial of Ian Brady and Myra Hindley, the Moors Murderers.
Right: the *Evening Chronicle*'s Johnnie Walker being attacked by Alfred Merrifield wielding a silver-topped cane. Merrifield and his wife Louisa (seen with him) were accused of poisoning an old lady in Blackpool, April 1953. Merrifield was released for lack of evidence but his wife was executed at Strangeways prison, Manchester, in September 1953, the last woman to hang there

Overleaf: Anti-capital punishment demonstration at Strangeways, on May 12 1936, the day Dr Buck Ruxton was hanged for murdering his wife and housekeeper. The loudspeaker van belonged to Violet Van der Elst, a prominent campaigner against the death penalty. A Fox Photos picture

up to the Second World War, and then with Rolls-Royce at Barnoldswick as a foreman on the Merlin jet engine line, before he was himself called up. Hallawell's engineering background helped him develop a lightweight long-lens plate camera after the war, his version of the so-called, unwieldy Long Tom cameras, which he installed at Old Trafford cricket ground, and cemented his relationship with Donald Campbell at Coniston where he worked on the Merlin engine Campbell had put in K7. His freelance career continued into the 1990s.

Dave Cooksey was one of the rising stars of the 1930s. He too began as a freelance but had become a staff photographer with the *Daily Express* by 1939. In an unpublished memoir "Rain for the Princess", written with Geoffrey Newson, Cooksey describes how he missed one of the scoops of the decade in 1935.

Covering the second day of a Grand National meeting at Aintree, the young Cooksey was in the paddock standing beside Tubby Abrahams, an experienced Keystone Press operator. As a modish couple sauntered by, Tubby remarked: "that's the Prince of Wales, but who's his girl?"

Reacting swiftly, both shot from about seven yards with their 9x12cm glass plate cameras. But a palace detective came straight over, grabbed Cooksey's camera, pulled out the sheath from the holder containing the exposed plate and crushed it into the grass. He then did the same to Abrahams' camera, and warned them he would evict them

Top left: volunteers sign on
to fight, Manchester 1941.
A Keystone picture.
Bottom left: Oldham slum
dwelling. Above: prostitution
in Manchester's Piccadilly.
A posed picture by
Johnnie Walker for an
Evening Chronicle feature.
Left: Manchester reporters
and photographers jostle
for a sight of Yuri Gagarin,
the Russian cosmonaut

both from the course if they attempted to take more pictures of the Prince.

Abrahams suggested they go for a drink. When Cooksey bemoaned his fate the Keystone photographer patted his pocket. Unnoticed, he had switched plates while the detective was destroying Cooksey's effort. His snatch photo of the Prince with Mrs Simpson went round the world.

Ironically, Cooksey was to become famous for his pictures of royalty. The shot of Princess Margaret smiling stoically through a rain-flecked limousine window was made at Stoke-on-Trent in June 1956, at the time when Margaret was herself involved with a disapproved divorcee, Peter Townsend. Cooksey was the only photographer present for her routine tour of the Potteries, and the pictures he sent back to Manchester were not much to the taste of the *Express's* then northern editor, Tim Hewat. Hewat disliked the "ugly duckling" image, choosing another in preference. But Cooksey, calling it "Smiling Through", submitted it for the 1956 Encyclopedia Britannica Kodak awards where it won first prize in the Royal section. He sent prints to the princess, who returned one signed simply "Margaret." By then it had become hot property and was all over the *Express* front pages. Invited to judge the 1957 Kodak awards, Cooksey found himself working alongside a young London photographer name of Anthony Armstrong-Jones, who was interested to know what the older man thought of Margaret.

Johnnie Walker, Cooksey's cousin, an *Evening Chronicle* and then *Daily*

Right: Princess Margaret through a rain-flecked limousine window, Stoke-on-Trent, 1956.
Dave Cooksey's *Daily Express* picture won national awards.
Clive Cooksey caught Sophia Loren for the *Evening News* on the tarmac of Manchester Airport, Johnnie Walker found Englebert Humperdink reflected in his Rolls-Royce

Mirror photographer at Withy Grove, has another Royal tour of the Potteries story. "Neil Morgan, the *Daily Express* photographer, and I had rota passes, which meant that we were covering the event for everyone and had a blue Buckingham Palace pass", he tells in a memoir written for his great grandchildren. "We stood at the church entrance, a line of people stretching to the lychgate. The Queen had just alighted from her limo and started to walk towards us. At the back of the crowd appeared the photo printer who wanted to collect our pictures to wire for the early editions. He called out in a loud whisper, 'Neil, Neil'. We split our sides laughing when some of people at the front actually started to kneel."

Donald Campbell's sequence of waterspeed record attempts on Ullswater and Coniston, beginning in 1949 and culminating in his spectacular 1967 death, was the classic northern story. Only Manchester-based reporters and photographers were close enough to home to keep an eye on these episodic events, and it was a strain even for them. Geoff Hallawell financed his freelance business by means of retainers, though these could be thin over the years. Hallawell, the long lens specialist, sacrificed professional advancement to a 17-year friendship with Campbell which saw him in the rescue boat, powerless to do anything, on that fateful January morning.

Campbell's close relationship with photographers, and his love of drama, is celebrated on these pages

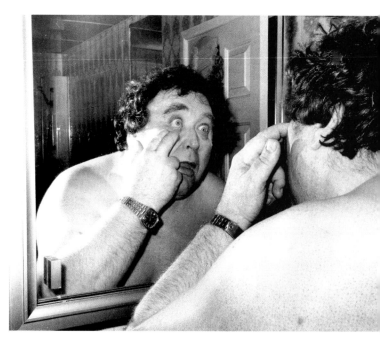

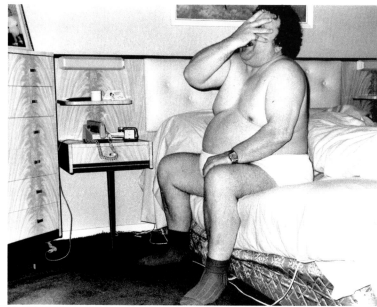

Bernard Manning, the Manche
club-owner comedian, shows
Johnnie Walker of the *Daily M*
his morning routines. Walker fo
showbiz of another sort at
Manchester's Whitworth Galle

study of the showman and his mechanics posing on K7; Johnnie Walker's signed cockpit portrait of Campbell, his wife Daphne and his chief mechanic Leo Vila; and Walker's group shot of the Coniston fancy dress party held over the Christmas-New Year break just days before the tragedy.

Cooksey was the founding father of a photographic dynasty. His son Clive worked for the *Manchester Evening News* for over 40 years as a photographer and later as picture editor. His grandson Christian is picture editor of the *Glasgow Evening Times*. Johnnie Walker's son Howard became a *Sunday Mirror* photographer. Cooksey and Walker were part of a very busy scene which Denis Thorpe, who arrived at the *Daily Mail* in March 1957, remembers vividly.

Thorpe joined a team of seasoned professionals led by Wilf Cross, who covered the 1945 Japanese surrender on the USS Missouri in Tokyo Bay and was to win an Encyclopedia Britannica award for his picture of a crash at the Isle of Man TT races with the bike in flames, the escaping rider running away with his boots on fire. Colleagues included Reg "Buddy" Flint, whose mother had started a picture agency in London and whose principal word of wisdom was "never use your last plate", Peter Howard – who was to survive the Manchester United Munich crash – and a gifted young man by the name of Graham Finlayson. Thorpe and Finlayson, both to become *Guardian* photographers, soon rubbed

up against what they considered to be the archaic practices of the *Mail's* Manchester office.

"Charles Madden, the Manchester art editor, must have been rather puzzled by this intrusion into his Northern empire," writes Thorpe. "Graham had a large selection of cameras including 35mm format. I had my beloved pre-war 35mm Contax II. (Robert Capa had taken two of these to cover the D-Day landings – not a bad recommendation). We both had high hopes for the new photojournalism. The work of the photographers from Magnum, *Picture Post*, and *Life* was our inspiration. We were in for a shock. The fact that Bert Hardy and Henri Cartier Bresson and all our heroes had made their names with the 35mm format cut no ice with Mr Madden. The awful truth was that in those days of endless 'collects' and 'doorstepping', art was in short supply.

"Although after several years on provincial papers I could handle any sort of equipment, I wanted the best gear for the job. Most of my portfolio had been achieved with the 35mm format. So at the *Daily Mail* in 1957 I was staggered to be told to dispose of this "toy" and I was hastily equipped with glass plates and a box-type camera which I was sure had belonged to W.H. Fox Talbot. Mr Talbot didn't mind: he had traded it in about a hundred years before."

It turned out that the main reason for the plate cameras' survival was a dark room equipped with Edwardian horizontal wood-and-brass enlargers which could not cope with 35mm technology. In 1957 Thorpe reluctantly

Donald Campbell's many attempts at the world water speed record on Ullswater and Coniston between 1949 and 1967 involved close relationships with photographers. Campbell needed them to sustain public interest in his exploits; they needed him as a source of stories. Johnnie Walker of the *Daily Mirror* took the signed cockpit portrait of Campbell, his wife Daphne and his chief engineer Leo Vila not long before the final attempt, as well as (page 170) the Christmas fancy-dress party for press and other supporters at Coniston and the earlier shot of fellow photographers using Long Tom plate cameras. Dave Cooksey of the *Daily Express* captured Campbell the showman with his engineers on K4 (page 171) using daylight flash to stress the team's exuberance

traded his Contax for a second-hand Rollieflex, whose bigger negatives the enlargers could handle. Rollies became standard issue to Manchester photographers within a year or so.

"The *Mail* had permanent offices around the north, all with darkrooms and wire facilities and staff photographers working to the Manchester office schedules. Len Forde was in Liverpool, Arthur Thompson in Leeds and Leo Dillon in Newcastle. In 1959 John Walters was given the chance to leave the Manchester darkroom to take over as the *Mail's* Northern Ireland staff photographer in Belfast. He gave unparalleled service for the *Mail* throughout The Troubles. Other *Mail*

From Russia to Jodrell with love: an *Express* scoop

The West was gripped by Cold War, Britain enthralled by James Bond. The Russians were at it again. Luna 9 had landed on the moon. At Jodrell Bank, which tracked the course of Sputnik a decade earlier, there was just a chance that radio signals picked up from the latest Russian spacecraft could be converted into pictures of the moon's surface. On its home patch, the *Daily Express* Manchester determined to be first in the newspaper race. Brian Stringer, night news editor, was coordinating a high-tech, top-secret operation. Now read on

Nightdesk to News Ed February 4 1966

"Luna 9 on the moon is transmitting TV pix back to its receiver station in Russia. Jodrell Bank tuned in but the radio telescope can pick up only SOUND signals and not PIX. But there is just a chance that by using a certain machine of a type owned by most newspapers Jodrell will be able to convert the sound signals into actual pictures.

The machine Jodrell need to try this experiment is called a facsimile receiver of standard type manufactured by Muirhead. After consulting our transmission dept and LN we learn that Jodrell wd also need a "Frequency Modulation Discriminator" machine... hereafter described as FMD. We have a facsimile receiver, our LN office has a portable FMD.

Eds in LN and MX say: get this gear to Jodrell and see if we can get them working so that we can turn the sound signals into pix usable in the DE...pix that wd show what it is like on the moon's surface. Lascelles, the Jodrell PRO, says he is willing to cooperate.

So this is what is happening: a car has left the LN office carrying the FMD machine and a member of the LN transmission staff, Bernard Nash. It is due to arrive at the Springfield Hotel, Congleton, around 6.30 to 7am. Waiting at the Springfield to meet Nash will be our office night car carrying the facsimile receiver gear and Jack Dobson (transmission dept) and George Moores (darkroom). After the meeting the two cars will go to the main entrance at Jodrell Bank. There at 8am they will meet Tony Brooks and John Hamshire whose jobs will be to a) ensure that PRO Lascelles keeps his word about trying our machines and b) do a story on the result. Last night Lascelles assured us that Jodrell wd be only too happy to make use of our gear and our transmission dept experts. But he pointed out that PA were also sending similar gear and theirs wd be used as well. We shd be there first, however, because our machine is moving overnight from LN whereas I understand PA don't set off until this am.

Eds in LN and MX both understand that there is only an outside chance we will succeed in turning the sound signals into pix, but say we must try. The idea is Derek Marks'.

Jodrell won't be tuning in to the moon until 2.50pm today but they have tapes of the signals picked up last night and they can be tried in our machines. See T.Pattinson copy enclosed which explains in quotes from Jodrell what they hope to do. For more informed technical info the man to talk to this am is Jack Dobson whose whereabouts is listed. At 12.30am today Lascelles was still at Jodrell so I do not expect he will be putting in too early an appearance this morning. However, he gave us to understand that the rest of the Jodrell staff would know the purpose of our mission and the experiment cd go ahead when we arrive with the necessary equipment."

As our picture shows, the operation was a success. Other papers which used the image were forced to credit Daily Express technology. Stringer duly received congratulations for the scoop from John McDonald, northern editor, who quoted a note from Sir Max Aitken: "It is a great joy for me to see the energy and efficiency of Manchester pushing through to the top."

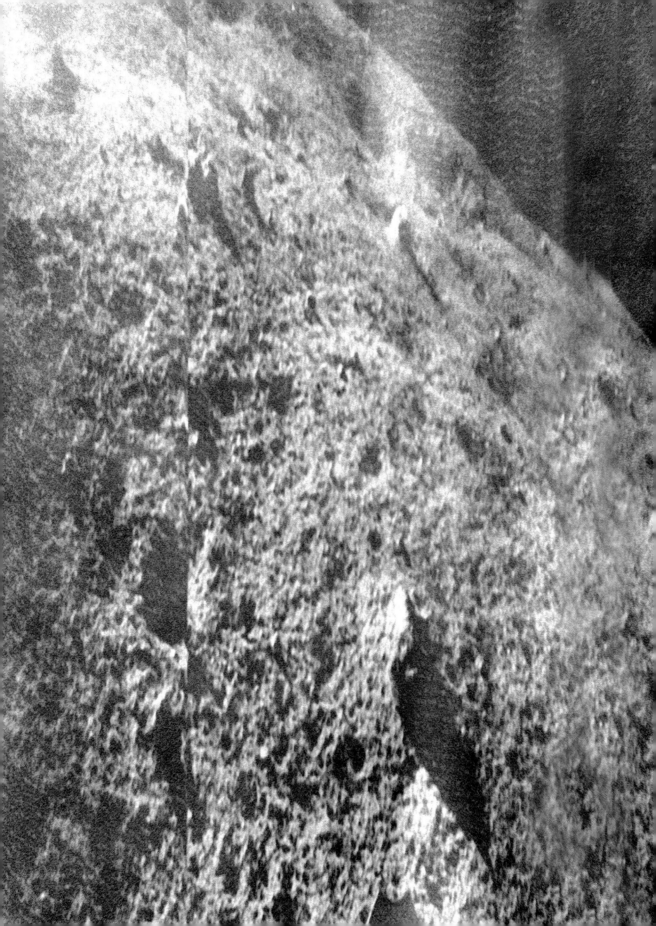

Denis Thorpe, a *Daily Mail* photographer at the time, portrays L.S.Lowry. He was to take a historic sequence of images of the artist's house after Lowry died, just before the removal men arrived. Thorpe's Hebden Bridge, West Yorkshire, is caught at twilight on a wintry February afternoon in 1978 (illustrating a feature by the author). The landscape remains the single most ordered print by *Guardian* readers. Tom Stuttard's eccentric Derbyshire couple is another *Guardian* favourite

stalwarts included John Smart and Gordon Priestley.

"Freelance coverage for the *Mail* from Sheffield came via Peter Elinskas. Born in Eastern Europe, he'd a wonderful way with the English language, using words not yet in everyday 1950s polite society. He had all the latest 35mm equipment, and a new AC Bristol car. When the infamous Woodhead Pass across the Pennines was blocked by snow, and people and vehicles were marooned in the blizzards, he told Tommy Woods on the desk: 'I ski across.' Tommy agreed and crossed his fingers. He need not have worried. Around tea time the call came: 'send car to Glossop, I've ******* done it!' A page one scoop with exclusive pictures of the wintry chaos. Herograms all round. The *Express* editor's reputed terse memo in response: 'Where were our skiing photographers?' In 1962 Peter won an Encyclopedia Britannica Award

Two faces of Manchester law and order: Moss Side rioting in 1981 by Clive Cooksey of the *Evening News*; New Year's Eve at Strangeways by Johnnie Walker of the *Daily Mirror*

with a sequence on Stirling Moss's crash. He became a London staff photographer for the Mail."

Finlayson joined the *Manchester Guardian* in 1959 when Robert Smithies was transferred to set up the photographic side of the new London operation. Thorpe himself went to the *Guardian* in 1974, several years after the retirement of Tom Stuttard, where he was to be Ilford Photographer of the Year in 1988. Of course as a Manchester photographer he worked alongside Stuttard on many occasions. "My main memory of Tom is when a great

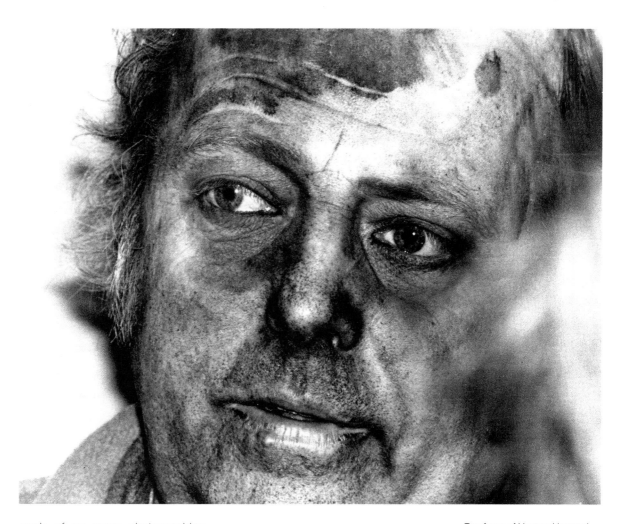

pack of us were photographing Sammy Davis Jnr in Albert Square. Sammy was leaping high into the air for us and being very patient and polite when Tom, the perfectionist, kept asking for a repeat performance. In the end Sammy took a close look at Tom's equipment and commented 'You want to get yourself a N'eye'kon!'"

Competition between the *Mail* and the *Express*, always fierce, tended to peak over northern institutions like Jodrell Bank. Denis Thorpe recalls being told by Madden to hire a de Havilland Rapide and fill airspace over the radio telescope, to which a

Two faces of Liverpool law and order: Anti-police protest during the Toxteth riots of 1981, by Johnnie Walker; football managers and players from Liverpool and Everton including Bob Paisley, Howard Kendall and Kenny Dalglish join police in a move to combat hooliganism. An unpublished freelance submission to the *Daily Mail*. Above: a miner surfaces after an unsuccessful attempt to rescue colleagues trapped in a pit disaster near Atherton in the East Lancashire coalfield. Picture by Johnnie Walker

part was being fitted by helicopter. Against Thorpe's better judgment he was ordered into the air well in advance of the planned manoeuvre so that before the helicopter arrived his light plane had to leave for a refuelling stop, allowing the competition in. Forced to shoot the telescope and the helicopter separately, his picture was somehow joined in the *Mail* darkroom – so successfully that Jodrell Bank used it on their next Christmas card.

By the time press photographers started using digital techniques Manchester publishing was long over. The darkroom and process routines which drove deadlines (see the description of *Daily Mail* coverage from 1911 of the Prince of Wales's Carnarvon investiture, page 31) are as obsolete today as hot metal itself. But the quality recorded on these pages is evident to all. Manchester photographers had nothing to prove to the rest of the world.

Love, Blackpool style. Pictures by Johnnie Walker

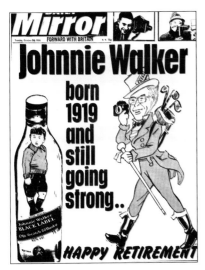

Johnnie Walker, whose images feature strongly in this chapter, started as a darkroom assistant for Fox Photos before the Second World War, becoming a staff photographer for the *Manchester Evening Chronicle* and then the *Daily Mirror*. Although never one to claim he was more than a craftsman, his photographs epitomise the professionalism of the Manchester national newspaper scene. We would like to thank Johnnie for offering his portfolio (some of which has not been published before) and Antony Schipani of Mirrorpix for agreeing to its use.

Whatever became of the *Manchester Guardian?*

Brian Redhead posed the question in the first issue of a *Guardian* promotional publication called "miscellany", published in July 1967, whose cover showed the *Guardian* being studied by an eager young businessman at a Parliament Square bus stop backed by Big Ben. The gist of his reply was that the *Guardian*, a fully national newspaper – indeed the only one to have become a national from the provinces – had not lost its Manchester roots. It enjoyed the best of both worlds.

"Every night, or more precisely every morning at 12.30 a.m., after the third edition with the late night theatre notices and parliamentary notes has gone to press in London and Manchester, the senior editorial staff in Manchester prepare the CITY EDITION. They reappraise the total content of the night's paper and introduce additional matter of moment to Manchester.

"The new content is not local trivia – no alleged chip-pan fires in Chorlton-cum-Hardy. It contains serious reporting and analysis of issues that directly concern people in Manchester. It is usually well-written, sometimes witty, always important. This is the *Guardian* on its home ground."

Then Redhead, northern editor at the time, quoted C.P.Scott himself:

Brian Redhead, northern editor of the Guardian between 1965 and 1968 when he moved across to edit the *Manchester Evening News*, wisecracking at his Cross Street farewell. Harry Whewell, northern news editor and Joe Minogue, his deputy, are on Redhead's right. Sitting behind him is Alastair Hetherington, editor, while Bill Taylor, northern night editor, is standing. Redhead made a failed bid to become editor in 1974 when Hetherington left

"The paper which has grown up in a great community, nourished by its resources, reflecting in a thousand ways its spirit and its interests, in a real sense belongs to it. How else except in the permanence of that association can it fulfil its duty or repay the benefits and the confidence it has received?"

Redhead concluded "How else, indeed?"

It was wishful thinking. There was anything but permanence in the association. The *Guardian's* Manchester City Edition of 1967 did not have a great deal of space for North West news. Plans were already afoot to leave Cross Street. Just nine years later the *Guardian* closed down "live" production in Manchester.

The battle for the north was already lost in 1967, and Redhead knew it. He was putting on a brave face. It gave some heart to those left behind. The day in February 1964 that the editor, Alastair Hetherington, moved his headquarters to London marked the conclusion of a process which had started some 15 years before. Manchester remained a convenient joint production centre until London had the premises and the technology to take that over too, in 1976.

Redhead had himself been at the centre of a Manchester-London spat when, in 1962, he resigned from the Manchester-based features editor's post to take up a job with the BBC in London. He assumed that his able deputy, Anthony Tucker, would be offered the features editor role. Instead Hetherington appointed John Rosselli, a London-based leader-writer. Legend has it that Redhead sent Hetherington a telegram expressing virulent disgust. Rosselli was himself a wise and conciliatory features editor before departing for academia in 1964; Tucker went to London in 1964 as science correspondent, a post he fulfilled with distinction until he retired in 1988; the features powerbase was consolidated in London; and Redhead scotched his prospects of one day editing the *Guardian*.

So, did the *Manchester Guardian* really have to leave Manchester – and has the switch proved worthwhile? What impact did developments in Cross Street have on the national newspapers who had made Manchester their second home? Does today's *Guardian* bear any trace of the newspaper C.P.Scott edited for 57 years, and does that matter anyway?

The most tantalising question is whether, in the modern world, a national must be edited from London. Geoffrey Taylor's view in "Changing Faces" is that Hetherington was catapulted to London by the *Guardian's* alleged misreading of the Profumo Affair. The Manchester-based leader writer (not Hetherington himself, who was out of the country on the night that Profumo admitted lying to the House of Commons) suggested that things should be left to blow over. Maybe the leader-writer was correct. The mood of Parliament and the country proved otherwise. Was that such a big deal?

"The paper which has grown up in a great community, nourished by its resources, reflecting in a thousand ways its spirit and its interests, in a real sense belongs to it. How else except in the permanence of that association can it fulfil its duty...?"

Bert Hardy's *Manchester Guardian*

The *Manchester Guardian* which Bert Hardy, the celebrated *Picture Post* photographer, explored in 1958 was an institution on the point of drastic change. Within a year the word Manchester would be dropped from the paper's masthead. Within three years London printing would have started, and with it the inexorable transfer of power south.

Alastair Hetherington, who became editor in 1956 and immediately made his mark by opposing Britain's Suez adventure, switched to the London office in Gray's Inn Road during February 1964. By that time the features department was already run

from London and Manchester's news editor, Harry Whewell, had been sidelined. The foreign editor remained Manchester-based until "live" printing finished there in 1976.

Hardy's *Manchester Guardian* still has the feel of the family newspaper it was. The journalists sitting around the evening conference table in the Cross Street boardroom headed by Hetherington (in cardigan) include Larry Montague, an assistant editor, son of the illustrious leader-writer C.E.Montague and a grandson of C.P.Scott, as well as Paddy Monkhouse, son of the *MG* literary editor A.N.Monkhouse.

Mary Crozier, daughter of W.P.Crozier, editor from 1932-1944, was radio critic for the *MG* from 1933 and became the newspaper's first television critic. She poses for Hardy beside her office tv set in her pigeonhole on the famous Corridor.

Paddy Monkhouse is seen discussing galley proofs with John Putz, the *MG's* chief sub editor later entrusted with supervising London production. Monkhouse, whose craggy features and erudite honesty characterised the *MG*, is the editor who never was. When Hetherington, the man chosen ahead of him, departed for London, Monkhouse looked after Manchester until Brian Redhead, another editor manqué, was tempted back from London as northern editor in 1965.

Redhead is captured by Hardy pipe-in-mouth characteristically showing Austin McCawley how to plan an industrial page. He was about to become features editor. Nesta Roberts, the very bright, very Welsh deputy news editor enthuses at her typewriter. She was to be the *Guardian's* first London news editor, and then Paris correspondent. The reporters' room she inhabited was a spartan place of shared typewriters, scrumpled paper and a few phone lines. Its dominant feature is the well-used coat rack

In the composing room Hardy found Denys Rowbotham, the paper's cricket correspondent, putting together a sports page with stone-hand Roy Litherland. Sports writers doubled as sub-editors. Rowbotham, a stylist as elegant as Cyril Washbrook, died in 1968 aged just 52.

Absent in body if hardly in spirit is the mastermind of the London move, Laurence Scott. As managing director he had no role in nightly production.

Bert Hardy's 1958 images were taken for Hulton Press. *Picture Post* had been closed by Edward Hulton the previous year, but well-known photographers like Hardy were retained on occasional jobs. It seems that the *Manchester Guardian* pictures were never used. The photographer's widow, Mrs Sheila Hardy, kindly consented to this, their first publication.

The *Guardian*, after all, was respected for taking a contrary, non-metropolitan view of life. One suspects that – at a time when the *Guardian* was losing money heavily, under pressure from Fleet Street for its provincialism and amateurism, and starting to lose touch with its Manchester roots – there was only one way for Hetherington to go.

Hetherington, Redhead, Peter Preston and others involved in the transition period have all been quick to point out that Scott, often an absentee editor, understood the limitations of Manchester and the importance of a presence in the capital. The *Manchester Guardian* had enjoyed a private wire arrangement with Fleet Street from the 1860s. A system of bicycle deliveries for *Manchester Guardian*s sent down by overnight train was organised for W1 and SW1 in the 1890s. Scott even considered London printing in the 1880s and again in 1914, when he apparently discussed it with Lloyd George. The *Manchester Guardian* might be better known than the *Daily Telegraph* in Washington or Moscow but it needed London's imprimatur. Before London printing started in 1961 it was classed as a provincial morning paper. It was not, for instance, tabulated with nationals in appendices to the first Royal Commission on the Press of 1947-1949, although the small-circulation, London-printed *Daily Worker* was.

Being a provincial meant exclusion from the NPA, the Newspaper Proprietors' Association, a national newspaper management club which negotiated with the unions and, among other things, organised newspaper trains. In Manchester, then, the *Guardian* found itself packaged with provincial dailies like those from Liverpool, Leeds and Sheffield while the *Daily Telegraph*, the *Daily Mail* and other Manchester-published morning newspapers were part of the NPA. Laurence Scott, grandson of C.P., managing director of the Manchester Guardian & Evening News Ltd, declared until the 1960s that he would prefer to stay outside the NPA. His actions, however, suggest otherwise.

Laurence Scott's activities between 1948, when he became managing director, and 1967 when he was relieved of executive duties, are recounted in the official *Guardian* biographies of David Ayerst and Geoffrey Taylor, as well as in

Hetherington's own book "*Guardian* Years." They are a catalogue of disaster which the *Guardian* was lucky to survive. Scott drove the quest for London printing, pioneering a page facsimile system to be used from Manchester to London which was never presented to the London unions. When London printing came he plumped for a simultaneous typesetting system called TTS, a Heath Robinson arrangement which used perforated tape sent by wire to be run into conventional linotype machines at the other end. TTS was designed for small-scale use between City offices and Fleet Street for stock prices, but had been "blacked" there by the unions. It was to stagger on as the nightly Manchester-London-Manchester link between 1961 and 1976, the years of *Private Eye's* "Grauniad."

Scott had done a poor deal with Roy Thomson for London offices at Gray's Inn Road; in 1961 he signed another which put G&MEN in control of the loss-making *Manchester Evening Chronicle*. The terms of the deal were so worded that when the company decided to close the *Evening Chronicle* in 1963 it was saddled with a payment of £1.8 million to Thomson for breaking the print contract. Then, during 1965 and 1966, Scott pushed the idea of amalgamating the *Guardian* with the *Times* while Thomson the predator looked on; after that deal failed, he considered amalgamation with the *Observer*, retreating to Manchester or even closure.

From the start of London printing the *Guardian* incurred heavy losses due to extra costs, lack of circulation increase, and poor advertising revenues. Manchester had lost confidence and interest in the *Guardian*; London remained blasé about the intruder. These were, commercially and editorially, wilderness years. The *Guardian* survived because the *Manchester Evening News* made more than enough profit to cover the losses of the *Guardian* (some £11.233 million between 1961-1975) and the costs of the broken Thomson contract.

The Scott Trust was established in 1936, at considerable personal cost to the Scott family, to ensure the *Manchester Guardian*'s future. The *Manchester Evening News*, a relative of the *Manchester Guardian* from John Edward Taylor days, had been brought fully into the company to provide a solid commercial basis for *Guardian* ambitions. Yet until he was removed from power, Laurence Scott put the *Guardian* at high risk while effectively nullifying Manchester's role and squeezing the *MEN* of development cash. The Scott Trust was brought to its senses in November 1966 by two trustees – Richard Scott, Laurence's elder brother, who was the *Guardian's* Washington correspondent, and Paddy Monkhouse. However, as Taylor chronicles, even when non-executive chairman Scott continued to push the idea of a merger with the *Times* as late as Summer 1970.

Laurence Scott's motives are hard to understand. In 1973, on his final retirement, he wrote to his successor Peter Gibbings, as quoted by Taylor: "I believe I was quite a good manager of a provincial newspaper, but when the *Guardian* went national I was neither inclined nor equipped to play a part on

Above: *Manchester Guardian* advertisement from 1938

Top left: Laurence Scott, architect of the *Guardian's* move to London, seen right foreground at a Cross Street event in the 1960s. His son Martin Scott is standing behind him

Bottom left: a Scott family group in the late 1940s. Picture by Tom Stuttard the Fleet Street stage…" It was as if he had taken no role in the decision to go national. Or, having taken the paper over the edge, he hadn't the guts to lead it to safety. The quote also suggests a conceptual misunderstanding of the *Manchester Guardian*. Though based a long way from London, it was not provincial. Even those who disliked the *Manchester Guardian*'s brand of holier-than-thou liberalism had to admit that its international reporting and its editorial stance on issues like the Boer War, Irish independence and the Suez crisis, were unique. The *Guardian* did not have to go to London to prove itself.

Neville Cardus summed it up in his "Autobiography", describing the dilemmas he faced around 1935 when offered a lot of money to transfer allegiances to the London *Evening Standard*, and why he decided to stay put: "you had only to tell any musician in Europe, any man of letters, artist – anybody who was anybody, in fact, that you belonged to the *Manchester Guardian* and at once they met you not as a pressman, not as a journalist, but as a writer, free and civilised." As long ago as 1917, Beaverbrook wrote – comparing the radicalism of the *MG* with the conservatism of the *Daily Telegraph* – "If the *Manchester Guardian* gets a readier recognition abroad it is due to the brilliant independence of its editorial attitude." (As quoted in "Peterborough Court" by Lord Burnham.)

Peter Preston, who in 1975 followed Alastair Hetherington as editor, holds to the view that Laurence Scott was right in his belief that the *Manchester Guardian* had to change. It did not have the circulation or advertising base to support its obvious potential. By the late 1940s readers living beyond the North West exceeded those living in the region for the first time. Was this a threat or an opportunity? For the very same reason that London nationals found they had to print in Manchester to offer northern readers an up-to-the-moment morning newspaper, the *Guardian* sought London printing to be seen as a national. So why was the page fax system which Laurence Scott had pioneered with Muirhead to transmit pages from Manchester to London (in principle the same system the *Guardian* used from London to Manchester in 1976) never proposed to the London unions? Preston makes the point that the weight of copy flow was from London to Manchester (even though the foreign desk remained in Manchester until 1976). In his view it made little sense for this to be wired, set in Manchester, and then page-faxed back to London.

All the same, Preston admits that the instigators didn't really know what they were undertaking. "The truth" he writes, in response to questions, "is that the decision to go to London meant that the *Guardian* had to become effectively the first 'new' newspaper of the hi-tech age. In costs, quality, competitiveness that took us almost 20 years to come to terms with. Did Laurence and Alastair realise this? Almost certainly not. They thought the paper was not merely great already – but great enough to take on the *Times* and the *Telegraph* as head-to-head nationals. It wasn't."

Preston's most telling point is this: if the *Manchester Guardian* had not become the *Guardian*, at whatever the cost at the time, it would now be struggling or worse. In response to a question on the subject he writes: "what I think you need to ask yourself is where we'd be if things, however painfully, hadn't worked as they did. Answer: in deep trouble. Just look at the middle-term future of evening newspapers. It doesn't exist. Just look at provincial mornings from Leeds to Liverpool to Sheffield, gone or shrinking fast, and owned by big groups who put cost-cutting first. Just think what the *Independent* and others would have done to us as an unchanged Manchester morning."

What indeed. From a Manchester point of view (and from a London one) any attempt to compare the *Manchester Guardian* of 1954 with today's *Guardian* is irrelevant. One way or another the transformation happened. Back in the 1960s, while the little dramas were being played out between Cross Street and Gray's Inn Road and Laurence Scott courted the *Times* and the *Observer*, the *Guardian* was supplanted by the *Daily Telegraph* as the paper which covered the North West with any pretence of seriousness. The *Daily Mail* and the *Daily Express* showed more interest in social change around the North – it was the 1960s after all – while the *Daily Mirror* was giving the region a new voice. As the *Guardian* slowly and painfully staked its claim to be a national newspaper it surrendered its home ground – to the other nationals.

This was, inevitably, a difficult time for the Manchester office. The flow of ambitious young reporters and features sub-editors dried up. Those who stayed on found that London had them pigeonholed. It was the old London-Manchester thing again, but with added rancour. Harry Whewell's newsroom imploded. Features staff continued to design and edit most pages, but it was increasingly a production department apart from Mary Stott's women's pages. Northern sportswriters, as ever, excelled themselves. David Irvine, northern rugby correspondent, became tennis correspondent; John Roberts, an import from the *Daily Mail* as a football writer, was exported to the *Independent* as tennis correspondent; Paddy Barclay also went to the *Independent* as football correspondent. The two Manchester-based photographers, Don McPhee and Denis Thorpe, continued to take the best images in the paper – working for the London picture desk after 1976. And there was a late flurry for the long-moribund *Guardian* Weekly. John Perkin,

From a Manchester point of view (and from a London one) any attempt to compare the Manchester Guardian of 1954 with today's Guardian is irrelevant. One way or another the transformation happened

its editor from 1969, created a successful international review whose scope included four pages from *Le Monde* and four from the *Washington Post*. It stayed a Manchester production until Perkin retired in 1994. Page film was flown each Tuesday lunchtime from Ringway to North America, where over half of its total circulation was printed – under the banner *Manchester Guardian Weekly*. Today it prints in centres around the world by page fax.

The *Guardian's* direct legacy to Manchester's nationals was hitch-free implementation of page faxing from London in August 1976. Preston, who says all the decisions had been made before he took over the editor's chair in 1975, recalls that the lead up to the period involved "some of the most difficult months of my life." He had the double task of easing the paper into the new London office at Farringdon Road while smoothing potential crises in Manchester. In the end, things went quietly. A rump of sub-editors took redundancy or moved to London (where the Manchester foreign desk stalwarts proved their worth). Whewell became northern editor, whatever that meant. Print-workers, reduced by natural wastage, were switched to the burgeoning classified sections or across to the *Manchester Evening News*. Industrial action was avoided.

Decked out for the 1953 Coronation, the *Manchester Guardian* office on Cross Street was at the centre of city life

It took the other nationals a further decade to close down "live" Manchester production, though both the *Daily Telegraph* and the *Daily Mirror* had signalled intentions by the mid-1970s. Fleet Street had more urgent preoccupations. By acting when they did, Laurence Scott and Alastair Hetherington unconsciously assured that the *Guardian* was well-placed to benefit from the battles of Warrington and Wapping. Innocents at Home – the phrase is from Geoffrey Taylor's book – they were. Somehow they prevailed. But "permanence" and "Manchester" were no longer associated in the *Guardian* vocabulary.

New beginnings, and the end

In the spring of 1974 Express Newspapers decided to close down its Albion Street plant in Glasgow – the third of Sir Owen Williams's celebrated Black Lubyankas – and transfer production of the *Scottish Daily Express* to Manchester. Some 50 sub-editors were detailed to move south, leaving behind a few feature writers, a news and a sports desk in Glasgow. Many predicted disaster. It duly happened. Before moving, the *SDE* was on a circulation high of 550,000 copies daily. In the charged, competitive environment of Scottish dailies – Glasgow was a mini Fleet Street of its own – it was head-to-head with the *Daily Record,* Mirror Group Newspapers' Scottish version of the *Daily Mirror.* The *Scottish Daily Mail,* which had already switched publishing to Manchester, was not in the frame, nor were other Manchester or London-produced dailies. But the *Glasgow Herald*, the *Scotsman*, the *Dundee Courier* and the *Aberdeen Press & Journal* all had loyal readerships which overlapped. At a time of resurgent nationalism, Scotland was particularly sensitive to its destiny. It did not take punters long to realise that "Scotland's *Daily News*paper" had gone to bed far too early to provide reports of the previous night's football, or updated news. Circulation sank swiftly to 250,000, then dropped again despite heroic efforts by journalists catapulted South of the Border.

Alan Mackenzie, a Scot who had worked several years in Manchester before he moved across to Great Ancoats Street, takes up the story: "I was the first non-Glaswegian hired – all the others were transplanted like the Plantation of Ulster. They were tremendous journalists – I learned all I know about copy editing from the *Scottish Daily Express*."

The Manchester edition had to close between 8-9pm each evening to catch trains. It was "quite costly to pretend to be a Glasgow paper." There was a real problem with evening football matches, for instance. Reports had to be on the breakfast table, but how?

Initially journalists were dispatched ahead of their wives but with a generous relocation package. "It was blood money", says Mackenzie. "Jobs were saved as part of the destruction of Glasgow. There was a culture problem. People lived a nomadic existence in hotels. They resented what had happened, while some in Glasgow resented them for betraying the cause. It was all highly emotional and hugely alcoholic. The quality of journalists was fantastic – tight and bright writing, headlines second to none for flair, wit and brevity. We worked essentially from 6-9 pm, it was very intense. English colleagues admired us and treated us with great respect, which was earned. But despite the very high quality of production it was a Titanic."

Bob Gray, another Mancunian Scot who had cut his teeth on the *Scottish Daily Express* in Glasgow in the early 1960s and became night editor at Great Ancoats Street when he moved across from the *Daily Mirror*, echoes the feelings: "It was a kind of death wish. Perhaps management didn't anticipate

In the spring of 1974 Express Newspapers decided to close down its Albion Street plant in Glasgow and transfer production of the Scottish Daily Express to Manchester. Many predicted disaster. It duly happened

that the Scottish people would be so upset at losing their national newspaper – it was the semi national newspaper then."

Meanwhile, English journalists in the same building were having culture problems of their own. "What the hell were they talking about?" asks Stanley Blenkinsop, then northern news editor. "We didn't understand their stories, either. What was so important about Irn Bru? Bruce McLeod was the liaison in Manchester with the news editor in Glasgow. He had no deputy. When he was off the desk nobody understood what the correspondents, who kept trying to interest us in Scottish stories, were saying. But the paper slowly died. In Dumfries a newsagent was asked, 'can I have the *Scottish Daily Express*?' The reply came – 'no, you can have the English *Daily Express*'."

Proprietor Victor Matthews at the launch of the *Daily Star* in November 1978. The "joke" was John Knill and Stanley Blenkinsop (with visor up) dressed as Beaverbrook crusaders

With hindsight, what happened to Glasgow would happen to Manchester. It was only a matter of time. But there were diversions. Towards the end of the 1970s, with the *Scottish Daily Express* petering out and a superfluity of journalists and production space on the Manchester presses, Trafalgar House, the new owners of Express Newspapers, created the *Daily Star*, a north-only tabloid to take on the might of the northern *Daily Mirror* and the growing power of Murdoch's *Sun*. The November 1978 launch was not a particularly auspicious event, overseen by Derek Jameson, who had been persuaded against his better judgment to keep an eye on Manchester from Fleet Street, where he was editing the *Daily Express*. Jameson made Peter Grimsditch editor of the *Star*; they had worked together before in Manchester on the *Sunday Mirror*. Grimsditch, who was to resurface in Manchester in 1988 as launch editor of the *Sport*, lasted just over a year and Jameson reluctantly moved north again to assume the editorship (see pages 78-79).

In his autobiography "Last of the Hot Metal Men" Jameson admits that it was bingo rather than journalism which kept the *Star* in business, though he notes Victor Matthews' generous blessing: "I do not believe this could have been done anywhere else in this country but in Manchester and I do not believe it could have been done anywhere else in the world but in this country."

DAILY STAR

Friday, November 3, 1978   2   BRITAIN'S BEST BUY ★

6P

DON'T MISS THE
TELLY BABIES
Centre Pages

WHY?
IT'S BRITAIN'S BEST BUY

THE BIRTH of the Daily Star was a rip-roaring success. We printed 1,400,000 copies of Britain's brightest newspaper and they were all snapped up in the North and Midlands by 10 a.m. yesterday. Thanks to everyone who joined us, and greetings to new readers who have reached for the Star today. Stay with us by ordering your copy today.

HOW ABOUT THIS FOR A BRIDE!

TURN TO PAGE 19 FOR THE GROOM

HANGMEN OF CELL 5 GET LIFE

Lynch-mob fears in grisly Risley prison —by the governor

by MAURICE RICHARDS

THE teenage lynch mob from Cell Five were b a c k behind bars last night.

Two were jailed for life.

And t w o others, aged 16, were ordered to be detained during Her Majesty's pleasure.

A jury found them guilty of murdering a cellmate after condemning to death at a mock trial.

Timid David Evans, 17, was hanged in a macabre midnight execution at Risley Remand Centre, Warrington.

And last night the grim centre's governor stood near the spot where David died and admitted.

"It could h a p p e n again."

Mr. Freddie Owens threw the doors of his centre to reporters to show the Pressures caused by understaffing and over-crowding.

Condemned

And he revealed that only one officer was available to guard 300 young offenders on the night of the execution in Cell Five.

The four thugs who condemned Evans to death were found guilty of murder after a 14-day trial at Mold Crown Court.

Ringleader Dennis Slater, 18, of Cumbran Road, Worsley Hall.

Turn to Page Four

David Evans . . . sentenced to death

Hard times

A selective diary of newspaper amalgamation and new technology issues as they affected Manchester, taken from *Daily Telegraph* cuttings in the Greater Manchester County Record Office

Daily Sketch to close by mid-May

March 9 1971

Losses said by Harmsworth to be £2.25 million in the year to March 1 1971. Associated announce 1,700 redundancies, with 6,000 jobs remaining.

Journalist redundancies:

Daily Sketch, London 92 of 150
Daily Sketch, Manchester 10 of 12
Daily Mail, London 132 out of 261
Daily Mail Manchester 27 of 144

New *Daily Mail* has 187 journalists in London, 121 in Manchester

Facsimile proposed at *Daily Mirror*

October 24 1975

Percy Roberts, general manager, announces plans for switch to facsimile pages from London to Manchester. Production halted of 1.4 million copies of the *Daily Mirror*, 200,000 copies of the *Daily Telegraph* and 75,000 copies of the *Sporting Chronicle* in protest. From October 1976 the *Daily Mirror*, the *Sunday Mirror* and the *People* to be produced in London. Out of 150 Manchester *Mirror* journalists, 50 sub-editors will move to London.

October 29 1975

Bill Duffy, chairman of the office section of NGA at Withy Grove: "We are not going to accept it. They are making a compost heap of the composing room. There is no overmanning in our department, but we are being sacrificed for others where there is."

Journalists' statement: "The company's announcement has totally failed to convince us that there is any financial justification for any major changes affecting journalists in Manchester"

Roberts: Modernisation is necessary for survival. "There is no way in the present economic climate…in which we can achieve substantial improvements in revenue."

October 30 1975

Scheme to transfer northern editions of MGN to London attacked by North West MPs and civic leaders. Winston Churchill (Stretford) says his regrets are tempered by excessive wage demands of some unions.

Churchill: "We are losing a national voice. That the whole of the paper should be produced in every way except the printing from London is a most regressive step from a regional standpoint."

Duffy: "We are not going to be kicked out on our arse. It appears to me that we are having a ritual blood-letting in Manchester to appease the gods in the Holborn palace." The NGA would not allow Manchester facsimile printing, either at the *Mirror* or elsewhere in Manchester.

November 6 1975

Production of the *Daily Mirror* northern editions halted by NUJ following NGA action on November 3. Plans are to transfer 45-50 of 174 *Daily Mirror* journalists to London, retaining 55-60 in Manchester and making 65-70 redundant.

NUJ chapel resolution attacked the "folly, inhumanity and impracticability" of the development plan

Unions wary of new technology

March 15 1976

Manchester Print Unions Action Group issues policy statement "The National Press in the North." It notes the success of Manchester editions of the *Daily Telegraph* and the *Daily Mirror* – both of which would transfer editing to London. The group is not opposed to new technology per se, even if jobs are lost. "When new technology can be used to maximise the selling points of a paper we will welcome it."

MGN recently yielded to journalists' demands for phased introduction of new technology over three years with retention of editing and production of some pages in Manchester.

NGA Manchester-London wrangle over launch of *Daily Star*

October 31 1978

NGA national council told Manchester that they should get improvements on the launch deal – Manchester NGA determined to go ahead.

Daily Telegraph reports: "One reason for the NGA council's rejection, however, is believed to be rivalry between London and Manchester, both over earnings and the prospect of Manchester increasing in importance as a print centre in relation to Fleet Street, where production of national newspapers is affected by industrial action every week."

Joe Wade, NGA general secretary, under heading 'Confidence trick' by Express Newspapers on NGA Manchester branch: "The only difference between the council and the Manchester branch is that we want more jobs, whereas they are prepared to accept 'ghost payments"

1.4m copies of *Daily Star* printed on first night on top of 1.1m copies of the *Daily Express* in Manchester. 124 new jobs involved for the NGA.

Withy Grove seeks parity with wages paid at *Daily Star*

April 11 1979

Future of *Sporting Chronicle* in jeopardy. George Dunn, managing director of Thomson Withy Grove: "We are not saying it will reappear again"

MGN says composing room action over the facsimile agreement is unofficial. It had been agreed previously that shifts covered by 64 staff would be covered by regular staff providing casual shifts or extra shift working. "But the real cause of the problem is a demand for parity with wages being paid by the *Daily Star* in Manchester." Increase of £41 per week sought.

Scottish *Daily Express* page facsimile plan abandoned

June 7 1980

Daily Express abandons plans to facsimile *Scottish Daily Express* and *Daily Star* to Inverness from Manchester. Jocelyn Stevens said in Manchester that the group faced "a crisis situation" with the *SDE* losing £50,000 a week (£2.6 million annually) and the Manchester-based *Daily Star* losing £12 million annually. Scottish SOGAT refuses to allow Inverness printing. Glasgow printing no longer possible.

Closed-shop dispute costs 20 NGA wire-room jobs

December 11 1982

20 members of the NGA working for MGN Manchester lose their jobs because of closed-shop agreement:

Wire-room men who disobeyed instructions to work normally during a manning dispute and refused to pay fines of £50 imposed by NGA, were deemed to be in arrears and then expelled from union – the

NEC turned down their appeals. Management then had to make the men redundant because of the closed-shop agreement.

Dispute began when telecoms chapel of NGA refused to fill two vacancies because of the effect they would have on overtime payments. This widened to 20 members who objected to cuts in editorial manning levels because they feared a drop in services, leading to earnings loss.

They were instructed to work normally in February 1982 but refused. Between June and Sept warnings were sent out by recorded delivery. They refused to attend appeal hearings and didn't contact NGA leaders. Expelled on November 27, dismissed from jobs two days later. They attempted to pay their fines at the last minute but the offer was refused by local officials because they no longer belonged to the union. Work now carried out by casuals.

SOGAT calls for guarantees on northern editions

March 9 1984

SOGAT 82 calls for assurances that printing northern editions will not be transferred from Manchester when Thomson House contracts terminate in 1985. Thomson Withy Grove gave notice to terminate its contract on December 31 1985. SOGAT wants "absolute guarantee" of continued Manchester printing as well as no job losses.

The *Daily Star* survived – without Jameson who had moved on to the *News of the World* – becoming a fully national paper edited from London. By that time, Manchester had seen the writing on the wall. The 1970s were worrying times. Page facsimile from London, successfully introduced by the *Guardian* in August 1976, had also been mooted by the *Daily Telegraph* in 1974 and the *Daily Mirror* in 1975. It was only a matter of time: the battles fought with the NGA first by Eddy Shah at Warrington in 1983 and crucially by Murdoch at Wapping in 1986 cleared the ground for introduction of new working practices throughout the industry. When the other nationals started to follow suit and move from Fleet Street to places like the Isle of Dogs the days of hot metal were over. Manchester could have originated much of the new-age production. It would have been cheaper and more hassle-free (in fact Maxwell prepared a computer-friendly floor in Withy Grove in case he had to bypass Holborn). But it didn't happen. One-centre production meant London.

Maxwell's arrival at Withy Grove in 1984 had left little doubt about his intentions. It is claimed that he had no wish to buy the plant but was forced to because Thomson Withy Grove declined to renew the *Daily Mirror*'s print contact. He eventually paid the Thomson International Organisation just £1 for it – the bargain of the millennium – and the building was renamed, extraordinarily, Maxwell House. According to Ken Martin, a NATSOPA representative, "Maxwell walked into a meeting of branch officials 50 minutes late, strolled to the platform and wolf-whistled: 'I'm talking now'. We were treated to effing and blinding. Someone got up to ask a question. Maxwell said, 'who are you? Sit down, you cunt'. That's how he spoke." Maxwell's message was that the days of demarcation were over. Anyone who wanted to stay in a job would play it his way. What he didn't tell people was that he also had his eyes on the Withy Grove Pension fund, a fact that of course still rankles with many.

Leo White, the *Daily Mirror* northern news editor, had been charged with making the arrangements for another Maxwell Manchester event as part of his infamous whistle-stop train tour of the country, though White declined to attend himself because he hated the man. On board the train, Maxwell again summoned the Manchester dignitaries he'd invited – by wolf-whistling. The story of how Maxwell acquired Withy Grove on Christmas Eve 1985 is described on page 202 in the words of Revel Barker, one of his assistants at the time. Maxwell sent employees a New Year 1986 greeting reminding them that the new House Agreement (which went with the Withy Grove acquisition) "requires the avoidance of inefficiency, over-manning and waste and the acceptance of flexible working." He had the unions cornered.

Over at the *Telegraph* there had also been turmoil. Ben Hurren, the assistant general manager of the *Daily Telegraph* in Manchester who became managing director of Trafford Park Printers, describes the panic on hearing, in December 1983, that the *Telegraph* had just two years to make alternative printing arrangements. Thomson Withy Grove wanted out by December 1985, when

"Maxwell walked into a meeting of branch officials 50 minutes late, strolled to the platform and wolf-whistled: 'I'm talking now'… Someone got up to ask a question. Maxwell said, 'who are you? Sit down, you cunt.' That's how he spoke"

contracts with Mirror Group and News International would also terminate.

"In London the *Telegraph* had taken the decision to quit Fleet Street and build a new printing plant at West Ferry Road in Docklands. Then came this sudden bombshell from the north. The options were to close Manchester and transfer all production to London; a possible joint venture with the *Mirror* (ruled out 'because of Maxwell'); or build our own plant. Alan Rawcliffe headed the company's project team which plumped for option three. West Ferry Road plans were cut in half: all that remained was to find a northern site, build the plant, install the presses and employ staff. The following 24 months were to prove interesting.

"I remember meeting up with Hugh Lawson (now Lord Burnham) and our northern manager, Peter Janes, to inspect a potential site in Skelmersdale. We arrived in separate cars, the only ones in a large pub car park. Entering the bar we were faced with a scene reminiscent of a wild west film. Four or five local lads surrounded a smallish pool table whilst the bar boasted no more than a handful of bottles and a single pump. We were not inconspicuous ourselves in our suits and ties. We sat in a corner nursing our halves of bitter and then escaped outside where Hugh produced a camera and proceeded to take shots of the surrounding fields. After that we all returned to our offices: I can't imagine what the pool players made of it.

"The *Telegraph* finally settled on a Enterprise Zone site in Trafford Park. In the 18 months from June 1984 the plant was built, machinery installed, new roads created and (most) staffing problems resolved after many difficulties and sleepless nights. London unions had made it clear that they were not prepared to allow northern editions of the *Sunday Telegraph* to be printed in Trafford Park, Manchester unions wanted the same numbers employed as at Withy Grove (despite the fact they were well aware that new technology inevitably meant the disappearance of many NGA jobs) and, for their part, journalists were insisting that their numbers be maintained in order keep the paper's 'northern flavour'.

"Just six months before the scheduled opening of the plant the NGA weren't speaking to us. The position worsened when we took on one of their Belfast-based members who had experience in running Goss Headliner presses – there was virtually no such experience among existing Withy Grove staff. Our 'sin' was to offer work to a member not in the Manchester branch; that set negotiations back another four weeks. With about four months to go agreements were hammered out although we were grossly overmanned, with initial numbers similar to Withy Grove."

Duff Hart-Davis records in his *Telegraph* biography "The House the Berrys Built" that Lord Hartwell was convinced that the unforeseen extra labour costs at Trafford Park were a major factor in the Berry family losing control of the Telegraph. The picture of a morose Hartwell pushing the button to start

"In the 18 months from June 1984 the (new Daily Telegraph) plant was built, machinery installed, new roads created and most staffing problems resolved after many difficulties and sleepless nights"

the new presses on January 1 1986, page one in the next morning's Telegraph, tells it all. When Conrad Black took over he stipulated what he needed, take it or leave it, just like Maxwell had done at Withy Grove and would do at Hollinwood, where he finally transferred *Mirror* operations in May 1988.

Black never visited Trafford Park. He was originally anxious to sell the plant, and almost shook hands on a deal three times with Maxwell – who, true to form, kept trying to bring the price down by £1 million. However, fortunes started to change for Trafford Park Printers when News International ran out of capacity at its Knowsley plant. Sections of the *Sunday Times* were switched to Trafford Park. Then along came a contract to print the *Guardian* and the *Manchester Evening News*, who were moving production from their Deansgate site. Associated, also moving from Deansgate, sought to print the *Daily Mail* there too, but finished up in Stoke-on-Trent at the Evening Sentinel plant. Trafford Park Printers, now jointly owned by Hollinger, News International and the Guardian Media Group, is the modern equivalent of Withy Grove. However, it employs only about 270 people.

What of the *Daily Mail*, the first and most constant of Manchester's national newspaper investors? The *Mail* had not seen the upheavals in ownership which blighted the *Daily Express* after Beaverbrook's death and afflicted the *Daily Mirror* following the King-Cudlipp IPC confrontation. It had absorbed the *News Chronicle* in 1960 and the *Daily Sketch* in 1971, while Manchester had benefited by the retreat from Edinburgh in 1968. In Larry Lamb it had seen one of the strongest of Northern editors. In the days of Ken Donlan and Harold Pendlebury it had an unrivalled news editor/chief reporter combination, and in Jim Stansfield the north's best-connected crime specialist. But things had changed, too, at the *Mail*. Associated's huge investment in the *Mail on Sunday* had bypassed Manchester; David English's success in taking the *Mail* past the *Express* was grounded in his understanding of affluent Middle England, an England of the South Midlands and the Home Counties. Manchester was increasingly peripheral to the *Mail's* ambitions. The move from Fleet Street was under way and a print complex at Surrey Docks under construction. But there was a Docklands cost overrun of £60 million. In September 1986, 100 Manchester journalists were put on notice that their jobs were in jeopardy.

In response, a Manchester staffer, Kevin Dowling wrote eloquently for the October 6 1986 edition of *UK Press Gazette*, the journalist's weekly: "The *Daily Mail* has been faithful to the traditional formula of national coverage for a national paper, and is only now threatening to become a London suburban morning."

He concluded: "New technology was supposed to benefit the Press. We in the North have never opposed it, but we have seen our deadlines shorten, the trivialisation of content in favour of slickness of presentation and the

"New technology was supposed to benefit the Press. We in the North have never opposed it, but we have seen our deadlines shorten, the trivialisation of content in favour of slickness of presentation and the emasculation of editorial budgets to cover capital debts"

emasculation of editorial budgets to cover capital debts.

"Until these issues are properly addressed we will be like the baker who tries to go on selling the same old traditional mince pies – and hopes his customers won't notice that he's missing out the currants."

The announcement, when it came in January 1987, only slightly alleviated the blow – 63 journalists were to go in closure of the "live" Manchester operation. This was presented in the *Daily Mail* itself as "a major investment programme in Manchester (by Mail Newspapers plc) to maintain and strengthen its position in the North." It was hard to see just how. A £15 million proposal to update the Deansgate facilities shared with the Guardian & Manchester Evening News Ltd eventually came to naught.

Nor were the words of Arthur Perrin, NGA branch secretary, prophetic: "We are not prepared to accept compulsory redundancy. We are also not prepared to accept that there will not be origination in Manchester," he was quoted in the *Mail* as declaring. "Every paper that has tried to pull out of Manchester has realised that there is a need for a paper that relates to the Northern heart of England."

To Mike Cuerden, *Daily Mail* northern news editor, the end began about a year out. "The first chunk of redundancies were subs and district reporters. Management started building a suite of offices capable of taking new

The suite of offices on a top floor of Withy Grove which Maxwell wired for computers in case he chose to switch all publication of Mirror Group Newspapers to Manchester to avoid industrial action. It did not happen

technology. Later the plan was revised and Manchester was shut. I was offered number four on the London news desk, with little extra money. I declined that one. I was 48, disappointed and bemused.

"At the final *Mail* chapel meeting the news-desk tv was switched on. Suddenly we found ourselves watching John Womersley, the northern editor, saying what a great day for the *Mail*…Then it was the night of the long envelopes. My memories are of people, not the building. Of great friends, great colleagues, of how lucky we were to be paid for doing things others would have given their eye teeth to do."

A kind of collective amnesia about the final days and months still grips Manchester journalists. We know that the last live editions of the *Daily Mirror* were published on Saturday May 8 1988, and that Maxwell House closed after publication of the *Sunday Mirror* the following day. The *Daily Mail* had already halted live Manchester production, in mid-May 1987, over 87 years after Northcliffe's emissary Kennedy Jones had seen the first northern editions off the improvised Gorton press. The *Daily Express* and *Star* struggled on into 1989, with increasing numbers of pages faxed from London. It was a messy process, and it was the end.

Below: the former Northcliffe House on Deansgate, site of the *Daily Mail* office for 85 years, in final stages of demolition to make way for office development

Opposite: A last goodbye to Manchester from the *Daily Telegraph* in September 1987, written by Michael Kennedy. Limited live production, using photocomposition and much-reduced staffing, had continued at Trafford Park after the *Telegraph's* contract at Withy Grove expired in December 1985

FOR SALE
Fleet of newspaper delivery vans
Any resonable offer accepted.

The Daily Telegraph

FINAL

No. 41,118. FRIDAY, SEPTEMBER 4, 1987 PRICELESS

WE WISH all our colleagues in the composing room all the very best for the future. We shall miss the repartee and light banter!

And a big thank you to the ever-cheerful Nobby Clark, who very kindly made up this commemorative page.

GOOD LUCK, LADS!

Sad day for Manchester journalists

THE END OF AN ERA

No whimpers after 47 proud years

By Michael Kennedy, Northern Editor 1960-86

"THIS IS THE WAY the world ends. Not with a bang but a whimper." That may be all right for the world and T. S. Eliot, but it won't do for the Manchester-produced *Daily Telegraph*. After 47 years, the editorial and composing-room functions will henceforward be based solely in London, but there will be no whimpers in Trafford Park—and, in the world of newspapers, all retirements are banged out.

In any case, it is a proud and honourable story. It began at Allied Newspapers, Withy Grove, with the issue of Oct 1, 1940. Believe it or not, the decision to print the paper in Manchester was taken only a week before production began. London was being bombed nightly, invasion was still a possibility even though the Battle of Britain had been won. Rail transport was disorganised. If Fleet Street was put out of action, how would our readers be served?

Allied Newspapers were owned by Lord Kemsley, whose brother Lord Camrose owned the Telegraph. So no contract was drawn up at first (or for quite a time afterwards, I believe). The presses could easily cope with the then small northern print. From that point of view, it was easy. What was not so easy was assembling a northern staff at a time when able-bodied men were all in the Services.

Night scene: A 1960s shot from Fennel Street. The now-demolished Douglas Hotel on the left—one of the many Telegraph watering holes—obscures our office but the wonders of the photographic touch-up department have moved our sign into view.

Camrose appointed one of London's assistant editors, Oscar Pulvermacher, as Northern Editor.

The manager was Harold Fish, the Circulation Manager Dan Weaver and Will Forman was Publisher. Only three sub-editors could be spared from London, Gilbert Yeats (chief sub), and two others. Three were recruited in Manchester. A trial run on a Sunday night was successful and full production began on Monday for Tuesday.

The first editorial room was the disused *Sporting Chronicle* room. It was dirty, small and the telephone's mouthpiece fell off every time it was used. By a miracle, the paper was produced on that first night. A spirit was born which I like to think has always persisted in the Manchester office. Everybody worked like mad, not least Pulvermacher.

All the copy had to come via Allied in those days. Our own wire-room was some time away. But there was a reporter, Freddie Perfect, who helped out as a sub, and a telephonist in liaison with London, Ronald Parkinson. He later joined the Army, returned, became Picture Editor and retired at the end of 1985. In the Circulation Department, Frank Taylor joined on Day One. He retired as Northern Publisher in July 1987. A copy boy who joined in November 1941 is the writer of this article and is still on the staff. The three of us have chalked up a total (so far) of 138 years' service.

Blitz stopped paper only once

Ironically, the Manchester operation was the first to be endangered by enemy action. Only once did the paper fail to appear, on the Sunday night before Christmas in 1940 when a 12-hour blitz hit Manchester and Withy Grove was surrounded by burning buildings and narrowly escaped a direct hit. On later occasions, we took over nearly all London's print during the 1941 blitz. The subs worked for 12 hours night after night.

After a few months the staff was increased. Others joined from London, including Hughie Dryden, who had only one arm and managed to smoke a cigarette almost to its last eighth of an inch, hardly ever moving it from his lips. He was revise sub, and his explosions of rage over errors of style could be heard all over the building. There was Johnnie Johnson, the only journalist I've ever seen wearing a green eyeshade, cinema-style. He had a Worcestershire accent as ripe as an apple, and a pretty daughter.

And there was P. Beaumont Wadsworth, former Berlin correspondent of the *Observer*, who had never in his life been involved in editorial production. He was sent to make up a page on the stone. Told by the compositor that they needed a filler, he walked to the random, picked up the type and carried it to the page. The astonished maker-up informed him that this was against all the rules. So he took it back. I remember two other recruits, who first came for a night "on trial." One was Jack Kirkby, of whom more anon; the other Frank Walker, who later went to London and became Deputy Managing Editor, a gentle, dear man.

But the outstanding figures of those first six years were "Pulver" and Gilbert Yeats. "Pulver" looked like a very prosperous solicitor or surgeon. He dressed immaculately and soberly, smoked very good cigarettes and lived throughout the war in a suite at the Midland. He was a music-lover and often entertained Malcolm Sargent to dinner after Hallé concerts.

Once the editorial team had settled into a routine he departed each night as soon as he'd seen a proof of the leader page. He was not to be disturbed, he announced, for anything less than the surrender of Germany (that, I may say, was in 1942). He had been, it was said, Northcliffe's hatchet man in the 1920s on the *Daily Mail* and I daresay he was. But he had a benevolent streak and had become Telegraphed by this time.

Sub-editor in shipwreck scoop

Yeats was his opposite—a big, red-faced man, Cockney, foul-mouthed, often terrifying but with a great sense of humour and an innate kindness if he knew you were trying. In swiftly re-making not only a page but a paper on receipt of big news (and that happened nightly in the war), I have never seen his equal. As a technician he was unsurpassed, and he gave good advice. At 16 I was stupid enough to make the sub's perennial complaint: "This won't cut any more, Mr Yeats". "Wot you say, son? Give it me. And remember this—there's nothing in the English language that won't cut with the possible exception of the first chapter of Genesis".

He could write poetry in the most complex and difficult of inner-rhyming schemes, and he could recite Kipling by the hour. When he left the *Telegraph* and ended up on the *Yorkshire Post* he trained another young man and sent him to his old paper in London—Andrew Hutchinson, now the Deputy Editor.

While Ronnie Parkinson was in the Army, another telephonist was engaged, a tiny little fellow from Eccles called Oates. Gilbert immediately nicknamed him Titus, and so that is how he was always known. He eventually became a sub. He took adventurous holidays, going voyages on small boats all over the place. On one of these he was shipwrecked and the story got into the paper. But nobody realised we had a scoop about one of our staff because the correspondent gave him his real name, Vincent Oates. Another telephonist—who in those days had to take down copious notes on page changes (usually ignored) from London—was Ken Tonge. As a hobby he built model trams which are probably worth quite a bit today if they exist.

When I returned from the Navy, "Pulver" and Yeats had gone. The editor was G. C. Hepburn Reid, who had been the "Manchester sub" in London, dictating to Ronnie Parkinson, Titus Oates and Ken Tonge. He had joined the *Telegraph* in 1937 when it absorbed the *Morning Post*. He was a remarkably cultured man and a brave one. His leg and hand had been disfigured at birth and he suffered cruelly from bronchial asthma, so that Mancunian fogs were no blessing to him.

Hepburn was a stickler for detail and had a keen nose for a story. I can't think how many times I've heard him say, about some down-column filler, "Keep that for the front or the middle—it's going to blow up into something big". He was invariably right. When he first came, he knew little about the stone, I think, *but he turned* himself into a first-class operator there. He rarely left the office till 4 a.m. and I never believed he was fully appreciated by London.

He had the ideal journalist's magpie mind. He knew something about everything and quite a lot about quite a lot. He loved gossip and when the rival papers came in, I noticed he always turned first to William Hickey in the *Express*. In the office he never seemed to eat much except corned-beef sandwiches or a meal fetched from the canteen, but he was quite a gourmet and at his home he produced for me the finest vintage port I've ever drunk in my life. He could drive you mad, but he was in the best old-fashioned sense a gentleman and many people owe him a lot. He was in his sixties when he died in May 1960. His salary then, I discovered later, was barely £2,000. He earned it 10 times over.

Hepburn Reid had his equivalent in the composing-room where the Kemsley Head Printer for most of his régime was Dan Gilder, truly a printer of the old school. He ruled that floor like a king—woe betide anybody who took a visitor into that room without first asking his permission. He was tall, thin (a diabetic) and eagle-eyed. He walked between the stones sizing up the position on each page. Then he would walk up to the editor or whoever was in charge: "That page is overdue, Mr Editor, please fill it within five minutes then it can go to press". He was, in his way, a great man.

Circulation doubled

He was also unflappable. The City Prices page, all hand-set, once tipped off the trolley on to the floor a few minutes before edition time. Disaster, for the paper could not be printed without it. Dan simply said: Mr Reid, please tell the Publisher the paper will be an hour late". He then got together all the proofs and gave them to various comps, telling them to start again. Meanwhile he sent taxis to the homes of the regular setters (whose shift had ended the minute they had completed the prices) and fetched them back to the office. Within an hour the page was being moulded.

Inevitably an article such as this must become a catalogue of names, so many of them in nearly 50 years, and I can mention only a few. There are many I will omit, not because they are forgotten or under-valued, but simply because I would need a book to do justice to all the characters and friends who have been part of the Manchester *Telegraph* story. They were not all journalists. We've had some marvellous messengers, both men and boys, who have cheered us up at rough moments. Harold Burley is fresh in our memories, the man who knew where everything could be purchased! His predecessor Jim Banks was less benevolent and ruled the boys like Mr Squeers, hurling objects at them if they failed to answer the cry of "Copy".

Then there is Betty Besso, editor's secretary for over 30 years, the soul of tact, loyal, ageless. And who can forget the day the news-desk secretary, an innovation, arrived? She turned out to be Diane McCartney, the only member of the Manchester staff to be sent vintage champagne by Peter Eastwood. Her charms could have no greater or more unlikely tribute. Then there was George Harvey, once the picture man, later the Librarian, ever-helpful, monosyllabic, with a wickedly dry sense of humour. He made consulting Crockford's into fun.

From 1960 to 1970 was fun too. We began, in 1960, with a dinner to mark the 20th anniversary with Michael Berry (later Lord Hartwell) as chief guest, in company with the then Editor, Sir Colin Coote. Then we really got the bit between our teeth and tried to show that *The Daily Telegraph* could have a "northern flavour" and still be *The Daily Telegraph*. We pioneered the news-feature, something that is commonplace now but was a bit daring then. We expanded the reporting staff. Tom Cooper was the News Editor and Deputy Editor. He recruited a fine team of reporters, several of whom are now "stars" of the London staff, like Maurice Weaver, Roland Gribben and Ken Clarke. There were many others too, notably Trevor Bates.

Knowledgeable legend

Everyone will have his favourite Tom Cooper story and many of them I probably don't know. He was tall and debonair and had his share of human weaknesses, like us all. But he was a superb newspaperman when the chips were down. I've seen him organise coverage of a big air crash in a matter of minutes while others were flapping around wondering what to do. Then he'd flop into a chair, or go for a pint, until further news came in.

I never met a man with a greater capacity for meeting celebrities on their off-days, so his tales of the famous nearly all had an element of black comedy. Nothing ordinary ever happened to Tom. He was a masterly smoother of ruffled feathers and he could persuade reporters to work on for hours extra by a blend of old-fashioned good manners and a steely look in his eyes. He was a terrible soft touch for a tale of woe, bless him, but that was what made him lovable.

Tom played a major part in what resulted in the doubling of our circulation in the North, and so did our sports staff. In 1947 the chief sports sub (no title of sports editor then) was Kingsley Wright, later London's sport editor, and even then devoted to the golf course. Then we had Frank Nicklin and after him T. H. "Bill" Evans-Baillie, formerly of the *Manchester Guardian*. Bill was tall, stooping and monocled. He could write like an angel, mainly on rugby, and he nightly did the crossword within about 10 minutes of the first edition arriving in the office. He was also a talent-spotter, hence his successor Bob Williams. Bob wrote of Bill that he drank beer "so lovingly he seemed to be listening to the froth".

After Bob's death I compiled a small anthology of his writings in the paper and I hope some are still around, because they are collector's pieces by now, nearly 20 years later. At a time when *Telegraph* sports writing was factually accurate but deadly dull (with one or two exceptions), Bob sparkled with wit. It was often too much for London, who cut him down to their size, but we printed him as written and how glad I am that we did. At the age of 42 he was drowned on holiday while attempting to save his son and a friend who were not, as it happened, in danger. A more dreadful waste is hard to imagine. He was the life and soul of whatever party he was in, and I still can't think of him without a lump coming into my throat. Nor am I alone, I suspect.

Bob was followed by Mil Shanks, wholly a production man and a more conscientious one could scarcely be found. He *had been on the News Chronicle*, and he brought to the paper, to succeed Bob as a football writer, Denis Lowe, also ex-News Chronicle, whose tragically early death is a painfully recent memory. The sports pages have always been part of the *Telegraph's* strength. We've been fortunate to have men like Baillie, Wright, Standring, Williams, Lowe, Chapman, Mackay and Shanks.

Some paragraphs back I mentioned Jack Kirkby, perhaps the Manchester office's most persistent legend. He was a tubby Lincolnshire man, a first-rate sub-editor, and he became Night Editor. Jack's failing was a lack of a sense of humour. But in conscientiousness, devotion to the paper and knowledge of what the *Telegraph* could and could not contain he was pretty well unbeatable. He was a stickler for style and found it hard to entertain any divergence from the style-book. He was not a disciplinarian and I suppose a lot of people didn't like him, which was a pity because he had so many good points. (Brevity in conversation was not one of them).

Among many Jack Kirkby stories three deserve repeating here. There was the night a sub was leaving the staff. Jack saw him preparing to depart and called him over: "Now Mr So-and-So, before you go, there's just one point of style..." (I often wonder if that really was deadpan). Then there was the sub to whom he said in exasperation: "I've taught you all I know and you still know f... all". And, after a long session on the phone with me during which he seemed to be changing every top in the paper, he emerged into the big room exclaiming: "The Editor says I've got to do less and I can't".

The reverse of Jack was Jim Nelson, a cancer victim in his forties. He *was* a disciplinarian, having been an army sergeant in the Western Desert and in Normandy. He was a splendid chief sub, impatient of fools but encouraging to the real triers. No nonsense about Jim, he naturally commanded respect. He and I drove to London at midnight in 1965 to walk past Churchill when he was lying in state in Westminster Hall.

Hector Preece, for years the home copytaster, had the best line in blarney I've ever heard for getting a sub to take on about six stories at once: "I know you've got that top, old chap, but this one's just up your street and I know you'll want to do it, so I'll leave it with you". Len Hart on the leader page, rushing round like a whirlwind; Ike Panner on Parliament, muttering imprecations under his breath ("Bastards, bastards", meaning London usually); Freddie Fenton, foreign copytaster and art critic, whose brilliant caricatures of Jack Kirkby nearly precipitated a civil war; Horace Pilling and Denis Trinick on the city pages, oblivious to everything except Wall Street; a sub called Gerry Elwood, not unlike Clark Gable or Cesar Romero, who had a classic retort when told his headline was not covered in the story—"It's covered by implication"; Harry Myers who, as chief sub, suddenly remembered in the Swan that none of the tops on Page 5 had been subbed and took everyone back into the office to clear the copy in five minutes so that drinking-time could be resumed. We also once had a sub who didn't seem to appreciate that RYL was the standard creed-room abbreviation for Royal and converted the Royal Philharmonic into the Rhyl Philharmonic.

We were lucky in the 60s to have Les Willis as circulation manager, silver-haired, a dandy, no stranger to the bottle, but what a man at his job, what drive, what organisational ability, what charm. With Jack Cooper as manager, too, the *Telegraph* rode high at that time, inside and outside the office. People knew we were here. I had the satisfaction of encouraging new talent among reporters and subs, John Williams, John Clarke, Kevin Lavelle, many besides.

New technology death-knell

I scarcely need to recount the tale of the last decade. The words "new technology" were the death-knell. We knew it had to come, that it might be a good thing, but all Mancunian journalists realised in their hearts that one day it would render them expendable. To those who disliked the idea of Manchester—and people do, in all sorts of professions, I don't know why—it was a godsend and troubles were created which nearly, but not quite, wrecked the camaraderie of the Manchester staff.

There were confrontations between management and the NUJ, unheard of in the first 35 years. Yet that redoubtable FoC (and outstanding stone-sub) Dave Taylor still calls to see us, the old battles now an occasion for nostalgic, unmalicious, reminiscence. Long meetings in the canteen must have been as boring for the participants as they were frustrating for those left down below. It's hard work subbing a paper by oneself, or with the help of so expert a friend and colleague as Ken Loran (the best Home Copytaster of my experience, by the way). But at least it showed London that Manchester could still produce the goods.

It was a bold decision to build Trafford Park and an amazing feat to put up so fine a building so fast. Sceptics doubted if the presses would roll on Jan. 1, 1986, there would have to be a hiatus, or a period of double-harness with Withy Grove. But they were proved wrong. We finished at Thomson House on Dec. 31 and we started at Trafford Park on Jan. 2. The paper looked clean, the pictures were a revelation, the closing prices were legible! It was a new start and perhaps the northern edition would expand even more. "Looks North", Ken Loran's brilliant innovation, pointed the way and set the seal on his succession to the editorship.

But we reckoned without the financial crisis which caused a change in control of the paper. To any management looking for economies, the Manchester operation would always present a tempting target and so it proved. If it was inevitable, it is still deeply distressing to those who have seen so much hard work and good spirit go into the Manchester edition. It is hard to see friends made redundant, to wonder if one's own contribution has been worthwhile and enough.

But doesn't it say something very special about the Manchester staff that they have planned this commemorative page? The end of an era, yes, but not the end of a spirit. That survives, and let us hope it will give London some ideas which will allow us still to be proud of the paper that comes out of Trafford Park. Farewell—and hail!

A happy team . .

Thomson House may have been old and draughty, but we all remember those hot-metal days with great affection. The atmosphere in the composing room—once the world's largest—will never be matched. So it was with mixed feelings that we left our home of 45 years, not least because we said farewell to 19 colleagues.

The latter years at Withy Grove had been difficult and uncertain and those of us who stayed saw Trafford Park as a new challenge. We had success: there was a healthy increase in circulation and our small editorial team was a happy band.

Ken Loran (*Northern Editor*)

Michael Kennedy (*Associate Editor*)

John Clarke (*Deputy Editor*)

Trevor Bates (*Assistant Editor*)

Dai Bridgman (*Assistant Night Editor*)

Norman Rigby (*Assistant Night Editor*)

Rob Firth (*Assistant Night Editor*)

Tony Mellor (*Assistant Night Editor*)

The Subs

Chris Moorhead

John Gaule

Dave Parkin

Bernard Pratt

Hilary Jones

Brian Baker

Frank Green

Eamonn Giblin

Steve Greaves

News Desk

John Williams

Stanley Goldsmith

Diane McCartney (*News desk secretary*)

Charles Henn

Mike Arron (*Freelance photographer*)

John Dunsford

Sports Desk

Eddie Giles (*Sports Editor*)

Graham Tait (*Deputy Sports Editor*)

George Mackay

Bill Johnson

John Whalley

David Keenan

Peter Sutton

Caroline Wainwright (*Editors' secretary*)

TELEGRAPH staffers who left at the end of 1985 were: Vic Belfield, Tony Bez, Bill Barton, Geoff Browne, Frank Chapman, John Corness, Mark Dickinson, Harley Gelling, Charles Henn, Peter Hilton, Tom Leeson, Fred Meachin, Michael Niblock, Paul Niblock, Ronnie Parkinson, Paul Rylance, Cyril Ritson, Denis Trinick and George Turnbull.

Phil Darbyshire, Mike Deary, Paul Nettleton and Mil Shanks had already taken an early out.

And with the end of Withy Grove it was goodbye, too, to a host of long-serving regulars who had been like a "second tranche" of staff for many years, although they were officially casuals: Colin Colebrook, Alan Curren, Brian Fitzgerald, Arthur Hunt, Alan Mackenzie, Barry Prescott, Malcolm Ryding and Duncan Williamson.

How Cap'n Bob bought Withy Grove for £1

Revel Barker writes: Christmas Eve, 1985. Midnight. Holborn. I was walking along the deserted ninth floor corridor towards the lifts and home when Maxwell came out of his office, obviously in high spirits.

"Come and celebrate with me," he said. "I've just got the NGA to sign the agreement. You understand how important that is. Come and help me celebrate it!

He ushered me into his office. "Open some champagne." I hesitated...

"What do you want to drink?"

"Perrier; I'm not drinking. It sparkles, at least. What have they accepted, exactly?"

"The whole deal. Who'd have believed, 18 months ago, that we could get all this? It just shows that people can see reason if they're handled properly."

"Who's accepted it? Tom [Tom Harrison, NGA convener]? Or the chapel?

"Tom has. And he can deliver. And I've bought Withy Grove for your mates in Manchester."

"Not before bloody time, either. The number of times that deal's been on and off..."

"But who gave in at the end? Thomson gave in, not me. Know what I paid for it? One pound. I've told you before, nobody plays poker with Robert Maxwell."

"It's a great game for you. But while you're playing brinkmanship there are people up north with families and mortgages who don't know from one day to the next whether they've got a job. It's all heart attack stuff."

"But it's worked. And now they've got their jobs. Mind you, if it hadn't – if I hadn't got Withy Grove and this agreement from Tom – I was going to close down and go on holiday at Christmas."

"Close what down?"

"Everything."

"You know, Bob, you've got it wrong. It's the captain who goes down with his ship; the captain doesn't sink the bloody thing and walk away across the water."

"It's the same thing."

"Not if you're a member of the bloody crew, it isn't."

Maxwell laughed. "I know what you mean. I had an uncle – this is when I was very young – and he sailed to America with a friend to join the gold rush. Well

he got all the gold he thought he would need for the rest of his life, but his pal wanted more. So my uncle waited while he dug for it. When they were coming home, just as the ship was leaving San Francisco harbour, the earthquake happened and the ship started to sink. Everybody had to get into lifeboats, so my uncle threw his gold into the sea, jumped in, and climbed into a lifeboat. But his friend jumped with his rucksack, full of gold, still strapped to his back. He went straight through the bottom of the lifeboat and was never seen again.

"Every time my uncle told us children that story he would say: ....And I always wonder – did he get the gold, or did the gold get him?' "

Barry Lord, property manager, was the final person to leave Withy Grove when newspaper production halted in May 1988

Ode on the passing of Thomson Graphics Chapel

So this is it – the die is cast
The age of craftsmanship is past
Hot metal feels the icy blast
Of cold technology

So now they say the time is ripe
To still the ancient Linotype
An era's slate cleaned in a wipe
Of new technology

The Ludlow and the old type case
The setting stick, the very chase
In one almighty fall from grace
For new technology

Out with the old and in the new
The laser and the VDU
I wonder, will it really do
This new technology?

So Thomson Graphics "passes on"
Hard on the heels of *Sporting Chron*
Who will remember when it's gone?
Not new technology

And as the members now disperse
Some for better, some much worse
We realise the bitter curse
Of new technology

Alan Lunn 1985

A sort of afterlife

The precipitate closure of Manchester's national newspaper offices threw numbers of highly-experienced journalists onto the market. Some headed for London, others took early retirement, but many wanted to stay in Manchester – and work. By chance, the spring of 1988 was the moment when a regional daily newspaper start-up project finally achieved funding. It's here that I must declare an interest. I was the instigator, and editor, of *North West Times*. With my colleagues James Lewis and David Bridgman, both ex-*Guardian*, I found, quite unexpectedly, that we had the pick of Manchester talent. Just 50 jobs were on offer: we could not employ everyone. We wanted an admix of younger journalists from evening newspapers, those whose ambitions would clearly take them much further but were keen to take the unusual opportunity of joining a regional morning start-up.

In little over a month we had appointed about a dozen former *Mirror* journalists, seven or eight who had been with the *Daily Telegraph*, a few from

Below: Winston Churchill, MP for Trafford, with Tory grandee Nicholas Ridley, at Old Trafford cricket ground toting the short-lived regional morning newspaper on October 29 1988. Picture by Howard Barlow.
Right: launch issue of the *Post*, Eddy Shah's equally short-lived "family" tabloid produced at Warrington on Apple Macs

the *Mail* and *Express*, plus a leavening of young hopefuls from provincial papers and old hands like R.W. (Bill) Shakespeare, the former *Times* northern industrial corr who had also worked for the *Guardian* and happened to be a playwright. Young worked with old, tabloid journalists were cast alongside broadsheet stalwarts, all no doubt making their own comparisons. The summer of 1988 was one of feverish preparation. *North West Times* was launched early in September but taken off the streets just seven weeks later when the company's lawyers advised directors, myself included, that it would be foolish to bank cash raised by public subscription because the paper was not performing commercially as per prospectus. Our bankers had, in any case, swiftly withdrawn a £500,000 overdraft agreement. The company was liquidated, with pain all round.

It is not for me to assess the project. David Yelland, a young business reporter with *North West Times* who came to be better-known as the editor of the Sun, contributed an

obituary for the November 14 1988 edition of *UK Press Gazette*. Under the heading 'Too good to live, too young to die' Yelland wrote: "The *North West Times* didn't deserve to die so young. It was a good paper, but it aimed at a market which remained tragically unaware of its existence…Jim Lewis, the deputy editor, was fond of talking about his 'crinklies and young bloods', the magical combinations we had of older ex-national staff and younger people like me. We learned from each other, we complemented each other. But many of the older staff have now been made redundant for the second time this year."

At *North West Times* we were half way to using new technology. Copy was assembled and edited on screen, then transmitted to contract printers in Wigan where it was film-set and pasted onto broadsheet page frames before being offset printed. It was a low-cost arrangement which involved page editors driving 25 miles and depended heavily on telephone lines. We were unable, in the short time we were there, to produce more than two editions a night, and sometimes just one. City prices were a particular problem.

The short life of *NWT* illustrated, as had *News of Sunday* before it, and as did Eddy Shah's *Post* soon after, that using new technology gave no guarantee of success. The nationals could make substantial cost savings while giving the illusion of covering their traditional markets. The newcomers needed to establish a market of their own, in what was a fiercely-competitive environment. Old enemies joined hands to see off the newcomers – whose resources they rightly suspected were very slim – before taking up the old battle positions again. It was a war which surprised even Roger Bowes, *NWT's* chairman and a former chief executive of Express Newspapers, by its ferocity.

The story of *News on Sunday* was ably charted by Peter Chippindale and Chris Horrie in their 1988 paperback "Disaster! The Rise and Fall of *News on Sunday*." *NoS* was the high-principled Socialist Sunday tabloid which began life as a brainchild of Ken Livingstone's Greater London Council, transferred to Manchester for cost reasons, was launched in April 1987 and died in November 1987, having been 'saved' in June of that year by the Blackpool entrepreneur Owen Oyston. Whatever its achievements, *NoS* like *NWT* failed dramatically to reach its proposed market. It lost £6.5 million of shareholder money within four weeks of launch, while Oyston is said to have sunk a further £2 million himself. Sundry redundant Manchester journalists who had found a haven at *NoS* were on the market again.

The *Post's* life was just as brief. It was particularly bitter for Shah, the man who had successfully defeated the NGA at Warrington in his Messenger skirmishes of 1983, then launched and nurtured *Today*, the first national newspaper fully embracing new technology. *Today's* turmoils are also well chronicled, with an insider's view from Brian MacArthur, the launch editor (and incidentally a former *Daily Mail* and *Guardian* man in Manchester). It was, of course, sold on to Rupert Murdoch and eventually closed after a short but honourable life. The *Post*, launched from Warrington in November 1988, came and went with such speed that – like Yelland's assessment of *NWT* – few were aware of its existence. A family-oriented tabloid, like a Socialist Sunday tabloid (and a regional morning broadsheet?) maybe stood little chance, anyway. But Shah seemed to stake most of his hopes in on-screen page design using networked Macintoshes. The system was slow, troubled – and of course no substitute for a marketplace. Launch editor Lloyd Turner, himself from the *Sun* and before that the *Daily Star*, boasted to *UK Press Gazette* "We have got some world-beating stories lined up for the coming weeks which will have our competitors running round chasing their tails." But Kelvin MacKenzie, the *Sun* editor of Gotcha! fame, was cruelly realistic. He sent a note to former *Sun* journalists on the *Post* saying "Having seen your first edition, I thought you would like to know that you can't have your job back."

David Sullivan knew his market – Fantasy and Sex: Sex and Fantasy. Existing tabloids, raunchy as maybe, were not cheek-to-cheek competition. This was top shelf stuff and would sell itself

So Manchester went into limbo, though there had been stirrings in Salford where a bizarre arrival called the *Sport* hatched. Unlike the three well-intentioned commercial failures, David Sullivan knew his market – Fantasy and Sex: Sex and Fantasy. Existing tabloids, raunchy as maybe, were not cheek-to-cheek competition. This was top shelf stuff and would sell itself. The time was right. The unions were vanquished. Sullivan could finance launch costs out of profits on other top-shelf publications, using one to promote the other. But was it a newspaper? Manchester journalists in full-flight from deceased titles liked to think so. Martin Regan, who had been a business reporter alongside David Yelland at *North West Times* and now runs his own Manchester-based business publishing empire, found himself on some strange missions when he did reporting shifts there:

"Peter Grimsditch, the editor, came over to me one day soon after I started. 'What the fuck is that?' he shouted, waving some copy I'd written at me. 'It's a semi-colon'. 'We don't do f-ing semi-colons'. One time a picture came over the wire claiming to be the smallest dog in the world. It was clearly false. I took it over to Grimsditch. What do I do with it? He looked at the calendar and said: 'Get it banned from Crufts' (which was due soon after); "I rang Crufts and told them we had the smallest dog in the world. 'Has it got a Kennel Club certificate?' 'No' 'Well it won't get into Crufts then'. So we ran the headline 'SMALLEST DOG IN THE WORLD BANNED FROM CRUFTS'.

"Sullivan came to Manchester (or Salford Precinct in fact) because more good tabloid journalists were available than anywhere else. We used to go in at 10am, write for an hour then depart for the pub until four or five pm. *The Sport* started on Mondays, but they had so many tabloid journalists they brought it out Mondays, Wednesdays and Friday, then they opened Sunday too. Sullivan's fortune was made on those early years. Mind you, they paid serious money, the equivalent of £300 a day in today's money.

"I have clippings at home with Martin Regan reporting from Rome. I was the Rome correspondent and I never left Salford. There was one incident which supposedly came over the wire. A crocodile had fallen out of a cargo plane carrying animals to a zoo, landed in a Turin swimming pool and eaten a girl it found in the water. I got a Turin date-line. Of course it was Grimsditch's idea. He was brilliant. He believed that journalists should entertain. The *Sport* never bothered about serious subjects. It held that the tabloid is itself an art form. And nowhere else but in Manchester did the tabloid art-form come to such a fruition. The stories we did like ELVIS FOUND ON THE MOON were pure Mancunian. At that stage there was virtually no sale in London. It appealed to people in the North East particularly. Southerners just didn't understand its humour.

"That was the beauty of the *Sport*. It was as if all tabloid journalists who had nothing better to do had come together and this was the last opportunity they had to work in Manchester. The last flowering of Manchester's journalistic

"Nowhere else but in Manchester did the tabloid art-form come to such a fruition. The stories we did like ELVIS FOUND ON THE MOON were pure Mancunian. At that stage there was virtually no sale in London"

talent. There were serious people there, in tabloid terms. The sad thing is that if you're a journalist with talent there's nowhere to go now but London."

What Sullivan did – and does, because the *Sport* today operates from offices in the former *Daily Express* building in Great Ancoats Street, and is moving back towards some 'real' news – was followed up by another top-shelf professional, Richard Desmond, whose company Northern & Shell bought the Express Group from Hollick in November 2000. Desmond is another convert to the North for reasons of cost and convenience. Bit by bit the *Daily Express*, the *Sunday Express*, the *Daily Star* and now the *Daily Star Sunday* are being sub-edited from, of all places, Broughton near Preston (rather disproving Regan's theory). Broughton started life on a new town grant-aided site as an offset printing plant for United Newspapers, and came to Desmond by simple inheritance. According to John Maddock, the boss there, Desmond didn't even know he owned Broughton until he'd done the deal with Hollick. "I told him that there were better journalists in the North at a cheaper price: he took it on board. He went one stage further with the *Daily Star Sunday*. 'If I start the *Sunday* can you produce it at Broughton, and at what cost?' he asked. The answer was yes, and much more cheaply than London."

Journalists – there are 56 staff/contract posts, supplemented by casuals, with work stations for 165 subs – work three-day, four-day or five-day weeks. Their average salary is about £28,000. Key players all have experience on nationals in London or Manchester. "They were searching for a sports editor for the *Daily Star Sunday* in London, for whom they would have had to pay £120,000. We found an entire sports desk here in a month." Maddock also brings in local journalists from evenings and weeklies to try them out. He has formed an association with the journalism school at Central Lancashire University in Preston. Already many students have passed through the plant, four at a time on a Thursday night. Two have been hired – and more will follow, he promises.

The *Daily Star Sunday* news operation is run from London but sub-edited in Broughton, while the sports sections are originated and edited from Lancashire. *The Sunday Express* sport is similar, with writing costs shared. More and more of the *Daily Star* is subbed at Broughton – including a new Welsh edition – and it is no secret that Desmond's proposed free London evening paper will be produced in its entirety at Broughton before being flicked back to London. Such are the wonders of today's technology, with open screens at both ends.

Things are slowly returning to the North, Maddock claims. "But we are having to overcome an awful lot of animosity in London." There is a now real fear in the south about losing jobs to the north. "Some London journalists try everything to sabotage Broughton – messy copy, altered facts, wrong crossword clues. We've been up to speed in spotting problems. People still think that the subs here are from the *Burnley Bugle* with straw in their hair. They get a shock…"

A London NUJ official who called Broughton "the George Formby appreciation society" was given a roasting. about a quarter of the journalists who work there are NUJ members

A London NUJ official who called Broughton "the George Formby appreciation society" was given a roasting, according to Maddock. Only about a quarter of the journalists who work for him are NUJ members.

Is Broughton a substantial new beginning or a fluke? It's impossible to say. There's a limit to the number of national-trained journalists currently available, even in the North West. Pay levels are so low that Northern exiles seeking to return home from the South must make some serious financial calculations. And if it can happen in Lancashire why not, say, in Devon or Dorset where many who took early retirement from Fleet Street might well fancy a little income supplement? But the greater the critical mass at Broughton, the tougher it will be to dislodge. Already *Express* and *Star* weekend colour magazines, as well as spin-offs like S2, are edited at Broughton. Express Newspapers' IT backup has also been transferred there from Glasgow with a £2 million investment. Maddock claims that all Northern & Shell titles could be produced from Broughton if London was not operational.

Desmond clearly has the *Evening Standard* and the *Daily Mail* in his sights. He has declared it his life's mission to topple the Harmsworth dynasty. The cost advantage Broughton gives him could be an important factor. In October 2002 the *Daily Mail* closed a Manchester office it had run for three years where up to 16 regional pages a day were written and produced. Ironically, considering its history, the *Mail* had discovered that it was proportionately weaker in the NW than anywhere in the country. The office was well run and sales increased slightly. Now the North West edition is being handled from London again, though a news desk and a limited sports desk survives in Manchester.

Front page picture on *North West Times's* final day of publication, November 9 1988

That appears to be the alternative model for national newspaper involvement in the regions. Invest where you want to, when you feel you have to. Keep the operation flexible and your options open. Manchester is just one of the places you might choose. *The Sun*'s decision to close its Manchester office in July 2004 is countered by the *Daily Mirror*'s recent vow to put more resources into the North. It's all part of marketing ebb and flow.

Since it thoroughly divested itself of its Manchester operation, you might have thought the same is true of the *Guardian*. Not so. Guardian Media Group's registered office remains 164 Deansgate. The group has a large classified advertising sales team there, with crossover between the *Guardian* and the *Manchester Evening News*. The *MEN* itself, despite being in decline like most evening papers, remains important, if only as a complement to the group's swathe of weekly free newspapers around the Manchester conurbation. Guardian Media Group is by far the biggest cheese in town. But what of the *Guardian* itself?

When Martin Wainwright took over as northern editor in 1995 he set out a series of aims and ambitions, which included proper use of the newspaper's history and a "modest increase of vigorous *Guardian* journalism in the North." He has found Alan Rusbridger, the *Guardian's* current editor, open to ideas. Rusbridger accepted Peter Preston's suggestion that more space and emphasis be given to northern stories. Thus was *Guardian* North born. Branding or something more? On a daily story count basis (sport, arts notices and readers' letters apart) *Guardian* North does not add up to a paper much different from the *Guardian*. The newspaper has three of the best senior reporters in the North – Wainwright himself based in Leeds, Peter Hetherington based in the North East and David Ward based in Manchester along with Don McPhee, a true *Guardian* photographer. It has also cultivated young talent sent from London – Angelique Chrisafis, Oliver Burkeman, Emma Brockes, Esther Addley – but lost them when it suited London to take them back.

Wainwright stays characteristically upbeat about it all:

"*Guardian* North is a flag-flying exercise and an important psychological declaration that we are here to stay. There have been moments since the 1980s when the *Guardian's* presence here has been very close to collapse, even – indeed mostly – when there was notionally quite a big editorial staff in Manchester. Its output was abysmal, considerably less than today's smaller but well-motivated group… We are a marginal operation, obviously, but we are no longer an irritation because – in marked contrast to the period of Manchester Moaning and decline – we are probably the most productive group of journalists on the entire paper."

So there. The *Guardian* lives. As do the other nationals – all of which, including the *Sun*, the *Times* and the *Financial Times*, now print somewhere in the North by facsimile from London. Regional circulation battles may wax and wane. Manchester may be seen as the place to invest in, or disinvest in. Just one thing is for sure. Like Fleet Street itself, The other Fleet Street will never happen again.

"Guardian North is… an important psychological declaration that we are here to stay. We are a marginal operation, but we are no longer an irritation because we are probably the most productive group of journalists on the entire paper"

A personal postscript

I took the train to Manchester's Central Station in June 1963, summoned for interview just before final exams by an unexpected telegram from the *Guardian*. A features subbing job was on offer, and as customary they were scouring Oxbridge. I didn't hold out much hope. I'd already been rejected by, among others, the BBC ("this is a studio position and you look like an outdoors type") and the *Western Daily Press* ("we're only taking geniuses this year, and you're obviously not one"). I had no university journalism to show for myself. I didn't read a daily paper, let alone the *Guardian*. I had simply decided that being a newspaperman was the least unpleasant of many unpleasant ways to earn a living. That was the extent of my ambition.

Dai Bridgman, Bob Waterhouse and Jim Lewis inspect the first "live" dummy issue of *North West Times*, July 14 1988

My interviewer turned out to have a sympathetic laugh, along with an RAF moustache and cravat (yes, he'd been a fighter pilot during the war). "Call me Phil", he said over a cup of tea in the Cross Street canteen. His wife knew him as Jimmy. His by-line was Anthony Tucker, his title northern features editor. I can't remember what we talked about, though it was pleasant enough. I later learnt Phil's first role at the *MG*, as a mature student from the Regional College of Art, had been to paint a canteen mural. On the way down the back stairs his deputy, John Course, told me how sorry he was I hadn't got the job.

So a return to finals, and much gloom. I had resigned myself to life outside journalism (probably without a degree) when, just as exams were finishing, another telegram arrived. Start next Monday, it said. Pay £17 per week. The only stipulation: I must live on an all-night bus route. I didn't appreciate my luck. These days, nobody gets near the back door of a national newspaper that easily.

I wasn't to know that a college acquaintance – yes, he got a First – had been offered the post and turned it down. He wanted to travel that summer. More fool him. I expect he found an academic niche somewhere. I showed my journalistic impulses by grabbing the job, though I found Manchester hard going. I loved language but knew nothing of editing. The Tucker style invited you to "look at" a story. No training, in fact, apart from standing at another's shoulder. No rules. No sanctions. No pressure, until one night about three months' later I found myself on my own looking after third edition, when the arts notices changed. I survived. Everyone drank to it. I was a member of the features team.

It was a team which included Mike McNay, the future assistant editor who supervised the new-look *Guardian* in 1988; Derek Malcolm, later the paper's illustrious film critic; Ian Breach, who became technology correspondent and then a correspondent for both ITV and the BBC; and Chris Dodd, who was to be rowing correspondent and founder of the Henley Rowing Museum. We worked, drank, drank, clubbed, ate early-morning curries together, even shared flats. I fell in love with Manchester. Young bloods, we had little interest in the traumas the *Guardian* underwent in the mid-sixties, although two later arrivals to the features department lost their jobs on a last-in, first-out basis. One by one we drifted off to London. The mood had been signalled by the departure south of the editor, Alastair Hetherington, in the early spring of 1964 – the very same week the *Guardian* ran a series entitled "Moving out of London."

My own destiny was to return to Manchester in April 1972 after rather less than four years away. Everything had changed. Not only did I bring a wife and young daughter, the *Guardian* had transferred from Cross Street to Deansgate, cosy Victorian clutter swapped for cold developer clutter. I was freelance, though largely dependant on *Guardian* commissions. It became increasingly obvious that the Manchester office was being abandoned. I felt anger and shame at what was happening – foolish emotions for a freelance. In 1976, shortly before "live" operations closed, I spoke my mind to the paper's new editor, Peter Preston. He said he needed my comments like a hole in the head. Then Harry Jackson, the London-based features editor, told to me that as from August 1976 Manchester no longer existed. I got the message.

All the same I'd been cashing-in on the wind-up process as a casual sub on the foreign desk, and happened to be stone sub on the last-ever *Guardian* foreign page in Manchester. After the edition had been duly banged out by the comps we all went to Press Club and got drunk. It was the only thing to do.

In December 1975 I had written to Harry Evans at the *Sunday Times* suggesting that the *Guardian's* forthcoming abdication of Manchester left the way open for a new North West regional daily. Could Thomson be interested? The reply came from David Cole, chief executive of Thomson Regional Newspapers. He pointed out that only four regional mornings in Britain (all in Scotland) were profitable and that there was little point thinking about a start-up until new technology had been accepted by the unions. It was a perceptive comment, and it put the kibosh on my plans for the next ten years or so.

If new regionals were out of the question, there were other possibilities. In 1978, while still freelancing spasmodically for the *Guardian* and subbing two days a week for the *Guardian* Weekly, three friends and I launched a fortnightly freesheet, the *Withington Reporter*. We were members of the local civic society and in despair at the *Manchester Evening News'* lack of coverage of serious issues in our ailing South Manchester suburb. It was a genuine community initiative. We had the 12-page tabloid typeset and printed

We worked, drank, drank, clubbed, ate early-morning curries together, even shared flats. I fell in love with Manchester. Young bloods, we had little interest in the traumas the Guardian underwent in the mid-1960s

professionally, but were all volunteers. I was the editor, my house was the office. With an initial distribution of 10,000 copies (we paid the delivery kids a pittance) we were in business for £500 each. After two editions we went monthly.

The travails of the *Reporter* are not relevant here. During those years I supplemented meagre freelance earnings by casualing first on the *Daily Telegraph* and then the *Daily Mirror* as their Manchester staffs were also run down. Eventually, converted to a weekly, with a free circulation of 48,000, a staff of about ten and an office in Didsbury, the *South Manchester Reporter* was sold to my friend Pat Quinn. This was 1987; I had edited the paper for five years and then passed the burden on to others, including Simon Inglis and Chris Benfield. I was more interested in activating my regional morning newspaper idea. Indeed, I'd worked full out on it from January 1986, garnering help and encouragement from an organisation called the Manchester Financial and Professional Forum.

Three MFPF members played a key role – Mel Harding, a partner in the ad agency HQO, Graham McInnes of the accountants Spicer & Pegler, and Soren Tattam of the lawyers March Pearson. All volunteered their services on account, with no fees due if the newspaper, which was to be called *North West Times*, did not transpire. Mel introduced me to Peter Coulton, former northern advertising manager of the *Daily Telegraph*, then crucially to Roger Bowes, a Fleet Street operator with a very impressive CV. Graham oversaw the business plan, Soren started the search for investment cash.

We eventually secured funding of a sort in May 1988. The rest of that particular story is told on pages 204-206. Following liquidation of the company I had to start again as a freelance. By mid 1989 there were, of course, no nationals publishing in Manchester (unless you count the *Sport*, which I don't). Ian Hamilton Fazey, then northern correspondent of the *Financial Times*, steered *FT* special reports towards me; together with a series of articles for the *Investors Chronicle*, they helped reincarnate me, this time as a business journalist. Then Alastair Balfour, managing director of Edinburgh-based Insider Publications, hired me in September 1990 to be launch editor of the monthly *North West Business Insider*.

In May 1992 my colleague Nick Jaspan and I were offered a management buyout of NWBI, which had cost the Scots a lot of cash. Nick raised the wherewithal via 3i, we founded Newsco Publications and, just before the millennium, sold it on to Regional Independent Media, publisher of the *Yorkshire Post*. As Newsco's editorial director I had the satisfaction of working with outstanding national newspaper journalists – John Flint, Trevor Bates and Ian Fazey among them. Once again, I benefited from The other Fleet Street.

Forty years and more on from my hesitant first arrival at Central Station, Manchester has become a very different sort of city. Its decline (evident even in the Swinging Sixties) has been halted. People live in the centre. There is bustle

At Newsco I had the satisfaction of working with outstanding national newspaper journalists – John Flint, Trevor Bates and Ian Fazey among them. Once again, I benefited from The other Fleet Street

in the streets, business in the air. Manchester's shops are the most interesting outside London, its airport the biggest. Hotels and restaurants lurk round every corner, finance professionals trip over each other hurrying across Barbirolli Square, students are ten a penny on Oxford Road. Weekends herald a 48-hour binge in bistros, bars and clubs from Oldham Street to Castlefield. High-speed trams connect Piccadilly and Victoria stations with the suburbs.

There's just one thing. Now that the newspaper factories have gone, rental values of the Withy Grove, Cross Street, Deansgate and Great Ancoats Street sites are much improved. Rental values are not quite all that matters.

The Printworks (formerly Withy Grove). Manchester's premier drinking and leisure venue. What's new?

A select bibliography

After I was Sixty
by Roy Thomson. Hamish Hamilton, 1975

Autobiography
by Neville Cardus. Collins, 1947

Beaverbrook
by A.J.P.Taylor. Hamish Hamilton, 1972

Changing Faces : A history of the *Guardian* 1956-88
by Geoffrey Taylor. Fourth Estate, 1993

Dear Bill
by W.F.Deedes. Pan Macmillan, 1997

Denis Thorpe Photographs 1950-2000
The *Guardian*, 2004

Disaster! The Rise and Fall of *News on Sunday*
by Peter Chippindale and Chris Horrie. Sphere Books, 1988

Eddie Shah and the Newspaper Revolution
by David Goodhart and Patrick Wintour. Coronet Books, 1986

Eddy Shah: Today and the Newspaper Revolution
by Brian MacArthur. David and Charles, 1988

Editor-in-Chief
by Denis Hamilton . Hamish Hamilton, 1989

Guardian: Biography of a Newspaper
by David Ayerst. Collins, 1971

***Guardian* Years**
by Alastair Hetherington. Chatto & Windus, 1981

Headlines all my Life
by Arthur Christiansen. Heinemann, 1960

In the News Manchester
by Chris Makepeace. W H Smith, 2002

Last of the Hot Metal Men
by Derek Jameson. Ebury Press, 1990

NATSOPA 75 years: A history of the National Society of Operative Printers and Assistants 1889-1964
by James Moran. Oxford, 1964

Of this our Time
by Tom Hopkinson. Hutchinson, 1982

On and off the Rails
by Peter Raynor. Novelangle, 1997

On home ground: photography
by Denis Thorpe. Lowry Press, 2001

Peterborough Court: The story of the *Daily Telegraph*
by Lord Burnham. Cassell, 1955

Press Gang
by Roy Greenslade. Macmillan, 2003

Royal Commission on the Press 1947-49, 1961-62, 1974
HMSO 1949, 1962, 1974

Shock! Horror! The tabloids in action
by S.J.Taylor. Bantam, 1991

Stick it up your Punter!
by Peter Chippindale and Chris Holmes. Heinemann, 1990.

The Autobiography of Howard Spring
Collins, 1972

The Great Outsiders: Northcliffe, Rothermere and the *Daily Mail*
by S.J.Taylor. Weidenfeld & Nicolson, 1996

The House the Berrys Built: Inside the *Telegraph* 1928-1986
by Duff Hart-Davis. Hodder & Stoughton, 1990

The *Mirror*: a political history
by Maurice Edelman. Hamish Hamilton, 1966

The Typographical Association: origins & history up to 1947
by A.E.Mason. Oxford, 1954

Towards the End of the Morning
by Michael Frayn. Collins, 1967/2000

Topical Budget: the great British news film
by Luke McKernan. BFI Publishing, 1992

Touched by Angels
by Derek Jameson. Ebury Press, 1988

Walking on the Water
by Hugh Cudlipp. Bodley Head, 1976

When I was a Child
by Edward Hulton. Cresset Press, 1952

A newspaper history website guide

This book would not have been possible in its present form without access to the worldwide web. What survives of Manchester's newspaper history is random and for the large part poorly documented. Although the web doesn't usually provide primary sources, it offers pointers to what is available or unavailable in the archives as well as making links to third-party sources via search-engines like Google

I have divided my guide into two: essential newspaper history links – and ones that I have come across by following my nose. There's a short personal assessment of both types. Neither list is exhaustive. New sites open each day while others close, but this guide attempts to be up-to-date on going to press

Essential sites

archiveshub.ac.uk

If you know what you're looking for you'll probably find it here. Interlinked listings describing hundreds of thousands of individual archive holdings at British universities

bopcris.ac.uk

BOPCRIS – the British Official Publications Collective Reader Information Service – is a lottery-funded body providing basic data on public documents in or out of print. Overviews of the three post-war Royal Commissions on the Press – 1948-49, 1961-62 and 1976-77 – are here

bjr.org.uk

Website of the British Journalism Review, the lively quarterly by and for media-into-academia buffs. Tasters only (you have to subscribe to the review to get it in full)

bl.uk.collections/newspapers

Overview of the massive British Library newspapers holding. Newspapers are listed by title, date and publication place on prodigi.bl.uk/nlcat, with a good search facility. The BL's Newsplan programme for archiving titles regionally is also described (not much value yet for Manchester, where Libraries North West is titularly in charge of the project – see nw.org.uk)

link.bubl.ac.uk/n/newspapers

Universal portal stuffed with useful links

gmcro.co.uk

Quick guide to the Greater Manchester County Record Office, listing an important newspaper archive

guardiancentury.co.uk

Key articles from the (Manchester) *Guardian's* coverage of the twentieth century, related decade by decade

guardian.co.uk/newsroom

Growing archive of *Guardian* and *Observer* source material, an introduction to the Newsroom archive opposite the newspaper's head office in Farringdon Road, London

hmc.gov.uk/nra

National Register of Archives maintained by the Historical Manuscripts Commission. Definitive overview of sources on press history (amongst everything else). The Archon regional directory of professional organisations and Archon portal is on hmc.gov.uk/archon

ketupa.net

500-page site developed by Australian-based Caslon Analytics with profiles of some 125 media groups. History section includes press barons. Good for links and for bibliographies

manchester.gov.uk/libraries/central/socsci/news

Titles and dates of archived newspapers

newspapersociety.org.uk

Overview and history of the NS, the provincial press proprietors' group

rylibweb.man.ac.uk/data2/spcoll/guardian

Description of the *Guardian* Archive held at the John Rylands University Library of Manchester

spartacus.schoolnet.co.uk/journalists

Basic but fairly comprehensive historical list of English-language journalists accompanied by selections of source material aimed at students

trinity-mirror.com/abouttrinitymirror/history

Potted history of the group

warwick.ac.uk/services/library/mrc

The Modern Records Centre at Warwick University, where most trades union archives are held. Info on the history of sundry print unions. Many archives still to be indexed

Other sites

btinternet.com/nigel.ellacott/ pantomimeannual

Richly-illustrated homage to the *Sunday Chronicle* Pantomime Annual published by Hulton and then Kemsley at Withy Grove from 1910

brad.ac.uk/library

Catalogue entries of *Reynolds News* and the *Sunday Citizen* holdings from the Co-operative Society in the Bradford University collections

bufvc.ac.uk/databases/newsreels/archives

Guide to the history of British newsreels

busterkeaton.com/Margaret/shop1

Luke McKernan's story of the 1922 Hulton film star competition linking the *Daily Sketch* to Topical Budget newsreels

carlscam.com

Full list of Hulton and Kemsley employees who lost their lives fighting in the First and Second World Wars as commemorated on plaques at the Printworks (Withy Grove). Compiled by Carl Rogerson for his series on North West war memorials

cudlipp.cf.ac.uk

Details of the Hugh Cudlipp (and Tom Hopkinson) archives at the Cardiff University School of Journalism, Media and Cultural Studies

encyclopedia-titanica.org

Everything to do with the sinking of the Titanic (a *Daily Sketch* triumph)

guardianlies.com

A former North West MP rants at the *Guardian*, not for leaving Manchester but for helping oust him from Parliament on the "cash for questions" issue

heritagecommercials.com/ jan02/feature2

Enthusiast magazine's celebration of the newspaper delivery van in the days of steam and hot metal

hffax.de/History/ hauptteil_faxhistory

Graphically-illustrated English-language history of the fax machine, invented by the Scot Alexander Bain in 1843

home.imprimus.com.au/ oseagram/creed2

History of the Creed telegraphic system used by the *Daily Mail* to transmit news between London and Manchester from 1912

manchesteronline.co.uk/ newspapers

Manchester portal with newspaper links and some history

northtrek.plus.com

Site created by Geoffrey Mather, a former assistant editor of the *Daily Express* in Manchester. An opinionated celebration of Northerness from a Lancastrian perspective, plus a homage to Arthur Christiansen

oddbooks.co.uk/oddbooks/kemsley

Jokey review of the Kemsley Manual of Journalism 1950 by one Alfred Armstrong on his own site which features a personal selection of obscure books

politicalcartoon.co.uk

A sadly under-represented art in Manchester newspapers

terramedia.co.uk

UK media history from a audiovisual perspective

the-shipman-inquiry.org.uk

Official site of the Manchester-based inquiry into Britain's most prolific mass murderer

tuc.org.uk/the tuc/tuc-2878-f0

Online text of the TUC's own version of the first TUC Congress, held in Manchester in 1868, the brainchild of two local compositors

2d53.co.uk/bangor/parcels

Enthusiast's illustrated history of the North Wales Coast Railway featuring newspaper trains from Manchester and Chester

A hot metal glossary

AEU Amalgamated Engineering Union (machine-room engineers)

Art editor Former title for picture editor, who dealt with engravings and drawings before photography became current

Art room Former title for picture desk

Backbench Night editor, chief sub-editor, deputy chief sub, copytaster etc who run the sub-editing team

Banging out Compositors' practice of marking special occasions by thumping metal on chases

Black Carbon copy of typescript

Block The metal base for process images, placed alongside type in chases. Shorthand for illustration

Brief Short news item

Bush machine Roneo-type contraption used in branch offices or mobile vans to add cricket and football scores to early editions before sales and distribution

Case room Area where compositors make up special pages like advertising inserts working from the slanted wooden cases where loose type is kept – capitals in the upper slots, lower-case or small letters in the lower rows (origin of the terms upper and lower case)

Casual Sub-editor or print-worker hired by the night

Catch-line Running indicator of story on copy

Chapel Union branch, or sub-branch (derives from the monastic origins of printing)

Chase Steel frame in which metal type and blocks are assembled, corrected and revised to fit, then locked up as a finished page

Compositor (or comp) NGA craftsman. Technically anyone who works in the composing room but usually a stone-hand as opposed to a lino-operator

Copy Edited story used by lino-operator to set material

Copy desk Composing room station where copy is collated and dispensed

Copyholder Reader who reads out loud from original copy for colleague to mark galley proofs

Copytaker Typist with telephone headset taking copy from staff journalists or agencies

Copytaster Production journalist who reads incoming copy and ascribes it to pages

Corrections Process of correcting setting mistakes via resetting from readers' proofs

Creed Trade-named fast wire room printer often connected to PA

Cutting in Cutting on the stone by subs to make page fit

Drop cap Capital letter, the depth of two or three lines, used to start stories or paragraphs

Em Measure for specifying column width. One em = a 12pt pica

En Half an em. Measure of lino operator's setting output

Filler Stories kept in type to fill holes on pages

Flong Fibre mat (originally papier-mâché) moulded to the completed chase or page of type and used to make a stereo

Flyhand Operative overseeing delivery of newsprint quires from folders

FoC Union branch leader (literally Father of the Chapel)

Foreigner Working informally for another organisation

Folder Cuts, folds and collates papers after printing. A measure of output, since its capacity dictates the press speed

Foundry Department where blocks used for printing plates are made and stereo is cast

Fount (font) Type specification, eg Times Roman or Bodoni Italic

Fudge Stop-press news on front or back pages

Full out Instruction to set copy without paragraph indent

Fustic Late edition material used as early edition material the next evening, then discarded

Galley Individual columns of type, separately stored

Galley-proof Proof from galleys for reading and correcting

Head printer The person in charge of the composing room, more important than the editor to the nighly performance of a newspaper

Hot metal Molten lead alloy used in linotype machines to form line slugs. Shorthand for the "steam" days of printing

Igranic Trade-named wire belt on which printed papers are transferred from machine room to publishing room

Jobbing printers General – as opposed to newspaper – printers, where most compositors serve their apprenticeship

Jobbing room Place where process images are stuck to pre-cast blocks

Lead Strips of metal, normally 1pt or 2pt thick, inserted between lines to space out paragraphs or fill out columns

Leading The process of spacing type with lead

Lemon Compositors' term for line with setting error(s)

Lemon random Desk from which corrections are distributed

Lift Instruction to use existing type matter

Lino Linotype machines, industry standard of hot-metal newspaper printing, setting line slugs from keyboards automatically collated into galleys

Lino operator Compositor who sets type on lino machines

Literal Journalists' and proofreaders' term for setting error(s)

Long Tom Plate camera with ultra long lens

LSP The London Society of Printers

Ludlow Machine for hand-set headlines

LX *Daily Express* shorthand for London

Machine room Department where presses print newspapers

Mangle Compresses flongs to imprint page matrices

Mark up Writing on printed papers to indicate amounts to be paid to correspondents or photographers

Mat The matrix, created on flongs, from which stereo pages are cast

Mat box Page-size box used to transport mats by train between Manchester and London

Measure The width, in ems, of a column

mf Reporter's/sub's mark at the bottom of a page indicating more copy is to come

mfl Mark indicating more is to follow later

Minders Quality-control operatives in the machine room

MG *Manchester Guardian*

MTS Manchester Typographical Society

MX *Daily Express* shorthand for Manchester

Mufax Muirhead facsimile machine used to wire images between centres. An ancestor of page faxing

NATSOPA National Society of Operative Printers and Assistants

NGA National Graphical Association

NPA Newspaper Proprietors' (later Publishers') Association

NUJ National Union of Journalists

NUPT National Union of Press Telegraphists

Nump, numple Abbreviation of nonpareil, the old name for 6pt leading

Nut indent Type indent of one en, or 6pt

Obits (or Morgue) Department where obituaries are prepared and stored

On a portable Dark room and wire room staff with portable printing and wiring facilities for transmitting pictures from remote events like football matches or party conferences

On the cobbles Printers' term to down tools, or strike

Overmatter (O/M) Galleys of unused (or cut) type

PA Press Association

Pica Old name for 12pt, equivalent to one em

Picture bender Alternative early term for picture editor

Pinch-run Van drivers making up time to catch newspaper trains

Point Size of type; normally 72 points to the inch

Process Department responsible for making photographic plates

Propping & cocking Juggling to meet distribution deadlines

Publishing room Department where printed papers are bundled, addressed and dispatched

Pull Proof of inked page or galley made on moist paper with a roller for reading/checking purposes

Putting over copy Dictating by phone to copytakers

Quire Standard order measure of 26 newspapers for publishing room (a quire is twice a baker's dozen)

Random Desk where set metal, including headlines, is ascribed to pages

A hot metal glossary

Readers Proof-readers marking galleys (or pages) with corrections

Retouching Process department's controversial custom of highlighting photographic images for stronger reproduction

Ruby Small type-face (five and a half point) used for City prices and advertisements. Lino machines grouped to set in this size known as Ruby Alley

Send up The process of sending subbed copy to the composing room

Setting for practice Head printer's caustic description of o/m

Spike Literally a metal spike with a wooden base used by subs for storing copy not sent to the composing room. Figuratively, stories which are rejected or not used

Squeeze A vice to compress type

SLADE Society of Lithographic Artists, Designers and Engravers

Slow drop Photographers' use of long exposure techniques on glass plates

SOGAT Society of Graphic and Allied Trades

Standing metal Set stories kept in reseve,principally obits

Stereo Department which creates curved stereotype printing plates from mats, plates which are then bolted to the rotary presses

Stone Work-bench on which pages are made up in chases, originally with marble top; shorthand for the composing room

Stone-hand Compositor who makes up pages

Sub-editors (subs) Journalists who edit others' copy

TA The Typographical Association

Take Portion of copy allotted to a lino operator for setting

Tick up Instruction to a sub to prepare copy for setting without changing the contents

TTS Tele-type setting, near simultaneous typesetting in two or more centres using perforated tape fed into lino machines

Tube Room Messengers' room where copy is organised and routed via belts or suction tubes

Wayzgooze Traditional printers' holiday outing and booze-up

wf Wrong font

White Generic term for space on page

Wire (or Creed) Room Where wired copy is transmitted, received and collated

Name index

Name index

Credits

Text credits

The author and publisher thank the following:

Sir Jocelyn Stevens for use of quotations and reproduction of pictures from his uncle's book "When I was a Child" by Sir Edward Hulton, Cresset Press, 1952

Geoffrey Taylor for use of a quotation from his book "Changing Faces: A history of the *Guardian* 1956-88", Fourth Estate, 1993

The Random House Group for quotations from "Walking on the Water" by Hugh Cudlipp, Bodley Head, 1976 and "Last of the Hot Metal Men" by Derek Jameson, Ebury, 1990

Harper Collins for quotations from "Autobiography" by Neville Cardus, Collins, 1947

David Higham Associates for quotations from "Headlines all my Life" by Arthur Christiansen, Heinemann, 1960

Orion Books for a quotation from "The Great Outsiders" by S.J.Taylor, Weidenfeld & Nicolson, 1996.

Penguin Books for a quotation from "After I was Sixty" by Lord Thomson, Hamish Hamilton, 1975

Nigel Hamilton for an extract from "Editor-in-Chief" by Denis Hamilton, Hamish Hamilton, 1989

All attempts to trace copyright of "Peterborough Court: The Story of the *Daily Telegraph*" by Lord Burnham, Cassell, 1955, proved unsuccessful

Picture credits

British Film Institute
44

British Library Newspapers
41,42

Clive Cooksey
156,157,158,164,165,171,176

Daily Mail (Associated Newspapers)
56,57,59,62,111,116,122,126,137, 174,178

Daily Express (Northern & Shell)
Front and back covers,
52-53,54,55,156-157,173

Getty Images, Hulton Archive
9,32,37,39,49,54,160-161,162

Guardian Media Group
13,28,59,77,123,127,135,
152-153,154-155,175,182,186,190

Sheila Hardy
184-185

Michael Kennedy
71,72,149

John Knill
130,192

Mirrorpix (images from the Kemsley and Thomson picture libraries)
2,12,14,23,26,46,57,58,60,61,
62,85,86,87,88-89,91,94,95,97,99,
100,101,128,163,199,203

Museum of Science and Industry Manchester
105

Stuart Neale
148

Sir Jocelyn Stevens
33,34,51

Denis Thorpe
114,200

Johnnie Walker (Mirrorpix)
120,122,134,137,138,140,159,
162,163,164,166,167,168-169,170,
177,178,179,180,181

Withy Grove Fellowship
24,93,98